W9-BFE-136

Glencoe

WORLD HISTORY

Modern Times

Active Reading
Note-Taking Guide
Student Workbook

Douglas Fisher, Ph.D.
San Diego State University

 Glencoe

New York, New York   Columbus, Ohio   Chicago, Illinois

About the Author

Douglas Fisher, Ph.D., is a Professor in the Department of Teacher Education at San Diego State University. He is the recipient of an International Reading Association Celebrate Literacy Award as well as a Christa McAuliffe award for excellence in teacher education. He has published numerous articles on reading and literacy, differentiated instruction, and curriculum design as well as books, such as *Improving Adolescent Literacy: Strategies at Work* and *Responsive Curriculum Design in Secondary Schools: Meeting the Diverse Needs of Students*. He has taught a variety of courses in SDSU's teacher-credentialing program as well as graduate-level courses on English language development and literacy. He has also taught classes in English, writing, and literacy development to secondary school students.

Glencoe

The McGraw-Hill Companies

Copyright © by The McGraw-Hill Companies, Inc. All rights reserved. Permission is granted to reproduce the material contained herein on the condition that such material be reproduced only for classroom use; be provided to students, teachers, and families without charge; and be used solely in conjunction with *Glencoe World History—Modern Times.* Any other reproduction, for use or sale, is prohibited without written permission from the publisher.

Send all inquiries to:
Glencoe/McGraw-Hill
8787 Orion Place
Columbus, OH 43240

ISBN 0-07-867561-8

Printed in the United States of America

12 RHR 13 12

Table of Contents

Letter to the Student vii

Chapter 1   The First Civilization and Empires, Prehistory–A.D. 500
Section 1 The First Humans 1
Section 2 Western Asia and Egypt 6
Section 3 India and China 14

Chapter 2   Ancient Greece and Rome, 1900 B.C.–A.D. 500
Section 1 Ancient Greece..21
Section 2 Rome and the Rise of Christianity 29

Chapter 3   Regional Civilizations, 400–1500
Section 1 The World of Islam 40
Section 2 Early African Civilizations 47
Section 3 The Asian World 52
Section 4 Emerging Europe and the Byzantine Empire 59

Chapter 4   Toward a New World, 800–1500
Section 1 Europe in the Middle Ages 67
Section 2 The Americas 77

Chapter 5   Renaissance and Reformation, 1350–1600
Section 1 The Renaissance..82
Section 2 The Intellectual and Artistic Renaissance 87
Section 3 The Protestant Reformation 92
Section 4 The Spread of Protestantism and the Catholic Response 97

Chapter 6   The Age of Exploration, 1500–1800
Section 1 Exploration and Expansion 103
Section 2 Africa in an Age of Transition 109
Section 3 Southeast Asia in the Era of the Spice Trade 113

Chapter 7   Crisis and Absolutism in Europe, 1550–1715
Section 1 Europe in Crisis: The Wars of Religion 117
Section 2 Social Crises, War, and Revolution 121
Section 3 Response to Crisis: Absolutism...126
Section 4 The World of European Culture 130

Table of Contents

Chapter 8   The Muslim Empires, 1450–1800

Section 1   The Ottoman Empire 135

Section 2   The Rule of the Safavids..141

Section 3   The Grandeur of the Moguls 145

Chapter 9   The East Asian World, 1400–1800

Section 1   China at Its Height 150

Section 2   Chinese Society and Culture 153

Section 3   Tokugawa Japan and Korea 157

Chapter 10   Revolution and Enlightenment, 1550–1800

Section 1   The Scientific Revolution 163

Section 2   The Enlightenment..168

Section 3   The Impact of the Enlightenment 173

Section 4   Colonial Empires and the American Revolution 178

Chapter 11   The French Revolution and Napoleon, 1789–1815

Section 1   The French Revolution Begins 183

Section 2   Radical Revolution and Reaction 188

Section 3   The Age of Napoleon 193

Chapter 12   Industrialization and Nationalism, 1800–1870

Section 1   The Industrial Revolution 199

Section 2   Reaction and Revolution 204

Section 3   National Unification and the National State....................209

Section 4   Culture: Romanticism and Realism................................215

Chapter 13   Mass Society and Democracy, 1870–1914

Section 1   The Growth of Industrial Prosperity 219

Section 2   The Emergence of Mass Society....................................223

Section 3   The National State and Democracy 228

Section 4   Toward the Modern Consciousness................................233

Chapter 14   The Height of Imperialism, 1800–1914

Section 1   Colonial Rule in Southeast Asia 238

Section 2   Empire Building in Africa 243

Section 3   British Rule in India 248

Section 4   Nation Building in Latin America....................................252

Table of Contents

Chapter 15 East Asia Under Challenge, 1800–1914
Section 1 The Decline of the Qing Dynasty 257
Section 2 Revolution in China 263
Section 3 Rise of Modern Japan 268

Chapter 16 War and Revolution, 1914–1919
Section 1 The Road to World War I 273
Section 2 The War 277
Section 3 The Russian Revolution 282
Section 4 End of the War 287

Chapter 17 The West Between the Wars, 1919–1939
Section 1 The Futile Search for Stability 290
Section 2 The Rise of Dictatorial Regimes 294
Section 3 Hitler and Nazi Germany 299
Section 4 Cultural and Intellectual Trends 304

Chapter 18 Nationalism Around the World, 1919–1939
Section 1 Nationalism in the Middle East 308
Section 2 Nationalism in Africa and Asia 313
Section 3 Revolutionary Chaos in China 318
Section 4 Nationalism in Latin America 322

Chapter 19 World War II, 1939–1945
Section 1 Paths to War 326
Section 2 The Course of World War II 330
Section 3 The New Order and the Holocaust 334
Section 4 The Home Front and the Aftermath of the War 338

Chapter 20 Cold War and Postwar Changes, 1945–1970
Section 1 Development of the Cold War 342
Section 2 The Soviet Union and Eastern Europe 347
Section 3 Western Europe and North America 351

Chapter 21 The Contemporary Western World, 1970–Present
Section 1 Decline of the Soviet Union 357
Section 2 Eastern Europe 361
Section 3 Europe and North America 365
Section 4 Western Society and Culture 369

Table of Contents

Chapter 22 Latin America, 1945–Present

Section 1 General Trends in Latin America 376

Section 2 Mexico, Cuba, and Central America 381

Section 3 The Nations of South America 385

Chapter 23 Africa and the Middle East, 1945–Present

Section 1 Independence in Africa 390

Section 2 Conflict in the Middle East 394

Chapter 24 Asia and the Pacific, 1945–Present

Section 1 Communist China 400

Section 2 Independent States in South and Southeast Asia 405

Section 3 Japan and the Pacific 409

Chapter 25 Challenges and Hopes for the Future

Section 1 The Challenges of Our World 413

Section 2 Global Visions 423

Dear Social Studies Student,

Can you believe it? The start of another school year is upon you. How exciting to be learning about different cultures, historical events, and unique places in your social studies class! I believe that this Active Reading Note-Taking Guide *will help you as you learn about your community, nation, and world.*

Note-Taking and Student Success

Did you know that the ability to take notes helps you become a better student? Research suggests that good notes help you become more successful on tests because the act of taking notes helps you remember and understand content. This *Active Reading Note-Taking Guide* is a tool that you can use to achieve this goal. I'd like to share some of the features of this *Active Reading Note-Taking Guide* with you before you begin your studies.

The Cornell Note-Taking System

First, you will notice that the pages in the *Active Reading Note-Taking Guide* are arranged in two columns, which will help you organize your thinking. This two-column design is based on the **Cornell Note-Taking System**, developed at Cornell University. The column on the left side of the page highlights the main ideas and vocabulary of the lesson. This column will help you find information and locate the references in your textbook quickly. You can also use this column to sketch drawings that further help you visually remember the lesson's information. In the column on the right side of the page, you will write detailed notes about the main ideas and vocabulary. The notes you take in this column

will help you focus on the important information in the lesson. As you become more comfortable using the **Cornell Note-Taking System**, you will see that it is an important tool that helps you organize information.

The Importance of Graphic Organizers

Second, there are many graphic organizers in this *Active Reading Note-Taking Guide*. Graphic organizers allow you to see the lesson's important information in a visual format. In addition, graphic organizers help you understand and summarize information, as well as remember the content.

Research-Based Vocabulary Development

Third, you will notice that vocabulary is introduced and practiced throughout the *Active Reading Note-Taking Guide*. When you know the meaning of the words used to discuss information, you are able to understand that information better. Also, you are more likely to be successful in school when you have vocabulary knowledge. When researchers study successful students, they find that as students acquire vocabulary knowledge, their ability to learn improves. The *Active Reading Note-Taking Guide* focuses

Copyright © by The McGraw-Hill Companies, Inc.

on learning words that are very specific to understanding the content of your textbook. It also highlights general academic words that you need to know so that you can understand any textbook. Learning new vocabulary words will help you succeed in school.

Writing Prompts and Note-Taking

Finally, there are a number of writing exercises included in this *Active Reading Note-Taking Guide*. Did you know that writing helps you to think more clearly? It's true. Writing is a useful tool that helps you know if you understand the information in your textbook. It helps you assess what you have learned.

You will see that many of the writing exercises require you to practice the skills of good readers. Good readers *make connections* between their lives and the text and *predict* what will happen next in the reading. They *question* the information and the author of the text, *clarify* information and ideas, and *visualize* what the text is saying. Good readers also *summarize* the information that is presented and *make inferences* or *draw conclusions* about the facts and ideas.

I wish you well as you begin another school year. This *Active Reading Note-Taking Guide* is designed to help you understand the information in your social studies class. The guide will be a valuable tool that will also provide you with skills you can use throughout your life.

I hope you have a successful school year.

Sincerely,

Douglas Fisher

Copyright © by The McGraw-Hill Companies, Inc.

Chapter 1, Section 1
The First Humans

(Pages 19–22)

Reason To Read

Setting a Purpose for Reading Think about these questions as you read:
- What important developments took place during the Paleolithic Age?
- What changes occurred during the Neolithic Revolution that made the development of cities possible?

Main Idea

As you read pages 19–22 in your textbook, complete the chart below by listing the six major characteristics of a civilization.

1.	4.
2.	5.
3.	6.

Sequencing Events

As you read, number the following events in the order in which they occurred.

_____ **Systematic agriculture develops**

_____ ***Homo sapiens sapiens* appear**

_____ **Paleolithic Age begins**

_____ **Neanderthals appear**

_____ **River valley civilizations develop**

Copyright © by The McGraw-Hill Companies, Inc.

 **Key Points**

 **Notes**

Before History *(pages 19–20)*

Monitoring Comprehension

As you read, write down one question from each subhead for a partner to answer. Exchange questions and see if you can answer your partner's questions.

Early Stages of Development

_____

_____

The Spread of Homo Sapiens Sapiens

_____

_____

Terms To Know

Define or describe the following key term from this lesson.

hominids

_____

_____

Academic Vocabulary

Write the letter of the correct definition next to each of these academic vocabulary words from this lesson.

____ **1.** construct

____ **2.** theories

____ **3.** crucial

a. important

b. build

c. statements devised to explain a group of facts

d. short essays on a current topic

The Hunter-Gatherers of the Old Stone Age *(page 20)*

Summarizing

As you read, complete the following sentences to help you summarize the lesson.

1. The _____ describes the period in human history from approximately 2,500,000 to 10,000 B.C. in which humans used simple _____ .

2. Humans lived in _____ and survived by hunting, _____ , and _____ .

Copyright © by The McGraw-Hill Companies, Inc.

3. Over time, Paleolithic people learned how to create

_____, how to use _____ , and how to

adapt to and change their physical _____ .

4. Paleolithic people created a human _____ that

included sophisticated _____ .

Terms To Know

Define or describe the following key term from this lesson.

nomads >

_____

_____

Academic Vocabulary

Use each of the following academic vocabulary words from this lesson in a sentence.

period >

_____

_____

adapt >

_____

_____

The Neolithic Revolution *(page 21)*

Identifying Cause and Effect

As you read, think about the Neolithic Revolution. Then write a paragraph describing the changes that occurred as a result of the development of systematic agriculture.

_____

_____

_____

_____

_____

Copyright © by The McGraw-Hill Companies, Inc.

Terms To Know

Write the letter of the correct definition next to each of these key terms from this lesson.

____ **1.** Neolithic Revolution

____ **2.** systematic agriculture

____ **3.** domestication

a. adaptation for human use

b. the keeping of animals and the growing of food on a regular basis

c. the period from around 3000 to 1200 B.C. characterized by the widespread use of bronze for tools and weapons

d. the shift from hunting and gathering to the keeping of animals and the growing of food on a regular basis

Academic Vocabulary

Define the following academic vocabulary words from this lesson.

revolution >

_____

_____

concentrated >

_____

_____

The Emergence of Civilization *(page 22)*

Drawing Conclusions

As you read, write down three details about the emergence of civilizations in Mesopotamia, Egypt, India, and China. Then write a conclusion you draw based on these details.

_____

_____

_____

_____

Terms To Know

Define or describe the following key term from this lesson.

civilization >

_____

_____

Copyright © by The McGraw-Hill Companies, Inc.

 **Key Points**

 **Notes**

Academic Vocabulary

Define the following academic vocabulary words from this lesson.

> significant

_____

_____

> feature

_____

_____

Section Wrap-up

Now that you have read the section, answer these questions from Setting a Purpose for Reading *at the beginning of the section.*

What important developments took place during the Paleolithic Age?

_____

_____

_____

_____

What changes occurred during the Neolithic Revolution that made the development of cities possible?

_____

_____

_____

_____

Copyright © by The McGraw-Hill Companies, Inc.

Chapter 1, Section 2
Western Asia and Egypt

(Pages 24–34)

Reason To Read

Setting a Purpose for Reading Think about this question as you read:

• How did geography affect the civilizations of western Asia and Egypt?

Main Idea

As you read pages 24–34 in your textbook, complete the chart below by listing the geographic locations of the civilizations of western Asia and Egypt.

Western Asia	Egypt

Sequencing Events

As you read, place the following events on the time line below.

• **Akkadian Empire falls**
• **Hammurabi comes to power**
• **Sargon overruns Sumerian city-states and sets up first empire**
• **King Menes unites Upper and Lower Egypt**
• **Sumerians establish independent city-states**

Copyright © by The McGraw-Hill Companies, Inc.

◆ 3500 B.C.   ◆ 3000 B.C.   ◆ 2500 B.C.   ◆ 2000 B.C.   ◆ 1500 B.C.

The City-States of Ancient Mesopotamia *(pages 24–25)*

Previewing

Preview the section to get an idea of what's ahead. First, skim the section. Then write a sentence or two explaining what you expect to learn. After you have finished reading, revise your statements as necessary.

_____

_____

_____

Terms To Know

Define or describe the following key term from this lesson.

_____

city-states

_____

Academic Vocabulary

Circle the letter of the word or phrase that is closest in meaning to the underlined word.

enabled

1. The abundance of food made possible by irrigation systems <u>enabled</u> large numbers of people to live together in cities.

   a. prevented   **b.** made possible   **c.** encouraged

devoted

2. The Sumerians <u>devoted</u> much of their wealth to building temples and elaborate houses for priests and priestesses.

   a. gave over to   **b.** earned   **c.** gained

Empires in Ancient Mesopotamia *(page 25)*

Evaluating

As you read, think about the geography of the Sumerian city-states. Why was it so easy for Sargon and his army to invade them?

_____

_____

_____

_____

Copyright © by The McGraw-Hill Companies, Inc.

Terms To Know

Define or describe the following key term from this lesson.

empire >

_____

_____

Academic Vocabulary

Use each of the following academic vocabulary words from this lesson in a sentence.

expanded >

_____

_____

conflicts >

_____

_____

The Code of Hammurabi *(pages 26–27)*

Responding

As you read, think about how you would feel living in ancient Mesopotamia under the Code of Hammurabi. What parts of that life do you find attractive? What parts would be difficult for you? Use the lines below to respond.

_____

_____

_____

_____

Terms To Know

Define or describe the following key term from this lesson.

patriarchal >

_____

_____

Copyright © by The McGraw-Hill Companies, Inc.

Academic Vocabulary

Choose one of these two academic vocabulary words from this lesson to fill in each blank.

> principle

> contract

1. Under the Code of Hammurabi, no one was considered legally married

without a _____ .

2. The _____ of retaliation was a fundamental part of
Hammurabi's system of justice.

3. Parents arranged marriages for their children, after which a

_____ was signed.

The Creativity of the Sumerians *(page 27)*

Connecting

As you read the descriptions of the many achievements and inventions of the Sumerians, ask yourself how these affect our lives today. Then write a paragraph describing how one of the Sumerians' inventions directly affects you.

_____

_____

_____

_____

Terms To Know

Define or describe the following key term from this lesson.

> cuneiform

_____

_____

Academic Vocabulary

Use the following academic vocabulary word from this lesson in a sentence.

> communicate

_____

_____

Copyright © by The McGraw-Hill Companies, Inc.

The Course of Egyptian History (pages 27–29)

Outlining As you read this lesson, fill in the outline below.

I. The Old Kingdom

A. _____

B. _____

II. The Pyramids

A. _____

B. _____

III. The Middle Kingdom

A. _____

B. _____

IV. The New Kingdom

A. _____

B. _____

Terms To Know Define or describe the following key term from this lesson.

dynasty >

_____

_____

Academic Vocabulary Define the following academic vocabulary word from this lesson.

unique >

_____

_____

Copyright © by The McGraw-Hill Companies, Inc.

Key Points

 Notes

Society in Ancient Egypt (pages 29–30)

Reviewing

After you have read the lesson, complete the chart below by listing the social classes of ancient Egypt and their roles in society.

Social Class	Role in Society

Academic Vocabulary

Write the letter of the correct definition next to each of these academic vocabulary words from this lesson.

_____ **1.** granted

_____ **2.** military

_____ **3.** labor

a. work

b. gave

c. armed force

d. political rule

Writing, Art, and Science (page 30)

Scanning

Before you read, scan the passage looking for descriptions of Egyptian innovations in writing, art, and science and the impact these had on life at that time. Use the lines below to note your findings.

_____

_____

_____

Terms To Know

Define or describe the following key term from this lesson.

> **hieroglyphics**

_____

Copyright © by The McGraw-Hill Companies, Inc.

New Centers of Civilization: The Israelites *(pages 30–33)*

Monitoring Comprehension

As you read, write down one question from each subhead for a partner to answer. Exchange questions and see if you can answer your partner's questions.

> The "Children of Israel"

_____

_____

> The Spiritual Dimensions of Israel

_____

_____

Terms To Know

Define or describe each of the following key terms from this lesson.

> Judaism

_____

_____

> monotheistic

_____

_____

Academic Vocabulary

Choose one of these two academic vocabulary words from this lesson to fill in each blank.

> migrated

1. The covenant, law, and prophets were three aspects of the Jewish religious _____ .

2. The Israelites _____ from Mesopotamia to the land that they referred to as Canaan.

> tradition

3. In Jewish _____ , God's wishes had all been written down.

Copyright © by The McGraw-Hill Companies, Inc.

The Rise of New Empires (pages 33–34)

Skimming   *Skim this lesson before you begin reading it, looking at headings and words in boldface type. Write a sentence below describing what you expect to learn. After reading, revise your sentence if needed.*

_____

_____

_____

Academic Vocabulary   *Use each of the following academic vocabulary words from this lesson in a sentence.*

internal

_____

_____

unify

_____

_____

Section Wrap-up   *Now that you have read the section, answer this question from* Setting a Purpose for Reading *at the beginning of the section.*

How did geography affect the civilizations of western Asia and Egypt?

_____

_____

_____

_____

_____

Copyright © by The McGraw-Hill Companies, Inc.

Chapter 1, Section 3
India and China
(Pages 36–45)

Reason To Read

Setting a Purpose for Reading Think about these questions as you read:
- How did the caste system influence the lives of people in ancient India?
- Why was the Mandate of Heaven important to Chinese rulers?

Main Idea

As you read pages 36–45 in your textbook, complete the graphic organizer below by showing the similarities and differences between Hinduism and Buddhism.

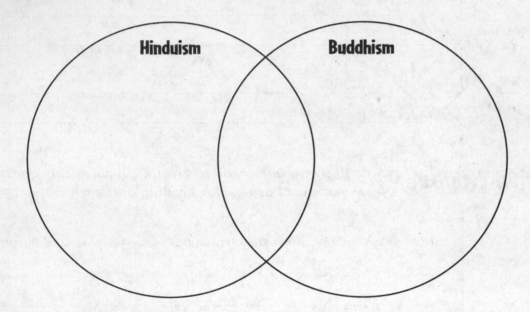

Hinduism   Buddhism

Sequencing Events

As you read, write the correct date next to each event on the time line below.

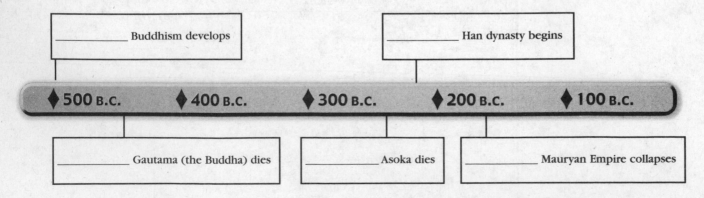

_____ Buddhism develops

_____ Han dynasty begins

◆ 500 B.C.   ◆ 400 B.C.   ◆ 300 B.C.   ◆ 200 B.C.   ◆ 100 B.C.

_____ Gautama (the Buddha) dies

_____ Asoka dies

_____ Mauryan Empire collapses

Copyright © by The McGraw-Hill Companies, Inc.

 **Key Points**

 **Notes**

Early Civilization in India (pages 36–39)

Summarizing

As you read, complete the following sentences to help you summarize the lesson.

1. Around 1500 B.C. the _____ moved across the _____ mountain range into northern India.

2. They invaded the _____ and developed a new Indian _____ based on _____ culture.

3. The _____ of ancient India included the _____ , who were at the top of the Indian social scale.

Terms To Know

Define or describe the following key term from this lesson.

caste system > _____

_____

Academic Vocabulary

Use the following academic vocabulary word from this lesson in a sentence.

apparent > _____

_____

Hinduism (pages 38–39)

Analyzing

How did the Hindu system of reincarnation support the Indian caste system? Write your answer on the lines below.

_____

_____

_____

_____

Copyright © by The McGraw-Hill Companies, Inc.

Terms To Know

Define or describe each of the following key terms from this lesson.

Hinduism _____
_____
_____

reincarnation _____
_____
_____

Academic Vocabulary

Circle the letter of the word or phrase that is closest in meaning to the underlined word.

goal
1. After a number of existences in the earthly world, the soul reaches its final <u>goal</u> in a union with Brahman.

   a. objective   **b.** score   **c.** task

status
2. A person's <u>status</u> is a result of his or her actions in a past existence.

   a. action   **b.** position   **c.** dishonor

Buddhism *(pages 39–40)*

Connecting

As you read this section, focus on the eight steps in the Middle Path. Write a paragraph describing which steps you think might apply to people's lives today.

_____
_____
_____
_____

Terms To Know

Define or describe the following key term from this lesson.

Buddhism _____
_____

Copyright © by The McGraw-Hill Companies, Inc.

Academic Vocabulary

Use each of the following academic vocabulary words from this lesson in a sentence.

ultimate

_____
_____

achieving

_____
_____

New Empires in India *(page 40)*

Sequencing

As you read this lesson, number the following events in the order in which they occurred.

____ Mauryan Empire collapses

____ Asoka dies

____ Gupta Empire begins

____ Mauryan Empire begins

____ Gupta Empire invaded by the Huns

____ Asoka's rule begins

Academic Vocabulary

Define the following academic vocabulary words from this lesson.

network

_____
_____

transport

_____
_____

Copyright © by The McGraw-Hill Companies, Inc.

Early Chinese Civilizations (pages 40–43)

Reviewing

As you read, complete the chart below about the early Chinese civilizations.

Dynasty	Time Period	Characteristics

Terms To Know

Define or describe the following key terms from this lesson.

Mandate of Heaven > _____

_____

Dao > _____

_____

Academic Vocabulary

Write the letter of the correct definition next to each of these academic vocabulary words from this lesson.

_____ **1.** obtain

_____ **2.** source

a. to get or gain

b. to take care of

c. one that supplies information

Copyright © by The McGraw-Hill Companies, Inc.

The Family in Ancient China (pages 43–44)

Determining the Main Idea

As you read, write down the main idea of the passage. Review your statement when you have finished reading and revise as needed.

_____

_____

_____

Terms To Know

Define or describe the following key term from this lesson.

filial piety

_____

_____

Academic Vocabulary

Use each of the following academic vocabulary words from this lesson in a sentence.

symbol

_____

_____

_____

subordinate

_____

_____

The Importance of Confucius (pages 44–45)

Evaluating

As you read, think about Confucius and his beliefs. How do you feel about the two main elements of the Confucian view of the Dao? Can it still apply today? Explain.

_____

_____

_____

_____

Copyright © by The McGraw-Hill Companies, Inc.

Key Points

Notes

Terms To Know

Define or describe the following key term from this lesson.

Confucianism ›

_____

_____

Academic Vocabulary

Define the following academic vocabulary words from this lesson.

elements ›

_____

_____

_____

consists ›

_____

_____

Section Wrap-up

Now that you have read the section, answer these questions from Setting a Purpose for Reading *at the beginning of the section.*

How did the caste system influence the lives of people in ancient India?

_____

_____

_____

Why was the Mandate of Heaven important to Chinese rulers?

_____

_____

_____

Copyright © by The McGraw-Hill Companies, Inc.

Chapter 2, Section 1
Ancient Greece

(Pages 51–60)

Reason To Read

Setting a Purpose for Reading Think about these questions as you read:
- Who lived in the polis?
- How did Athens and Sparta differ?

Main Idea

As you read pages 51–60 in your textbook, complete the graphic organizer below by showing the elements that contributed to the Classical Age of Greece.

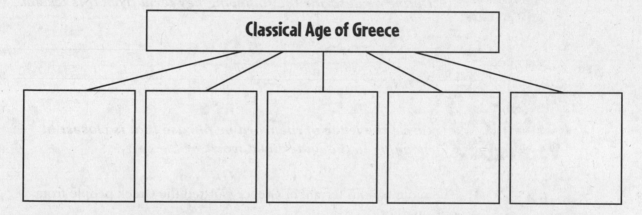

Classical Age of Greece

Sequencing Events

As you read, number the following events in the order in which they occurred.

_____ **Classical Age begins**

_____ **Peloponnesian War ends**

_____ **Mycenaean civilization peaks**

_____ **Alexander takes possession of the Persian Empire**

_____ **Dark Age of Greece begins**

Copyright © by The McGraw-Hill Companies, Inc.

 **Key Points**

 **Notes**

Early Greek Civilization (pages 51–53)

Monitoring Comprehension

As you read, write down one question from each subhead for a partner to answer. Exchange questions and see if you can answer your partner's questions.

The First Greek State: Mycenae >
_____
_____

The Dark Age and Homer >
_____
_____

Terms To Know

Define or describe the following key term from this lesson.

epic poem >
_____
_____

Academic Vocabulary

Circle the letter of the word or phrase that is closest in meaning to the underlined word.

isolated >

1. The mountainous terrain of Greece <u>isolated</u> the Greek people from one another.

   a. set apart   **b.** pulled together   **c.** endangered

site >

2. The <u>site</u> of Mycenae was discovered by a German archaeologist.

   a. capital   **b.** city   **c.** location

Terms To Review

Use each of these terms, which you studied earlier, in a sentence that reflects the term's meaning in this lesson.

consist
(Chapter 1, Section 3) >
_____
_____

period
(Chapter 1, Section 1) >
_____
_____

Copyright © by The McGraw-Hill Companies, Inc.

The Polis: Center of Greek Life (page 53)

Visualizing

As you read, try to imagine how life differed for men, women and children, and slaves and resident aliens in the Greek city-states. Then choose one of these groups, and describe what life in the city-states must have been like for them.

_____

_____

_____

Terms To Know

Write the letter of the correct definition next to each of these key terms from this lesson.

_____ **1.** polis

_____ **2.** acropolis

_____ **3.** democracy

_____ **4.** oligarchy

a. a fortified gathering place at the top of a hill

b. government by the people

c. long poem that tells the deeds of a hero

d. rule by the few

e. city-state

Academic Vocabulary

Define the following academic vocabulary word from this lesson.

assemble >

_____

_____

Sparta (page 54)

Identifying Cause and Effect

After you have read the lesson, write a brief paragraph summarizing the effects of the restrictions on Spartan males.

_____

_____

_____

_____

Copyright © by The McGraw-Hill Companies, Inc.

Key Points

Notes

Academic Vocabulary

Define the following academic vocabulary word from this lesson.

likewise ❯

_____

_____

Terms To Review

Use the following term, which you studied earlier, in a sentence that reflects the term's meaning in this lesson.

military
(Chapter 1, Section 2) ❯

_____

_____

Athens (pages 54–55)

Analyzing

As you read, think about the changes Cleisthenes made in Athens after he took over power from Solon. How did his reforms create the foundation for democracy in Athens?

_____

_____

_____

_____

Academic Vocabulary

Choose one of the following academic vocabulary words from this lesson to fill in each blank.

reacted ❯

1. The reforms of Cleisthenes created the _____ for Athenian democracy.

2. Ruling Athenian aristocrats _____ to political turmoil by giving full power to Solon.

foundations ❯

3. Cleisthenes _____ to the issue of land for poor peasants by passing new reforms.

Copyright © by The McGraw-Hill Companies, Inc.

Terms To Review

Write the definition of the following term that you studied earlier.

unified
(Chapter 1, Section 2)

_____

_____

Classical Greece (pages 55–56)

Drawing Conclusions

As you read, write down three details about the Age of Pericles. Then write a conclusion based on these details.

_____

_____

_____

_____

_____

Terms To Know

Define or describe the following key term from this lesson.

direct democracy

_____

_____

Academic Vocabulary

Define the following academic vocabulary word from this lesson.

participated

_____

_____

Terms To Review

Use the following term, which you studied earlier, in a sentence that reflects the term's meaning in this lesson.

expanded
(Chapter 1, Section 2)

_____

_____

Copyright © by The McGraw-Hill Companies, Inc.

The Culture of Classical Greece (pages 56–59)

Outlining

As you read this lesson, fill in the outline below.

I. The Classical Ideals of Greek Art

    A. _____

    B. _____

    C. _____

II. Greek Drama

    A. _____

    B. _____

III. Greek Philosophy

    A. _____

    B. _____

    C. _____

Academic Vocabulary

Write the letter of the correct definition next to each of these academic vocabulary words from this lesson.

_____ **1.** dominated   **a.** appropriate

                        b. agreeable

_____ **2.** relevant   **c.** influenced

Terms To Review

Define the following term that you studied earlier.

principles
(Chapter 1, Section 2)

_____

_____

Copyright © by The McGraw-Hill Companies, Inc.

Alexander the Great *(pages 59–60)*

Sequencing

As you read, number the following events in the order in which they occurred.

_____ Philip II becomes king of Macedonia

_____ Alexander crosses the Indus River into India

_____ Alexander takes possession of the Persian Empire

_____ the Macedonian army defeats the Greeks at the Battle of Chaeronea

_____ Philip II is assassinated and Alexander becomes king

Academic Vocabulary

Define the following academic vocabulary words from this lesson.

undertake >

_____

_____

task >

_____

_____

The Hellenistic Era *(page 60)*

Skimming

Skim this lesson before you begin reading it, looking at headings and words in boldface type. Write a sentence below describing what you expect to learn in this lesson. After reading, revise your sentence if needed.

_____

_____

_____

Copyright © by The McGraw-Hill Companies, Inc.

Key Points

Notes

Academic Vocabulary

Use each of the following academic vocabulary words from this lesson in a sentence that shows you understand the word's meaning.

derived

_____

_____

evident

_____

_____

Section Wrap-up

Now that you have read the section, answer these questions from Setting a Purpose for Reading *at the beginning of the section.*

Who lived in the polis?

_____

_____

_____

_____

_____

How did Athens and Sparta differ?

_____

_____

_____

_____

_____

Copyright © by The McGraw-Hill Companies, Inc.

Chapter 2, Section 2
Rome and the Rise of Christianity

(Pages 66–76)

Reason To Read

Setting a Purpose for Reading Think about these questions as you read:
- Why did Rome become an empire?
- Why did Christianity grow so quickly?

Main Idea

As you read pages 66–76 in your textbook, complete the chart below by listing the government officials and the legislative bodies of the Roman Republic.

Officials	Legislative Bodies

Sequencing Events

As you read, place the following events on the time line below.
- *Pax Romana* begins
- Visigoths sack Rome
- Western Roman Empire falls
- Constantine proclaims official tolerance of Christianity
- *Pax Romana* ends

◆ A.D. 1   ◆ A.D. 100   ◆ A.D. 300   ◆ A.D. 500

Copyright © by The McGraw-Hill Companies, Inc.

The Emergence of Rome (pages 66–67)

Reviewing

As you read, think about the events that led Rome to become master of the Mediterranean Sea. Then write a paragraph summarizing these events.

_____

_____

_____

_____

Terms To Know

Define or describe the following key term from this lesson.

republic

_____

_____

Academic Vocabulary

Define the following academic vocabulary words from this lesson.

maintains

_____

_____

founded

_____

_____

Terms To Review

Choose one of these two terms, which you studied earlier, to fill in each blank.

tradition
(Chapter 1, Section 2)

1. Under the Roman Confederation, loyal allies could improve their

   _____ by providing soldiers for the Roman army.

status
(Chapter 1, Section 3)

2. Roman _____ says that early Rome was under the control of seven kings.

3. Rome's political _____ changed after Pergamum became Rome's first province in Asia.

Copyright © by The McGraw-Hill Companies, Inc.

The Roman State (pages 67–68)

Evaluating

As you read, think about the differences between patricians and plebeians. Then write a paragraph describing how these differences prevented Rome from becoming a true democracy.

_____

_____

_____

_____

Terms To Know

Define or describe the following key terms from this lesson.

patrician

_____

_____

plebeian

_____

_____

Academic Vocabulary

Define the following academic vocabulary word from this lesson.

civil

_____

_____

Terms To Review

Use the following term, which you studied earlier, in a sentence that reflects the term's meaning.

ultimately
(Chapter 1, Section 3)

_____

_____

 Notes

 Key Points

Copyright © by The McGraw-Hill Companies, Inc.

Key Points / Notes

From Republic to Empire (pages 68–69)

Summarizing

After you have read this lesson, summarize the factors that contributed to disorder and civil war in the Roman Republic during the second and first centuries B.C.

_____

_____

_____

_____

_____

Terms To Know

Define or describe the following key term from this lesson.

imperator

_____

_____

Academic Vocabulary

Use the following academic vocabulary word from this lesson in a sentence that shows you understand the word's meaning.

creating

_____

_____

The Early Empire (pages 69–70)

Reviewing

As you read, focus on the actions of the five good emperors. Then write a paragraph identifying the ways their actions benefited the Early Empire.

_____

_____

_____

_____

_____

Copyright © by The McGraw-Hill Companies, Inc.

Academic Vocabulary

Circle the letter of the word or phrase that is closest in meaning to the underlined word.

arbitrary

1. During the *Pax Romana* rulers maintained peace in the empire and ended <u>arbitrary</u> executions.

   a. necessary

   b. based on individual preference

   c. based on a majority vote

domestic

2. During the *Pax Romana* rulers supported <u>domestic</u> policies that were helpful to the empire.

   a. relating to a country's internal affairs

   b. relating to international affairs

   c. relating to affairs between two different countries

Roman Law (pages 70–71)

Connecting

As you read, think about the Roman system of law. Then identify at least two principles in the Law of Nations that are still recognized today.

_____

_____

_____

_____

Academic Vocabulary

Define the following academic vocabulary word from this lesson.

generations

_____

_____

Copyright © by The McGraw-Hill Companies, Inc.

Key Points | Notes

Slavery in the Roman Empire *(page 71)*

Identifying Cause and Effect

After you have read the lesson, write a paragraph describing the effects the Roman conquest of the Mediterranean had on slavery in the Roman world.

_____

_____

_____

_____

Academic Vocabulary

Choose one of the following academic vocabulary words from this lesson to fill in each blank.

relied

1. No people had more slaves or _____ so much on slavery as the Romans did.

estates

2. Slaves in the Roman Empire built roads and buildings and farmed the large _____ of the wealthy.

3. Some Romans _____ on Greek slaves to tutor their children.

Daily Life in the City of Rome *(pages 71–72)*

Analyzing

As you read, think about the gap that existed between the rich and the poor in Rome. Then write a paragraph describing the differences in the daily lives of these two groups of people.

_____

_____

_____

_____

Copyright © by The McGraw-Hill Companies, Inc.

Academic Vocabulary

Use the following academic vocabulary word from this lesson in a sentence.

resided

_____

_____

Roman Culture _(page 72)_

Scanning

Before you read, scan the passage looking for examples of Roman culture and its impact on the world. Use the lines below to jot down notes as you scan.

_____

_____

_____

Academic Vocabulary

Define the following academic vocabulary words from this lesson.

overall

_____

_____

thereby

_____

_____

Terms To Review

Write the letter of the correct definition next to each of these terms that you studied earlier.

____ **1.** features
(Chapter 1, Section 1)

____ **2.** network
(Chapter 1, Section 3)

a. a system of interconnected pieces

b. a telephone system

c. elements

Copyright © by The McGraw-Hill Companies, Inc.

 **Key Points**

 **Notes**

The Emergence of Christianity (pages 72–73)

Skimming   *Read the title and quickly look over the passage to get a general idea of its content. Then write a sentence or two explaining what you think the passage is about.*

_____

_____

_____

_____

Academic Vocabulary   *Use each of the following academic vocabulary words from this lesson in a sentence.*

considerable >   _____

_____

decades >   _____

_____

The Spread of Christianity (pages 73–74)

Summarizing   *As you read, complete the following sentences to help you summarize the lesson.*

1. Christianity began as a _____ movement within

_____ .

2. _____ was recognized as the _____

of the apostles.

3. Between A.D. 70 and 100, the _____ about Jesus

became the basis of the written _____ .

4. These writings, along with the _____ and

teachings, became the basis of the _____ .

Copyright © by The McGraw-Hill Companies, Inc.

5. Many Romans came to view Christians as _____ ,

and the government began _____ Christians.

Terms To Know

Define or describe the following key term from this lesson.

Christianity > _____

_____

Academic Vocabulary

Circle the letter of the word or phrase that is closest in meaning to the underlined word.

major > **1.** By 100, Christian churches had been established in most of the <u>major</u> cities of the eastern hemisphere.

    a. less populated

    b. greater in rank or importance

    c. protected by the military

contrast > **2.** In <u>contrast</u> to their treatment in the first century, the persecution of Christians in the second century diminished.

    a. comparison   **b.** similarity   **c.** identity

The Triumph of Christianity (page 74)

Evaluating

As you read, think about how Christianity triumphed even after being persecuted by the Romans. What benefits did Christianity offer to individuals and to Roman society as a whole?

_____

_____

_____

_____

Copyright © by The McGraw-Hill Companies, Inc.

Key Points

Notes

Terms To Know

Define or describe each of the following key terms from this lesson.

clergy

_____

_____

laity

_____

_____

The Decline (pages 74–75)

Analyzing

As you read, think about the reforms of Diocletian and Constantine. Then write a paragraph comparing the short-term effects and the long-term effects of their policies.

_____

_____

_____

_____

Academic Vocabulary

Define the following academic vocabulary word from this lesson.

revenues

_____

_____

The Fall (page 76)

Sequencing

As you read, number the following events in the order in which they occurred.

_____ The Western Roman Empire collapses

_____ The Visigoths move south and west across the Danube River into Roman territory

_____ The Huns move into eastern Europe

_____ The Visigoths sack Rome

Copyright © by The McGraw-Hill Companies, Inc.

 Key Points  Notes

Academic Vocabulary

Use the following academic vocabulary word from this lesson in a sentence.

 series

_____

_____

Section Wrap-up

Now that you have read the section, answer these questions from Setting a Purpose for Reading *at the beginning of the section.*

Why did Rome become an empire?

_____

_____

_____

_____

_____

Why did Christianity grow so quickly?

_____

_____

_____

_____

_____

Copyright © by The McGraw-Hill Companies, Inc.

Chapter 3, Section 1
The World of Islam

(Pages 89–95)

Reason To Read

Setting a Purpose for Reading Think about these questions as you read:
- What are the major beliefs and principles of Islam?
- What major developments occurred under the Umayyads and Abbasids?

Main Idea

As you read pages 89–95 in your textbook, complete the chart below by identifying the achievements of the Islamic civilization.

Achievements of Islamic Civilization

Sequencing Events

As you read, place the following events on the time line below.

- **Umayyads establish Islamic Empire**
- **Mongols capture Baghdad**
- **Abbasid dynasty comes to power**
- **Muhammad receives first message**
- **Abbasids build new capital city at Baghdad**

| ◆ 600 | ◆ 800 | ◆ 1000 | ◆ 1200 |

Copyright © by The McGraw-Hill Companies, Inc.

The Arabs *(pages 89–90)*

Identifying Cause and Effect

As you read, think about life for people living on the Arabian Peninsula. Then write a paragraph describing the factors that contributed to the growth of towns in this region.

_____

_____

_____

_____

Academic Vocabulary

Define the following academic vocabulary word from this lesson.

survival

_____

_____

The Life of Muhammad *(page 90)*

Scanning

Before you read, scan the passage looking for important events in the life of Muhammad. On the lines provided below, write down notes on how these events affected the Muslim religion.

_____

_____

_____

_____

Terms To Know

Define or describe each of the following key terms from this lesson.

Islam

_____

_____

Hijrah

_____

Copyright © by The McGraw-Hill Companies, Inc.

Key Points

Notes

Academic Vocabulary

Circle the letter of the word or phrase that is closest in meaning to the underlined word.

convince

1. Muhammad tried to <u>convince</u> the people of Makkah to accept his message.

   a. discourage   **b.** persuade   **c.** change

converted

2. Eventually, many of the people in Makkah <u>converted</u> to Islam.

   a. returned   **b.** translated   **c.** changed

The Teachings of Muhammad (pages 90–91)

Connecting

As you read, compare Islam to Judaism and Christianity. Summarize your thoughts in a paragraph below.

_____

_____

_____

_____

Academic Vocabulary

Use each of the following academic vocabulary words from this lesson in a sentence.

similar

_____

_____

rejected

_____

_____

Terms To Review

Write the definition of the following term that you studied earlier.

monotheistic
(Chapter 1, Section 2)

_____

_____

Copyright © by The McGraw-Hill Companies, Inc.

Creation of an Arab Empire *(pages 91–92)*

Sequencing

As you read, number the following events in the order in which they occurred.

_____ Arabs, unified under Abu Bakr, defeat the Byzantine army

_____ Abu Bakr named caliph

_____ Egypt and areas of North Africa added to the Arab Empire

_____ Islamic movement begins to grow

_____ Muhammad dies

Terms To Know

Define or describe the following key term from this lesson.

caliph

_____

_____

Academic Vocabulary

Choose one of the following academic vocabulary words from this lesson to fill in each blank.

1. The death of Muhammad left his followers with a problem—he had

never named a _____ .

successor

2. The courage of the Arab soldiers was _____ by their

belief that they were assured a place in Paradise if they died in battle.

enhanced

3. After his death, some of Muhammad's followers chose Abu Bakr as his

_____ .

Terms To Review

Write the definition of the following term that you studied earlier.

series
(Chapter 2, Section 2)

_____

_____

Copyright © by The McGraw-Hill Companies, Inc.

Successors of the Arab Empire (pages 92–93)

Outlining   *As you read this lesson, fill in the outline below.*

I. The Umayyads

A. _____

B. _____

II. The Abbasid Dynasty

A. _____

B. _____

III. The Seljuk Turks

A. _____

B. _____

IV. The Mongols

A. _____

B. _____

Terms To Know   *Define or describe the following key term from this lesson.*

sultan

_____

_____

Academic Vocabulary   *Define the following academic vocabulary word from this lesson.*

occupied

_____

_____

Terms To Review   *Use the following term, which you studied earlier, in a sentence that reflects the term's meaning in this lesson.*

major
(Chapter 2, Section 2)

_____

_____

Copyright © by The McGraw-Hill Companies, Inc.

Economy and Social Structure (page 95)

Responding

As you read, think about how you would feel living in a city in the Arab Empire. What parts of that life do you think you would find attractive? Which elements would be difficult for you? Use the lines provided below to respond.

_____

_____

_____

_____

Academic Vocabulary

Use the following academic vocabulary word from this lesson in a sentence.

contributed

_____

_____

Terms To Review

Write the definition of the following term that you studied earlier.

dynasty
(Chapter 1, Section 2)

_____

_____

The Brilliance of Islamic Culture (pages 94–95)

Monitoring Comprehension

As you read, write down one question from each subhead for a partner to answer. Exchange questions and see if you can answer your partner's questions.

Philosophy and Science

_____

_____

Art and Architecture

_____

Copyright © by The McGraw-Hill Companies, Inc.

Key Points

Notes

Terms To Know

Define or describe each of the following key terms from this lesson.

astrolabe >
_____
_____

mosques >
_____
_____

Academic Vocabulary

Write the letter of the correct definition next to each of these academic vocabulary words from this lesson.

____ **1.** aware

____ **2.** available

____ **3.** accompanied

a. accessible

b. burdened

c. supplemented

d. knowledgeable

Section Wrap-up

Now that you have read the section, answer these questions from Setting a Purpose for Reading *at the beginning of the section.*

What are the major beliefs and principles of Islam?

_____
_____
_____
_____

What major developments occurred under the Umayyads and Abbasids?

_____
_____
_____
_____

Copyright © by The McGraw-Hill Companies, Inc.

Chapter 3, Section 2
Early African Civilizations
(Pages 97–101)

Reason To Read

Setting a Purpose for Reading Think about these questions as you read:
- What are the four distinct climate zones of Africa and where are they located?
- What factors led to the spread of Islam in Africa?

Main Idea

As you read pages 97–101 in your textbook, complete the chart below by listing the African kingdoms discussed in this chapter and whether they were in north, south, east, or west Africa

Kingdom	Location

Sequencing Events

As you read, number the following events in the order in which they occurred.

_____ **Arab forces take control of Egypt**

_____ **Mansa Musa begins reign**

_____ **Muhammad Ture expands Songhai**

_____ **Kush declines as Axum emerges**

_____ **Ghana emerges as a trading state**

Copyright © by The McGraw-Hill Companies, Inc.

Key Points

Notes

The Emergence of Civilization (pages 97–98)

Monitoring Comprehension

After you have read the lesson, write a paragraph describing the first three civilizations in Africa.

_____

_____

_____

_____

_____

_____

Terms To Know

Define or describe the following key term from this lesson.

savanna

_____

_____

Academic Vocabulary

Circle the letter of the word or phrase that is closest in meaning to the underlined word.

located

1. Axum was <u>located</u> in the highlands of present-day Ethiopia.

   a. attacked   **b.** situated   **c.** planned

impact

2. The rise of Islam in the Arabian Peninsula had an <u>impact</u> on Africa.

   a. effect   **b.** help   **c.** reaction

region

3. Kush emerged as a major trading state in the <u>region</u>.

   a. country

   b. urban area with 100,000 people

   c. geographic area with similar characteristics

Copyright © by The McGraw-Hill Companies, Inc.

The Royal Kingdoms of West Africa (pages 98–100)

Reviewing

As you read the lesson, complete the chart below by listing the royal kingdoms of West Africa and describing the accomplishments of each.

Kingdom	Accomplishments

Academic Vocabulary

Define the following academic vocabulary words from this lesson.

emerged >

_____

_____

secure >

_____

_____

Terms To Review

Use the term below, which you studied earlier, in a sentence that reflects the term's meaning in this lesson.

adapted >
(Chapter 1, Section 1)

_____

_____

Copyright © by The McGraw-Hill Companies, Inc.

Societies in East and South Africa (page 100)

Summarizing

As you read, complete the following sentences to help you summarize the lesson.

1. Farming peoples who spoke dialects of _____

   began to move from the region of the Niger River into the

   _____ River basin.

2. Muslims from the _____ Peninsula and the

   _____ Gulf began to settle at such ports as

   Mogadishu and _____ .

3. _____ was the wealthiest and most powerful

   state in southern Africa, prospering from the _____

   with traditional communities on the _____ coast.

Terms To Know

Define or describe the following key term from this lesson.

Bantu

_____

_____

Academic Vocabulary

Use each of the following academic vocabulary words from this lesson in a sentence that shows you understand the word's meaning.

communities

_____

_____

illustrate

_____

_____

Copyright © by The McGraw-Hill Companies, Inc.

Key Points

Notes

African Society and Culture (page 101)

Responding

As you read this lesson, think about what grabs your attention as you read. Write down two facts you find interesting or surprising.

_____

_____

_____

_____

Terms To Know

Define or describe the following key term from this lesson.

lineage groups

_____

_____

Academic Vocabulary

Write the letter of the correct definition next to each of these academic vocabulary words from this lesson.

____ **1.** rigid

____ **2.** varied

a. differed

b. matched

c. strict

Section Wrap-up

Now that you have read the section, answer these questions from Setting a Purpose for Reading at the beginning of the section.

What are the four distinct climate zones of Africa and where are they located?

_____

_____

_____

What factors led to the spread of Islam in Africa?

_____

_____

_____

Copyright © by The McGraw-Hill Companies, Inc.

Chapter 3, Section 3
The Asian World
(Pages 103–111)

Reason To Read

Setting a Purpose for Reading Think about these questions as you read:
- Why did Japan not develop a centralized government like China's?
- What impact did Muslim rule have on India?

Main Idea

As you read pages 103–111 in your textbook, complete the graphic organizer below by identifying all the civilizations that were affected by Mongol expansion.

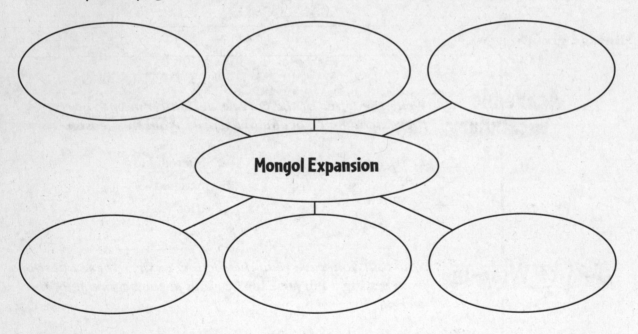

Mongol Expansion

Sequencing Events

As you read, write the correct date next to each event on the time line below.

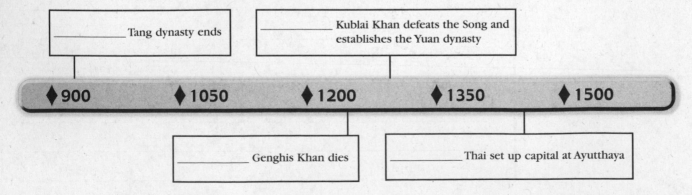

_____ Tang dynasty ends

_____ Kublai Khan defeats the Song and establishes the Yuan dynasty

♦ 900   ♦ 1050   ♦ 1200   ♦ 1350   ♦ 1500

_____ Genghis Khan dies

_____ Thai set up capital at Ayutthaya

Copyright © by The McGraw-Hill Companies, Inc.

China Reunified (pages 103–105)

Summarizing

As you read, think about the changes that took place in China in the era from the beginning of the Sui dynasty to the end of the Song dynasty. Then summarize the political and economic changes that occurred.

_____

_____

_____

_____

Academic Vocabulary

Define the following academic vocabulary word from this lesson.

economy >

_____

_____

Terms To Review

Use the following term, which you studied earlier, in a sentence that reflects the term's meaning.

civil
(Chapter 2, Section 2) >

_____

_____

The Mongol Empire (pages 105–107)

Monitoring Comprehension

As you read, write down one question from each subhead for a partner to answer. Exchange questions and see if you can answer your partner's questions.

The Mongol Dynasty in China >

_____

_____

_____

Religion >

_____

_____

Copyright © by The McGraw-Hill Companies, Inc.

Key Points / Notes

A Golden Age in Art and Literature

_____

_____

Terms To Know

Define or describe the following key term from this lesson.

khanates

_____

_____

Academic Vocabulary

Choose one of these academic vocabulary words from this lesson to fill in each blank.

undergone

1. Confucianism became dominant at court during the Song dynasty, a position it _____ until the early twentieth century.

retained

2. By the time the Mongols established their dynasty in China, religious preferences had _____ a number of changes.

3. The poem "Quiet Night Thoughts" has been _____ and recited by Chinese schoolchildren over many years.

The Rise of the Japanese State *(pages 107–108)*

Sequencing

As you read, number the following events in the order in which they occurred.

_____ Civil war destroys Kyoto and central authority disappears

_____ Shotoku Taishi attempts to unify the various Japanese clans

_____ Political power falls into the hands of the Fujiwara clan

_____ Centralized government under the shogun is created

_____ New class of military servants emerges

Copyright © by The McGraw-Hill Companies, Inc.

Terms To Know

Write the letter of the correct definition next to each of these key terms from this lesson.

_____ **1.** samurai

_____ **2.** Bushido

_____ **3.** shogun

_____ **4.** daimyo

a. the key to proper behavior under Confucianism

b. the strict code by which Japanese samurai were supposed to live

c. Japanese warriors similar to the knights of medieval Europe

d. heads of noble families in Japan who controlled vast landed estates and relied on samurai for protection

e. a powerful military leader in Japan

Academic Vocabulary

Define the following academic vocabulary word from this lesson.

challenge

_____

_____

Terms To Review

Use the following term, which you studied earlier, in a sentence that reflects the term's meaning.

dominated
(Chapter 2, Section 1)

_____

_____

Life and Culture in Early Japan (pages 108–109)

Connecting

As you read, compare the art and architecture of early Japan with the art and architecture in the United States today. Summarize your thoughts in a paragraph.

_____

_____

_____

_____

Copyright © by The McGraw-Hill Companies, Inc.

Key Points

Terms To Know

Shinto

_____
_____

Academic Vocabulary

items

_____
_____

Terms To Review

maintain
(Chapter 2, Section 2)

_____
_____

resided
(Chapter 2, Section 2)

_____
_____

India after the Guptas (pages 109–110)

Reviewing

Notes

Define or describe the following key term from this lesson.

Use the following academic vocabulary word from this lesson in a sentence that shows you understand the word's meaning.

Write the definition of each of the following terms that you studied earlier.

As you read, think about Muslim rulers in India. Then write a paragraph describing how these rulers viewed themselves.

_____
_____
_____
_____
_____

Copyright © by The McGraw-Hill Companies, Inc.

 **Key Points**

 **Notes**

Academic Vocabulary

Use each of the following academic vocabulary words from this lesson in a sentence.

> **brief**

_____
_____
_____

> **nevertheless**

_____
_____

Terms To Review

Define the following term that you studied earlier.

> **overall**

_____
_____

Civilization in Southeast Asia (pages 110–111)

Synthesizing

India and China strongly influenced the culture of Southeast Asia. As you read, think of what cultures have influenced different aspects of your community. Summarize your thoughts in a paragraph.

_____
_____
_____
_____

Terms To Know

Define or describe the following key term from this lesson.

> **archipelago**

_____
_____

Copyright © by The McGraw-Hill Companies, Inc.

 **Key Points**

 **Notes**

Academic Vocabulary

Define the following academic vocabulary word from this lesson.

techniques

_____

_____

Terms To Review

Use each of the following terms, which you studied earlier, in a sentence.

unique
(Chapter 1, Section 2)

_____

_____

founded
(Chapter 2, Section 2)

_____

_____

Section Wrap-up

Now that you have read the section, answer these questions from Setting a Purpose for Reading *at the beginning of the section.*

Why did Japan not develop a centralized government like China's?

_____

_____

_____

_____

What impact did Muslim rule have on India?

_____

_____

_____

_____

Copyright © by The McGraw-Hill Companies, Inc.

Chapter 3, Section 4
Emerging Europe and the Byzantine Empire
(Pages 116–123)

Reason To Read

Setting a Purpose for Reading Think about these questions as you read:
- What led to the development of feudalism?
- What was the impact of the Crusades?

Main Idea

As you read pages 116–123 in your textbook, complete the chart below by listing the differences between the systems of feudalism and empires.

Feudalism	Empires

Sequencing Events

As you read, place the following events on the time line below.

- **Battle of Hastings is fought**
- **Magna Carta is signed**
- **Charlemagne is crowned Roman emperor**
- **Clovis establishes Frankish kingdom**
- **Justinian becomes emperor of the Eastern Roman Empire**

◆ 500   ◆ 800   ◆ 1100   ◆ 1300

Copyright © by The McGraw-Hill Companies, Inc.

Key Points

 Notes

The New Germanic Kingdoms (pages 116–117)

Previewing

Preview the lesson to get an idea of what's ahead. First, skim the passage. Then write a sentence or two explaining what you expect to learn. After you have finished reading, revise your statements as necessary.

_____

_____

_____

Terms To Review

Write the definition of the following term that you studied earlier.

elements
(Chapter 1, Section 3)

_____

_____

The Role of the Church (page 117)

Monitoring Comprehension

As you read, think about the Christian church. Then write a paragraph explaining how it was organized in the Roman Empire.

_____

_____

_____

_____

Terms To Know

Define or describe the following key terms from this lesson.

pope

_____

_____

monk

_____

_____

Copyright © by The McGraw-Hill Companies, Inc.

 **Key Points**

 **Notes**

Academic Vocabulary

Use each of the following academic vocabulary words from this lesson in a sentence.

defined > _____

_____

_____

pursues > _____

_____

_____

Charlemagne and the Carolingians (pages 117–118)

Analyzing

As you read, think about Charlemagne and his actions. Then write two or three sentences explaining the significance of Charlemagne's coronation as Roman emperor.

_____

_____

_____

_____

Academic Vocabulary

Choose one of the following academic vocabulary words from this lesson to fill in each blank.

dynamic >

1. Although he was unable to read or write, Charlemagne was

_____ and was a patron of learning.

2. Charlemagne was the _____ and powerful ruler of the Frankish kingdom.

intelligent >

3. The Carolingian Empire was _____ ; it grew to cover much of western and central Europe.

 Copyright © by The McGraw-Hill Companies, Inc.

Terms To Review

Write the definition of the following term that you studied earlier.

empire
(Chapter 1, Section 2)

> _____

> _____

Feudalism (pages 118–119)

Synthesizing

As you read, focus on the relationship between lords and vassals. Then write a brief help wanted advertisement for a job as a vassal. The advertisement should summarize the requirements and roles of a vassal.

_____

_____

_____

_____

Terms To Know

Write the letter of the correct definition next to each of these key terms from this lesson.

____ **1.** feudalism

____ **2.** vassal

____ **3.** fief

a. a man who pursues a life of total dedication to God

b. a man who served a lord in a military capacity

c. the grant of land made to a vassal

d. political and social system that developed during the Middle Ages

Academic Vocabulary

Define the following academic vocabulary word from this lesson.

capacity

> _____

> _____

Copyright © by The McGraw-Hill Companies, Inc.

 **Key Points**

 **Notes**

Terms To Review

Use each of the following terms, which you studied earlier, in a sentence that reflects the term's meaning.

granted
(Chapter 1, Section 2)

_____

_____

contract
(Chapter 1, Section 2)

_____

_____

The Growth of European Kingdoms (pages 119–121)

Outlining   *As you read this lesson, fill in the outline below.*

I. England in the High Middle Ages

   A. _____

   B. _____

II. The French Kingdom

   A. _____

   B. _____

III. The Holy Roman Empire

   A. _____

   B. _____

IV. Central and Eastern Europe

   A. _____

   B. _____

V. Russia

   A. _____

   B. _____

Copyright © by The McGraw-Hill Companies, Inc.

Terms To Know

Define or describe each of the following key terms from this lesson.

common law

_____

_____

Magna Carta

_____

_____

Academic Vocabulary

Define the following academic vocabulary word from this lesson.

eventually

_____

_____

The Byzantine Empire (pages 122–123)

Identifying Cause and Effect

As you read, think about the Eastern Roman Empire. Then write a paragraph describing the effects of the rise of Islam on the empire.

_____

_____

_____

_____

Academic Vocabulary

Define the following academic vocabulary words from this lesson.

achieved

_____

_____

legal

_____

_____

Copyright © by The McGraw-Hill Companies, Inc.

Key Points

Notes

Terms To Review

Use each of the following terms, which you studied earlier, in a sentence that reflects the term's meaning in this lesson.

achieved
(Chapter 1, Section 3)

_____
_____

contrast
(Chapter 2, Section 2)

_____
_____

The Crusades *(page 123)*

Drawing Conclusions

As you read, write down three details about the Crusades. Then write a conclusion you draw based on these details.

_____
_____
_____
_____

Terms To Know

Define or describe the following key term from this lesson.

Crusades

_____
_____

Academic Vocabulary

Define the following academic vocabulary words from this lesson.

responded

_____
_____

benefited

_____
_____

Copyright © by The McGraw-Hill Companies, Inc.

Now that you have read the section, answer these questions from Setting a Purpose for Reading *at the beginning of the section.*

What led to the development of feudalism?

_____

_____

_____

_____

_____

What was the impact of the Crusades?

_____

_____

_____

_____

_____

Copyright © by The McGraw-Hill Companies, Inc.

Chapter 4, Section 1
Europe in the Middle Ages
(Pages 129–138)

Reason To Read

Setting a Purpose for Reading Think about these questions as you read:
- Why were church leaders often at odds with European rulers?
- How did the Black Death impact European society?

Main Idea

As you read pages 129–138 in your textbook, complete the graphic organizer below by showing the effects of the growth of towns on medieval European society.

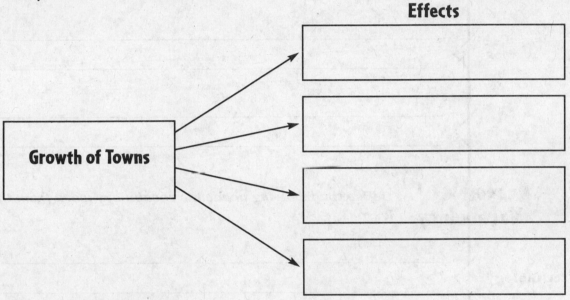

Effects

Growth of Towns

Sequencing Events

As you read, write the correct date next to each event on the time line below.

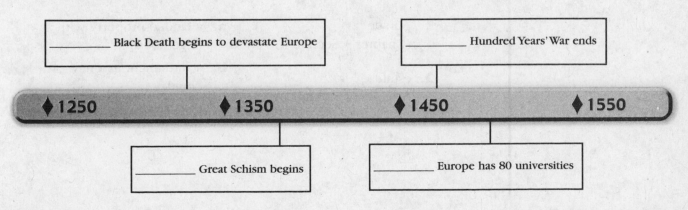

_____ Black Death begins to devastate Europe

_____ Hundred Years' War ends

♦ 1250   ♦ 1350   ♦ 1450   ♦ 1550

_____ Great Schism begins

_____ Europe has 80 universities

Copyright © by The McGraw-Hill Companies, Inc.

The New Agriculture (pages 129–131)

Identifying Cause and Effect

As you read this lesson, focus on why the European population increased dramatically during the High Middle Ages (1000–1300). Summarize the causes in a paragraph.

_____

_____

_____

_____

Terms To Know

Define or describe each of the following terms from this lesson.

manor

_____

_____

serfs

_____

_____

Academic Vocabulary

Define the following academic vocabulary word from this lesson.

technology

_____

_____

Terms To Review

Write the letter of the correct definition next to each of these terms that you studied earlier.

_____ **1.** pursue
(Chapter 3, Section 4)

_____ **2.** estate
(Chapter 2, Section 2)

a. a landed property with a large house

b. a settlement in a new country

c. to engage in

Copyright © by The McGraw-Hill Companies, Inc.

The Revival of Trade *(page 131)*

Responding

As you read, think about the fairs in the Middle Ages and compare them with arts and crafts shows or festivals in your community. Are the purposes the same? How do the items for sale or the music compare? Summarize your thoughts in a paragraph.

_____

_____

_____

_____

_____

Terms To Know

Define or describe each of the following key terms from this lesson.

> money economy

_____

_____

> commercial capitalism

_____

_____

Terms To Review

Use each of the following terms, which you studied earlier, in a sentence that reflects the term's meaning in this lesson.

> foundation
> (Chapter 2, Section 1)

_____

_____

> emerge
> (Chapter 3, Section 2)

_____

_____

Copyright © by The McGraw-Hill Companies, Inc.

The Growth of Cities (pages 131–132)

Analyzing

As you read, notice the connection between trade and cities. Think about how new homes and new stores or shopping malls are connected. In your town or city, was a mall built first and then homes built later, or was it the reverse? In a short paragraph, explain why homes and stores are connected.

_____

_____

_____

_____

Terms To Know

Define or describe the following key term from this lesson.

guilds

_____

_____

The Papal Monarchy (pages 132–133)

Interpreting

As you read the lesson, ask yourself why Pope Gregory VII believed that he had the right to tell the king of Germany what to do. Write a paragraph explaining Pope Gregory's ideas about the relationship between heaven and earth.

_____

_____

_____

_____

Academic Vocabulary

Define the following academic vocabulary words from this lesson.

administrators

_____

_____

Copyright © by The McGraw-Hill Companies, Inc.

 **Key Points**

 **Notes**

inclined >

_____
_____
_____

authority >

_____
_____

Terms To Review

Use the following term, which you studied earlier, in a sentence that reflects the term's meaning.

convinced >
(Chapter 3, Section 1)

_____
_____

New Religious Orders *(pages 133–134)*

Analyzing

After you read this lesson, write a paragraph describing how the Franciscans and the Dominicans affected the lives of the people they worked among.

_____
_____
_____
_____

Terms To Know

Define or describe each of the following key terms from this lesson.

heresy >

_____
_____

Inquisition >

_____
_____

Copyright © by The McGraw-Hill Companies, Inc.

Terms To Review

Circle the letter of the word or phrase that is closest in meaning to the underlined term that you studied earlier.

impact
(Chapter 3, Section 2)

1. The Franciscans and the Dominicans had a strong <u>impact</u> on the lives of people.

   a. impression   **b.** resemblance   **c.** collision

undertook
(Chapter 3, Section 1)

2. The Franciscans <u>undertook</u> missionary work first in Italy, then in the rest of Europe, and the Muslim world.

   a. refused   **b.** committed to   **c.** finished

Popular Religion in the High Middle Ages *(pages 134–135)*

Evaluating

As you read, think about the role that saints played in the life of a peasant. Then write a brief paragraph explaining why saints were so important to Christians in the High Middle Ages.

_____

_____

_____

_____

Terms To Know

Define or describe the following key term from this lesson.

sacraments

_____

_____

Academic Vocabulary

Use the following academic vocabulary word from this lesson in a sentence that shows you understand the word's meaning.

intensely

_____

_____

Copyright © by The McGraw-Hill Companies, Inc.

 **Key Points**

 **Notes**

Terms To Review

Define the following term that you studied earlier.

significance
(Chapter 1, Section 2)

_____

_____

The Rise of Universities *(pages 135–136)*

Connecting

As you read, notice what subjects the liberal arts curriculum for students in the Middle Ages included. On the lines below, list three courses you have studied in high school. Then in a sentence, explain how your courses are related to or entirely different from the liberal arts curriculum.

_____

_____

_____

_____

Terms To Know

Define or describe the following key term from this lesson.

theology

_____

_____

Academic Vocabulary

Choose one of these two academic vocabulary words from this lesson to fill in each blank.

logic

1. Few students could afford books, so teachers read from the basic

_____ and then added their own explanations.

text

2. The traditional liberal arts curriculum included grammar,

_____ , music, and astronomy.

3. Teaching at a medieval university was done by the lecture method in

which students depended on their teacher's lectures rather than on

the written _____ .

Copyright © by The McGraw-Hill Companies, Inc.

Architecture (page 136)

Reviewing

As you read this lesson, focus on the advances of architecture made during the High Middle Ages. Summarize these advances and their benefits in a paragraph.

_____
_____
_____
_____
_____

Academic Vocabulary

Define the following academic vocabulary words from this lesson.

innovation

_____
_____

distribute

_____
_____

structures

_____
_____

The Late Middle Ages (pages 136–138)

Outlining

As you read the lesson, fill in the outline below.

I. The Black Death

    A. _____

    B. _____

II. The Decline of Church Power

    A. _____

    B. _____

Copyright © by The McGraw-Hill Companies, Inc.

III. Political Crisis and Recovery

  A. _____

  B. _____

Terms To Know

Define or describe the following key term from this lesson.

new monarchies

_____

_____

Academic Vocabulary

Define the following academic vocabulary words from this lesson.

percent

_____

_____

recovery

_____

_____

Terms To Review

Use each of the following terms, which you studied earlier, in a sentence that reflects the term's meaning in this lesson.

challenged
(Chapter 3, Section 3)

_____

_____

economic
(Chapter 3, Section 3)

_____

_____

Copyright © by The McGraw-Hill Companies, Inc.

Now that you have read the section, answer these questions from Setting a Purpose for Reading *at the beginning of the section.*

Why were church leaders often at odds with European rulers?

_____

_____

_____

_____

How did the Black Death impact European society?

_____

_____

_____

_____

Copyright © by The McGraw-Hill Companies, Inc.

Chapter 4, Section 2
The Americas
(Pages 140–144)

Reason To Read

Setting a Purpose for Reading Think about these questions as you read:
- Who were the first inhabitants of the Americas?
- What forces ended the Aztec and Incan civilizations?

Main Idea

As you read pages 140–144 in your textbook, complete the chart below by describing the characteristics of Mayan, Aztec, and Incan cultures.

	Maya	**Aztec**	**Inca**
People			
Location			
Religion			
Architecture			
Year/Reason Declined			

Sequencing Events

As you read, number the following events in the order in which they occurred.

_____ **Incan ruler Pachacuti builds empire**

_____ **Mayan civilization begins**

_____ **Toltec civilization declines**

_____ **Olmec civilization emerges**

_____ **Aztec build capital city at Tenochtitlán**

Copyright © by The McGraw-Hill Companies, Inc.

 **Key Points**

 **Notes**

Early Americans (pages 140–141)

Summarizing — *As you read, complete the following sentences to help you summarize the lesson.*

1. The _____ extends about nine thousand miles from

   the _____ in the north to

   _____ at the tip of South America.

2. _____ crossed the land bridge in the

   _____ into _____ in search of

   bison and caribou.

3. These people created different _____ that responded

   to the conditions of their _____ .

Academic Vocabulary — *Define the following academic vocabulary words from this lesson.*

enormous >
_____
_____

culture >
_____
_____

Terms To Review — *Use each of the following terms, which you studied earlier, in a sentence that reflects the term's meaning.*

communities
(Chapter 3, Section 2) >
_____
_____

responded
(Chapter 3, Section 4) >
_____
_____

Copyright © by The McGraw-Hill Companies, Inc.

The Maya and Toltec *(pages 141–142)*

Drawing Conclusions

As you read, write three details about the Maya and the Toltec. Then write a conclusion you draw based on these details.

_____

_____

_____

_____

_____

_____

Terms To Know

Define or describe the following key term from this lesson.

_____

Mesoamerica

_____

Academic Vocabulary

Define the following academic vocabulary word from this lesson.

_____

cycle

_____

Terms To Review

Write the letter of the correct definition next to each of these terms that you studied earlier.

_____ **1.** internal
(Chapter 1, Section 2)

_____ **2.** theory
(Chapter 1, Section 1)

a. inside the group or culture

b. international

c. a set of statements to explain an event

Copyright © by The McGraw-Hill Companies, Inc.

Key Points

The Aztec (pages 142–143)

Evaluating

After you have read this lesson, imagine that you were among Montezuma's advisers who saw Spanish explorer Hernán Cortés march into the Aztec capital of Tenochtitlán. Montezuma asks you to weigh the advantages and disadvantages of fighting the Spaniards. Write your advice on the lines below.

_____

_____

_____

_____

_____

Academic Vocabulary

Define the following academic vocabulary words from this lesson.

linking

_____

_____

established

_____

_____

The Inca (pages 143–144)

Questioning

As you read, write two questions about the main ideas presented in the text. After you have finished reading, write the answers to these questions.

_____

_____

_____

_____

Copyright © by The McGraw-Hill Companies, Inc.

 **Key Points**

 **Notes**

Terms To Know

Define or describe the following key term from this lesson.

epidemic

_____

_____

Academic Vocabulary

Define the following academic vocabulary word from this lesson.

required

_____

_____

Terms To Review

Use the following term, which you studied earlier, in a sentence that reflects the term's meaning.

successors
(Chapter 3, Section 1)

_____

_____

Section Wrap-up

Now that you have read the section, answer these questions from Setting a Purpose for Reading *at the beginning of the section.*

Who were the first inhabitants of the Americas?

_____

_____

_____

_____

What forces ended the Aztec and Incan civilizations?

_____

_____

_____

_____

Copyright © by The McGraw-Hill Companies, Inc.

Chapter 5, Section 1
The Renaissance

(Pages 157–163)

Reason To Read

Setting a Purpose for Reading Think about these questions as you read:
• What was the Renaissance?
• Describe the political world that existed in the Italian states.

Main Idea

As you read pages 157–163 in your textbook, complete the graphic organizer below by identifying the major principles of Machiavelli's work, *The Prince*.

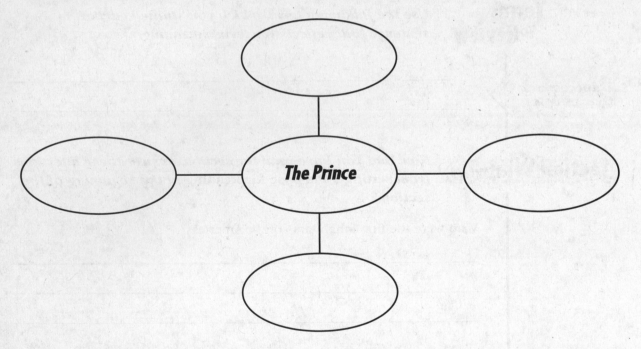

The Prince

Sequencing Events

As you read, number the following events in the order in which they occurred.

_____ **Machiavelli writes *The Prince***

_____ **Charles VIII of France invades Naples**

_____ **Cosimo de' Medici takes power in Florence**

_____ **Invading armies sack Rome**

_____ **Last Visconti ruler of Milan dies**

Copyright © by The McGraw-Hill Companies, Inc.

The Italian Renaissance (pages 157–158)

Monitoring Comprehension

As you read the lesson, think about what a city-state is. Recall that the term city-state *first appeared when you read about ancient Greece in Chapter 4. After you have finished reading, write a short description of a city-state, and name at least one ancient Greek city-state.*

_____

_____

_____

Terms To Know

Define or describe each of the following key terms from this lesson.

urban society

_____

_____

secular

_____

_____

Academic Vocabulary

Define the following academic vocabulary words from this lesson.

visible

_____

_____

individuals

_____

_____

Terms To Review

Write the definition of the following term that you studied earlier.

period
(Chapter 1, Section 1)

_____

_____

Copyright © by The McGraw-Hill Companies, Inc.

 Key Points

 Notes

The Italian States (pages 158–160)

Reviewing

As you read the lesson, fill in the chart below by describing the characteristics of these three Italian city-states. Review your chart when you have finished reading and revise as needed.

Italian State	Characteristics
Milan	
Venice	
Florence	

Terms To Know

Define or describe the following key term from this lesson.

mercenaries | _____
_____

Terms To Review

Use each of the following terms, which you studied earlier, in a sentence that reflects the term's meaning in this lesson.

crucial
(Chapter 1, Section 1) | _____
_____

economy
(Chapter 3, Section 3) | _____
_____

Copyright © by The McGraw-Hill Companies, Inc.

Machiavelli and the New Statecraft (pages 160–161)

Connecting

As you read, think about Machiavelli's belief that most people were selfish and self-centered. Do you think today's political leaders act as if they agree with Machiavelli? Do political speeches and TV ads appeal to people's morality or to their self-interest? Write a short paragraph below stating your opinion.

_____

_____

_____

_____

Academic Vocabulary

Define the following academic vocabulary words from this lesson.

attitude

_____

_____

behalf

_____

_____

Renaissance Society (pages 161–163)

Evaluating

As you read, think about how The Book of the Courtier set standards for noble behavior and education. Today, who sets the standards for your behavior and education? Write your answer on the lines below.

_____

_____

_____

Copyright © by The McGraw-Hill Companies, Inc.

Key Points

Notes

Terms To Know

Define or describe the following key term from this lesson.

dowry

_____

_____

Terms To Review

Use each of the following terms, which you studied earlier, in a sentence that reflects the term's meaning.

evident
(Chapter 2, Section 1)

_____

_____

estates
(Chapter 2, Section 2)

_____

_____

Section Wrap-up

Now that you have read the section, answer these questions from Setting a Purpose for Reading *at the beginning of the section.*

What was the Renaissance?

_____

_____

_____

_____

_____

Describe the political world that existed in the Italian states.

_____

_____

_____

_____

_____

Copyright © by The McGraw-Hill Companies, Inc.

The Intellectual and Artistic Renaissance

(Pages 164–169)

Reason To Read

Setting a Purpose for Reading Think about these questions as you read:
- What were the characteristics of Italian Renaissance humanism?
- What were the chief achievements of European Renaissance painters?

Main Idea

As you read pages 164–169 in your textbook, complete the chart below by describing the three pieces of literature and their primary importance.

Divine Comedy	The Canterbury Tales	The Book of the City of Ladies

Sequencing Events

As you read, place the following events on the time line below.
- **Christine de Pizan writes** *The Book of the City of Ladies*
- **Dante writes the** *Divine Comedy*
- **Leonardo da Vinci paints the Mona Lisa**
- **Chaucer writes** *The Canterbury Tales*

◆ 1300   ◆ 1400   ◆ 1500

Copyright © by The McGraw-Hill Companies, Inc.

Key Points

 Notes

Italian Renaissance Humanism (pages 164–165)

Determining the Main Idea

As you read, write down the main idea of the passage. Review your statement when you have finished reading and revise as needed.

_____

_____

_____

_____

Terms To Know

Define or describe the following key term from this lesson.

humanism

_____

_____

Academic Vocabulary

Write the definition of the following academic vocabulary word from this lesson.

philosophy

_____

_____

Vernacular Literature (page 165)

Previewing

Preview the lesson to get an idea of what's ahead. First, skim the passage. Then write a sentence or two explaining what you think you will be learning. After you have finished reading, revise your statements as needed.

_____

_____

_____

_____

Copyright © by The McGraw-Hill Companies, Inc.

 **Notes**

Academic Vocabulary

Define the following academic vocabulary word from this lesson.

format

_____

_____

Terms To Review

Use the following term, which you studied earlier, in a sentence that reflects the term's meaning in this lesson.

consists
(Chapter 1, Section 3)

_____

_____

Education in the Renaissance *(pages 165–166)*

Evaluating

As you read this lesson, make a list of the subjects the Renaissance humanists studied. Then make a list of a few subjects you think are important to your education. Write a sentence explaining why you might study something that a Renaissance humanist did not.

_____

_____

_____

Academic Vocabulary

Define the following academic vocabulary word from this lesson.

liberal

_____

_____

Terms To Review

Write the letter of the correct definition next to each of these terms that you studied earlier.

_____ **1.** enabled
(Chapter 1, Section 2)

a. bring into existence

b. gave the ability to do something

c. act of asking for something

_____ **2.** create
(Chapter 2, Section 2)

Copyright © by The McGraw-Hill Companies, Inc.

The Artistic Renaissance in Italy (pages 166–168)

Visualizing

Look at the illustrations of the Renaissance paintings in your textbook. Then find an image of a modern-day piece of art, and write a short paragraph identifying two differences you see between the Renaissance style and the modern style you found.

_____

_____

_____

_____

Terms To Know

Define or describe the following key term from this lesson.

fresco

_____

_____

Academic Vocabulary

Use the following academic vocabulary word from this lesson in a sentence that reflects the word's meaning.

design

_____

_____

The Northern Artistic Renaissance (pages 168–169)

Summarizing

As you read, complete the following sentences to help you summarize the lesson.

1. Like the Italian artists, the artists of northern Europe were interested

   in portraying things _____ .

2. The most important school of art in northern Europe was located in

   _____ .

Copyright © by The McGraw-Hill Companies, Inc.

Key Points

Notes

Academic Vocabulary

Define the following academic vocabulary words from this lesson.

approach

_____

_____

perspective

_____

_____

Terms To Review

Write the definition of the following term that you studied earlier.

theories
(Chapter 1, Section 1)

_____

_____

Section Wrap-up

Now that you have read the section, answer these questions from Setting a Purpose for Reading *at the beginning of the section.*

What were the characteristics of Italian Renaissance humanism?

_____

_____

_____

_____

What were the main accomplishments of European Renaissance painters?

_____

_____

_____

_____

Copyright © by The McGraw-Hill Companies, Inc.

Chapter 5, Section 3
The Protestant Reformation

(Pages 171–175)

Reason To Read

Setting a Purpose for Reading Think about these questions as you read:
• What were the beliefs of Christian humanists?
• Explain what is meant by justification by faith alone.

Main Idea

As you read pages 171–175 in your textbook, complete the graphic organizer below by identifying the steps that led to the Reformation.

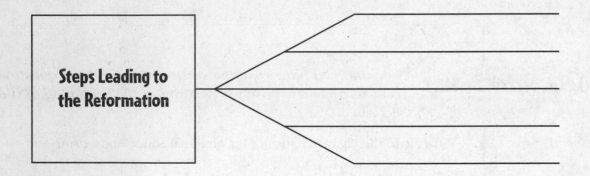

Steps Leading to the Reformation

Sequencing Events

As you read, write the correct date next to each event on the time line below.

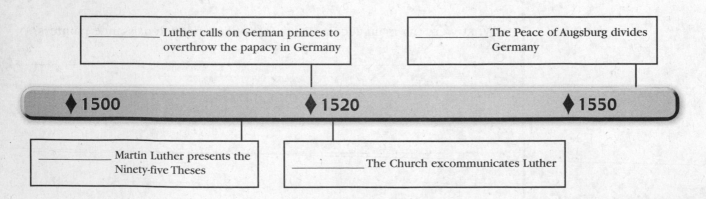

_____ Luther calls on German princes to overthrow the papacy in Germany

_____ The Peace of Augsburg divides Germany

♦ 1500   ♦ 1520   ♦ 1550

_____ Martin Luther presents the Ninety-five Theses

_____ The Church excommunicates Luther

Copyright © by The McGraw-Hill Companies, Inc.

 **Key Points**

 **Notes**

Erasmus and Christian Humanism *(pages 171–172)*

Skimming

Skim this lesson before you begin reading it, looking at headings and words in boldface or colored type. Write a sentence or two below explaining what you expect to learn in this lesson. After reading, revise your work if needed.

_____

_____

_____

Terms To Know

Define or describe the following key term from this lesson.

Christian humanism

_____

_____

Academic Vocabulary

Use each of the following academic vocabulary words in a sentence.

widespread

_____

_____

precise

_____

_____

Terms To Review

Define each of the following terms that you studied earlier.

major
(Chapter 2, Section 2)

_____

_____

goal
(Chapter 1, Section 3)

_____

_____

Copyright © by The McGraw-Hill Companies, Inc.

Key Points

 **Notes**

Religion on the Eve of the Reformation *(pages 172–173)*

Evaluating

Write a paragraph describing the state of religion before the Reformation, and explaining why Erasmus and others were calling for reform.

_____

_____

_____

_____

_____

Terms To Know

Define or describe the following key terms from this lesson.

salvation

_____

_____

indulgence

_____

_____

Academic Vocabulary

Define the following academic vocabulary words from this lesson.

assurance

_____

_____

process

_____

_____

Terms To Review

Use the following term, which you studied in an earlier chapter, in a sentence that reflects the term's meaning.

clergy
(Chapter 2, Section 2)

_____

_____

Copyright © by The McGraw-Hill Companies, Inc.

Martin Luther *(pages 173–174)*

Analyzing

As you read, think about Martin Luther's theory of salvation. How did it differ from what the Catholic Church believed was necessary for salvation? Write down your response on the lines below.

_____

_____

_____

_____

Academic Vocabulary

Circle the letter of the word or phrase that is closest in meaning to the underlined word.

amend

1. Pope Leo X thought that Martin Luther would eventually <u>amend</u> his views and stop his attacks on the Catholic Church.

   a. to change or correct **b.** to make stronger **c.** to make known

justifies

2. Martin Luther believed that faith alone <u>justifies</u> salvation.

   a. discourages **b.** proves to be right **c.** denies

Terms To Review

Define the following term that you studied earlier.

grant
(Chapter 1, Section 2)

_____

_____

Politics in the German Reformation *(page 175)*

Questioning

As you read this lesson, write two questions about the main ideas of the passage. After you have finished reading, write the answers to these questions.

_____

_____

_____

_____

Copyright © by The McGraw-Hill Companies, Inc.

Key Points

Notes

Terms To Review

Use each of the following terms, which you studied earlier, in a sentence that shows you understand the term's meaning.

conflict
(Chapter 1, Section 3)

_____

_____

legal
(Chapter 3, Section 4)

_____

_____

Section Wrap-up

Now that you have read the section, answer these questions from Setting a Purpose for Reading *at the beginning of the section.*

What were the main beliefs of Christian humanists?

_____

_____

_____

_____

_____

Explain what is meant by justification by faith alone.

_____

_____

_____

_____

_____

Copyright © by The McGraw-Hill Companies, Inc.

Chapter 5, Section 4
The Spread of Protestantism and the Catholic Response
(Pages 177–183)

Reason To Read

Setting a Purpose for Reading Think about these questions as you read:
- What different forms of Protestantism emerged in Europe?
- What were the contributions of the Jesuits, the papacy, and the Council of Trent to the revival of Catholicism?

Main Idea

As you read pages 177–183 in your textbook, complete the graphic organizer below by listing some of the church reforms the Council of Trent made. Beside each reform, list the Protestant viewpoint that inspired the reform.

Council of Trent	Protestant Viewpoint

Sequencing Events

As you read, number the following events in the order in which they occurred.

_____ The Act of Supremacy is passed in England

_____ Mary Tudor, "Bloody Mary," becomes Queen of England

_____ War between the Protestant and Catholic states in Switzerland

_____ John Calvin publishes the *Institutes of the Christian Religion*

_____ The Council of Trent meets

Copyright © by The McGraw-Hill Companies, Inc.

The Zwinglian Reformation *(pages 177–178)*

Connecting

As you read about the religious reformer Ulrich Zwingli, think about what happened to early Christians in Roman times. How does Zwingli's experience compare to the experience of early Christians? Was it the same or different? Write a brief paragraph in the spaces provided below.

_____

_____

_____

_____

Academic Vocabulary

Use the following academic vocabulary word from this lesson in a sentence.

removed

_____

_____

Terms To Review

Write the definition of the following term that you studied earlier.

authority
(Chapter 4, Section 1)

_____

_____

Calvin and Calvinism *(pages 178–179)*

Interpreting

As you read about John Calvin, think about what you have learned about the Puritans in the New England colonies. After you have finished reading, write a sentence or two comparing the lives of the Calvinists in Geneva, Switzerland, and the colonial Puritans in America.

_____

_____

_____

_____

Copyright © by The McGraw-Hill Companies, Inc.

Terms To Know

Define or describe the following key term from this lesson.

predestination

_____

_____

Academic Vocabulary

Define each of the following academic vocabulary words from this lesson.

summary

_____

_____

emphasis

_____

_____

Terms To Review

Use each of these terms, which you studied earlier, in a sentence that reflects the term's meaning in this lesson.

achieve
(Chapter 1, Section 3)

_____

_____

dynamic
(Chapter 3, Section 4)

_____

_____

The Reformation in England *(pages 179–180)*

Sequencing

As you read, number the following events in the order in which they occurred.

_____ Act of Supremacy declares that the king is head of the Church in England

_____ King Henry VIII's marriage to Catherine of Aragon is annulled

_____ Mary becomes the Queen of England

_____ Queen Anne gives birth to a daughter

Copyright © by The McGraw-Hill Companies, Inc.

Key Points

Notes

Terms To Know

annul

Define or describe the following key term from this lesson.

_____

_____

Academic Vocabulary

Write the definition of each of the following academic vocabulary words from this lesson.

restore

_____

_____

policies

_____

_____

The Anabaptists (pages 180–181)

Summarizing

As you read, complete the following sentences to help you summarize the lesson.

1. Anabaptists believed in _____ baptism and the complete separation of _____ and _____ .

2. Anabaptists refused to hold _____ or bear _____ .

3. Both Protestants and Catholics _____ Anabaptists.

Academic Vocabulary

Define the following academic vocabulary word from this lesson.

excluded

_____

_____

Copyright © by The McGraw-Hill Companies, Inc.

Key Points

Notes

Terms To Review

Write the definition of each of the following terms that you studied earlier.

undergone
(Chapter 3, Section 3)

_____

_____

communities
(Chapter 3, Section 2)

_____

_____

Effects on the Role of Women (pages 181–182)

Responding

As you read this lesson, think about the attitudes of Luther and Calvin toward married women. Use the lines below to write down the ideas you find interesting or surprising.

_____

_____

_____

_____

Academic Vocabulary

Define the following academic vocabulary word from this lesson.

function

_____

_____

Terms To Review

Define or describe each of the following terms that you studied earlier.

traditional
(Chapter 1, Section 2)

_____

_____

overall
(Chapter 2, Section 2)

_____

_____

Copyright © by The McGraw-Hill Companies, Inc.

 Key Points

 Notes

The Catholic Reformation *(pages 182–183)*

Drawing Conclusions

What was the result of the Council of Trent? How was the Roman Catholic Church affected?

_____

_____

_____

_____

Terms To Review

Write the letter of the correct definition next to each of these terms that you studied earlier.

____ **1.** founded
(Chapter 2, Section 2)

____ **2.** sacraments
(Chapter 4, Section 1)

____ **3.** unified
(Chapter 1, Section 2)

a. Christian rites

b. formed into a unit

c. brought into existence

d. existing in reality

Section Wrap-up

Now that you have read the section, answer these questions from **Setting a Purpose for Reading** *at the beginning of the section.*

What different forms of Protestantism emerged in Europe?

_____

_____

_____

What were the contributions of the Jesuits, the papacy, and the Council of Trent to the revival of Catholicism?

_____

_____

_____

Copyright © by The McGraw-Hill Companies, Inc.

Chapter 6, Section 1
Exploration and Expansion
(Pages 189–195)

Reason To Read

Setting a Purpose for Reading Think about these questions as you read:
- Why did Europeans travel to Asia?
- What impact did European expansion have on the conquerors and the conquered?

Main Idea

As you read pages 189–195 in your textbook, complete the chart below by listing reasons why Melaka, a port on the Malay Peninsula, was important to the Portuguese.

Importance of Melaka

Sequencing Events

As you read, place the following events on the time line below.
- **Spanish gain control of northern Mexico**
- **The Treaty of Tordesillas divides the Americas**
- **Bartholomeu Dias rounds the Cape of Good Hope**
- **Vasco da Gama arrives off the port of Calicut, India**

| ◆1480 | ◆1495 | ◆1510 | ◆1525 | ◆1540 | ◆1555 |

Copyright © by The McGraw-Hill Companies, Inc.

 Key Points

 Notes

Motives and Means (pages 189–191)

Connecting

As you read about the explorers of the 1400s and 1500s, think about exploration today. Are there still places to explore on earth? Are there other kinds of exploration? Summarize your thoughts on the lines below.

_____

_____

_____

_____

Academic Vocabulary

Define the following academic vocabulary words from this lesson.

overseas

_____

_____

motives

_____

_____

Terms To Review

Write the letter of the correct definition next to each of these terms that you studied earlier.

_____ **1.** civilization
(Chapter 1, Section 1)

_____ **2.** undertake
(Chapter 2, Section 1)

a. a large political unit, usually under a single leader, that controls many people and territories

b. to attempt or take upon oneself

c. complex culture in which large numbers of people share common elements

Copyright © by The McGraw-Hill Companies, Inc.

The Portuguese Trading Empire (pages 191–192)

Sequencing
As you read, number the following events in the order in which they occurred.

____ Bartholomeu Dias rounds the Cape of Good Hope

____ Portuguese gain control of the spice trade

____ Portuguese fleets begin probing southward along the western coast of Africa

____ Vasco da Gama arrives at coast of India

____ Portuguese warships defeat Turkish and Indian ships off the coast of India

Academic Vocabulary
Use the following academic vocabulary words from this lesson in a sentence that shows you understand the word's meaning.

range
_____
_____

route
_____
_____

Terms To Review
Write the definition of the following terms that you studied earlier.

sources
(Chapter 1, Section 3)
_____
_____

percent
(Chapter 4, Section 1)
_____
_____

Copyright © by The McGraw-Hill Companies, Inc.

Voyages to the Americas (pages 192–194)

Drawing Conclusions

Complete the following sentences. Then write a concluding paragraph below supporting your position.

The greatest impact of Columbus's voyages on the Americas was _____

_____ .

The greatest impact of Columbus's voyages on Europe was _____

_____ .

_____

_____

_____

_____

Academic Vocabulary

Define the following academic vocabulary words from this lesson.

spheres >
_____

_____

sought >
_____

_____

Terms To Review

Use the following term, which you studied earlier, in a sentence that reflects the term's meaning in this lesson.

established
(Chapter 4, Section 2) >
_____

_____

Copyright © by The McGraw-Hill Companies, Inc.

The Spanish Empire (page 194)

Identifying Cause and Effect

After you have read this lesson, write a brief paragraph summarizing the effects of the Spanish settlement on Native Americans.

_____

_____

_____

_____

Terms To Know

Define or describe the following key term from this lesson.

conquistadors >

_____

_____

Economic Impact and Competition (pages 194–195)

Evaluating

As you read this lesson, describe three ways in which the European colonists transformed world economic activity.

_____

_____

_____

Terms To Know

Write the letter of the correct definition next to each of these terms from this lesson.

_____ **1.** colony

_____ **2.** mercantilism

_____ **3.** balance of trade

a. a set of principles that dominated economic thought in the seventeenth century

b. Spanish conquerors

c. the difference in value between what a nation imports and what it exports over time

d. a settlement of people living in a new territory, linked with the parent country

Copyright © by The McGraw-Hill Companies, Inc.

Key Points

Notes

Academic Vocabulary

Define the following academic vocabulary word from this lesson.

subsidies ⟩ _____

_____

Terms To Review

Choose one of these two terms, which you studied earlier, to fill in each blank.

benefits
(Chapter 3, Section 4) ⟩

1. By 1700, the English _____ the eastern seaboard of North America.

dominated
(Chapter 2, Section 1) ⟩

2. Portuguese expansion into Asia resulted in economic

_____ .

3. One of the _____ of the colonies to European governments was that they provided a market for finished goods.

Section Wrap-up

Now that you have read the section, answer these questions from **Setting a Purpose for Reading** at the beginning of the section.

Why did Europeans travel to Asia?

_____

_____

_____

_____

What impact did European expansion have on the conquerors and the conquered?

_____

_____

_____

_____

Copyright © by The McGraw-Hill Companies, Inc.

Chapter 6, Section 2
Africa in an Age of Transition

(Pages 197–200)

Reason To Read

Setting a Purpose for Reading Think about these questions as you read:
- How did European expansion affect Africa's peoples and cultures?
- How were the African states structured politically?

Main Idea

As you read pages 197–200 in your textbook, complete the chart below by identifying economic and political factors that caused the slave trade to be profitable. List the economic and political effects of the trade.

Economic/Political Factors	Economic/Political Effects

Sequencing Events

As you read, number the following events in the order in which they occurred.

_____ **King Afonso of Congo writes a letter to the king of Portugal about the impact of the slave trade**

_____ **Moroccan forces defeat the Songhai army**

_____ **A Spanish ship carries the first boatload of African slaves to the Americas**

Copyright © by The McGraw-Hill Companies, Inc.

The Slave Trade (pages 197–199)

Visualizing

As you read this lesson, focus on how the slave trade changed many African societies. European merchants and African leaders wanted to make money by finding young African men to sell into slavery. Imagine you are a teenager living in a West African village. Use the lines below to describe some specific things that have changed in your village because of the slave trade.

_____

_____

_____

_____

Terms To Know

Define or describe the following key terms from this lesson.

plantations

_____

_____

triangular trade

_____

_____

Middle Passage

_____

_____

Academic Vocabulary

Use the following academic vocabulary word from this lesson in a sentence.

portion

_____

_____

Copyright © by The McGraw-Hill Companies, Inc.

Key Points

Terms To Review

Use each of the following terms, which you studied earlier, in a sentence that reflects the term's meaning in this lesson.

domestic
(Chapter 2, Section 2)

_____

_____

_____

culture
(Chapter 4, Section 2)

_____

_____

_____

Political and Social Structures (pages 199–200)

Questioning

As you read, ask yourself questions about the text to help understand it better. Write your questions and answers on the lines below.

1. What is the main idea of the passage?

_____

_____

2. Are there any parts of the passage I do not understand? What are they?

_____

_____

3. How can I go about clarifying the information I do not understand?

_____

_____

Terms To Review

Define the following terms that you studied in an earlier chapter.

subordinated
(Chapter 1, Section 3)

_____

_____

Copyright © by The McGraw-Hill Companies, Inc.

 **Key Points**

 **Notes**

Copyright © by The McGraw-Hill Companies, Inc.

nevertheless
(Chapter 3, Section 3)

 **Section Wrap-up**

Now that you have read the section, answer these questions from Setting a Purpose for Reading *at the beginning of the section.*

How did European expansion affect Africa's peoples and cultures?

_____

_____

_____

_____

_____

How were the African states structured politically?

_____

_____

_____

_____

_____

Chapter 6, Section 3
Southeast Asia in the Era of the Spice Trade

(Pages 201–204)

Reason To Read

Setting a Purpose for Reading Think about these questions as you read:
- How did the power shift from the Portuguese to the Dutch in the control of the spice trade?
- What religious beliefs were prevalent in Southeast Asia?

Main Idea

As you read pages 201–204 in your textbook, complete the chart below by listing reasons the destructive effects of European contact in Southeast Asia were only gradually felt.

European Contact in Southeast Asia

Sequencing Events

As you read, write the correct date next to each event on the time line below.

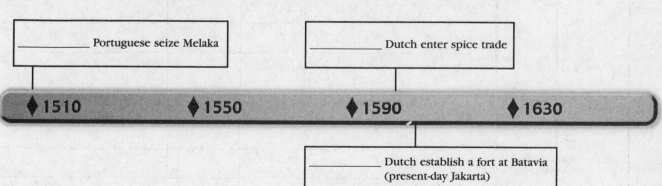

_____ Portuguese seize Melaka		_____ Dutch enter spice trade

♦ 1510   ♦ 1550   ♦ 1590   ♦ 1630

_____ Dutch establish a fort at Batavia (present-day Jakarta)

Copyright © by The McGraw-Hill Companies, Inc.

Key Points / Notes

Emerging Mainland States (pages 201–202)

Scanning

Before you read, scan the passage, looking for the names of emerging states in mainland Southeast Asia and the conflicts that erupted among them. Use the lines below to write down notes.

_____

_____

_____

Terms To Review

Write the definition of the following terms that you studied earlier.

successor
(Chapter 3, Section 1)

_____

_____

secured
(Chapter 3, Section 2)

_____

_____

The Arrival of Europeans (pages 202–204)

Skimming

Skim this lesson before you begin reading it, looking at headings and words in boldface or colored type. Write a sentence below describing what you expect to learn. After reading, revise your sentence as needed.

_____

_____

_____

Terms To Know

Define or describe the following key term from this lesson.

mainland states

_____

_____

Copyright © by The McGraw-Hill Companies, Inc.

 Notes

Academic Vocabulary

Use each of the following academic vocabulary words from this lesson in a sentence that shows you understand the word's meaning.

impose

_____
_____
_____

area

_____
_____

Terms To Review

Circle the letter of the word or phrase that is closest in meaning to the underlined word.

authority
(Chapter 4, Section 1)

1. The Portuguese lacked the resources to impose their <u>authority</u> over large areas.
   - **a.** the right and power to control people or things
   - **b.** military rule
   - **c.** control by a dictator

occupied
(Chapter 3, Section 1)

2. After 1600, the Dutch <u>occupied</u> most of the coastal forts along trade routes in the Indian Ocean.
   - **a.** took away
   - **b.** performed the functions of
   - **c.** took possession or control of

Religious and Political Systems (page 204)

Monitoring Comprehension

As you read, write a sentence to describe each of the four styles of monarchy that evolved in Southeast Asia.

_____
_____
_____
_____

Copyright © by The McGraw-Hill Companies, Inc.

Terms To Know

Define or describe the following key term from this lesson.

bureaucracy

_____

_____

Terms To Review

Use each of the following terms, which you studied earlier, in a sentence that reflects the term's meaning in this lesson.

adapted
(Chapter 1, Section 1)

_____

_____

converts
(Chapter 3, Section 1)

_____

_____

Section Wrap-up

Now that you have read the section, answer these questions from Setting a Purpose for Reading at the beginning of the section.

How did the power shift from the Portuguese to the Dutch in the control of the spice trade?

_____

_____

_____

_____

What religious beliefs were prevalent in Southeast Asia?

_____

_____

_____

_____

Copyright © by The McGraw-Hill Companies, Inc.

Chapter 7, Section 1
Europe in Crisis: The Wars of Religion
(Pages 211–214)

Reason To Read

Setting a Purpose for Reading Think about these questions as you read:
- What were the causes and results of France's wars of religion?
- How do the policies of Elizabeth I of England and Philip II of Spain compare?

Main Idea

As you read pages 211–214 in your textbook, complete the chart below by comparing the listed characteristics of France, Spain, and England.

	France	Spain	England
Government			
Religion			
Conflicts			

Sequencing Events

As you read, number the following events in the order in which they occurred.

_____ **Philip II becomes king of Spain**

_____ **Spain defeats Turks in Battle of Lepanto**

_____ **Edict of Nantes recognizes rights of Huguenots in France**

_____ **French wars of religion begin**

_____ **England defeats the Spanish Armada**

Copyright © by The McGraw-Hill Companies, Inc.

The French Wars of Religion (pages 211–212)

Drawing Conclusions

As you read, write down three details about the French wars of religion. Then write a conclusion based on these details.

_____

_____

_____

_____

Terms To Know

Define or describe the following key term from this lesson.

militant

_____

_____

Terms To Review

Write the definition of the following term that you studied earlier.

dynasty
(Chapter 1, Section 2)

_____

_____

Philip II and Militant Catholicism (pages 212–213)

Reviewing

This lesson discusses the role the Spanish king, Philip II, played in fighting Protestantism. As you read, think about Spain's long history of defending Catholicism. In the space below, list two examples from earlier history of Spain's loyalty to the Church.

_____

_____

_____

_____

_____

Copyright © by The McGraw-Hill Companies, Inc.

Academic Vocabulary

Choose one of these two terms from this lesson to fill in each blank.

conformity

1. Although Spain had controlled a large region at one time, power soon _____ from Spain to England and France.

shifted

2. To strengthen his control over the lands he had inherited from his father, Philip II insisted on strict _____ to Catholicism.

3. When power _____ from Charles V to Philip II, the lands under Philip's control were consolidated.

The England of Elizabeth (pages 213–214)

Interpreting

As you read the lesson, think about the challenges Queen Elizabeth faced from stronger powers, like Spain and France. Use the lines below to describe the Queen's strategies regarding foreign policy.

_____

_____

_____

_____

Terms To Know

Define or describe the following key term from this lesson.

armada

_____

_____

Academic Vocabulary

Use the following academic vocabulary word from this lesson in a sentence.

reveals

_____

_____

Copyright © by The McGraw-Hill Companies, Inc.

Terms To Review

Use the following term, which you studied in an earlier chapter, in a sentence.

foundations
(Chapter 2, Section 1)

_____

_____

Section Wrap-up

Now that you have read the section, answer these questions from Setting a Purpose for Reading *at the beginning of the section.*

What were the causes and results of France's wars of religion?

_____

_____

_____

_____

_____

How do the policies of Elizabeth I of England and Philip II of Spain compare?

_____

_____

_____

_____

_____

Copyright © by The McGraw-Hill Companies, Inc.

Chapter 7, Section 2
Social Crises, War, and Revolution

(Pages 216–221)

Reason To Read

Setting a Purpose for Reading Think about these questions as you read:
- What problems troubled Europe from 1560 to 1650?
- How did the Glorious Revolution undermine the divine right of kings?

Main Idea

As you read pages 216–221 in your textbook, complete the chart below by identifying conflicts prompted by religious concerns. Next to each conflict, list the country or region where it occurred.

Religious Conflicts	Country/Region

Sequencing Events

As you read, write the correct date next to each event on the time line below.

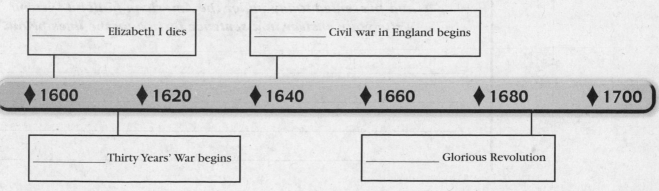

_____ Elizabeth I dies

_____ Civil war in England begins

♦ 1600   ♦ 1620   ♦ 1640   ♦ 1660   ♦ 1680   ♦ 1700

_____ Thirty Years' War begins

_____ Glorious Revolution

Copyright © by The McGraw-Hill Companies, Inc.

Economic and Social Crises (pages 216–217)

Skimming

Read the lesson title and quickly look over the passage to get an idea of its content. Then write a sentence describing what you expect to learn in this lesson.

_____

_____

_____

Terms To Know

Define or describe the following key term from this lesson.

> **inflation**

_____

_____

Terms To Review

Write the definition of each of the following terms that you studied in an earlier chapter.

> **economy**
> (Chapter 3, Section 3)

_____

_____

> **creation**
> (Chapter 2, Section 2)

_____

_____

The Witchcraft Trials (page 217)

Connecting

As you read this lesson, think about the kind of evidence that was used to convict women charged with witchcraft. How does this compare to the way evidence is gathered and presented today under the American judicial system? Write your answer in a sentence or two on the lines below.

_____

_____

_____

_____

Copyright © by The McGraw-Hill Companies, Inc.

Key Points

Notes

Terms To Know

Define or describe the following key term from this lesson.

witchcraft

_____
_____

Terms To Review

Write the definition of the following term that you studied earlier.

attitudes
(Chapter 5, Section 1)

_____
_____

The Thirty Years' War *(pages 217–218)*

Identifying Cause and Effect

After you have read this lesson, write a paragraph summarizing the effect the Peace of Westphalia had on the Holy Roman Empire.

_____
_____
_____
_____

Academic Vocabulary

Use each of the following academic vocabulary words from this lesson in a sentence that shows you understand the word's meaning.

entity

_____
_____

conduct

_____
_____

Copyright © by The McGraw-Hill Companies, Inc.

Terms To Review

Define or describe the following term that you studied earlier.

emerged
(Chapter 3, Section 2)

_____

_____

Revolutions in England (pages 219–221)

Interpreting

As you read this lesson, focus on the issues the King of England and Parliament were fighting over. Was it religion or political power—or perhaps a bit of both? Write your answer on the lines below.

_____

_____

_____

Terms To Know

Define or describe the following key terms from this lesson.

divine right of kings

_____

_____

commonwealth

_____

_____

Academic Vocabulary

Circle the letter of the word or phrase that is closest in meaning to the underlined word.

consent

1. During the reign of Charles I, Parliament did not want any taxes levied without its <u>consent</u>.

   a. rejection   **b.** help   **c.** permission

suspend

2. King Charles II <u>suspended</u> some laws that Parliament had passed.

   a. did away with   **b.** started up again   **c.** introduced

Copyright © by The McGraw-Hill Companies, Inc.

Terms To Review

Use each of the following terms, which you studied earlier, in a sentence that reflects the term's meaning.

series
(Chapter 2, Section 2)

_____
_____

impose
(Chapter 6, Section 3)

_____
_____

republic
(Chapter 2, Section 2)

_____
_____

Section Wrap-up

Now that you have read the section, answer these questions from Setting a Purpose for Reading *at the beginning of the section.*

What problems troubled Europe from 1560 to 1650?

_____
_____
_____
_____
_____

How did the Glorious Revolution weaken the idea that kings ruled by divine right?

_____
_____
_____
_____

Copyright © by The McGraw-Hill Companies, Inc.

Chapter 7, Section 3
Response to Crisis: Absolutism

(Pages 223–229)

Reason To Read

Setting a Purpose for Reading Think about these questions as you read:
• What is absolutism?
• Besides France, what other European states practiced absolutism?

Main Idea

As you read pages 223–229 in your textbook, complete the chart below by summarizing the accomplishments of Peter the Great.

Reforms	Government	Wars

Sequencing Events

As you read, number the following events in the order in which they occurred.

_____ **Louis XIV comes to the French throne at age four**

_____ **Romanov dynasty begins in Russia**

_____ **Peter the Great dies**

_____ **Construction of St. Petersburg begins**

Copyright © by The McGraw-Hill Companies, Inc.

France Under Louis XIV (pages 223–226)

Reviewing

As you read the lesson, focus on Louis XIV. Summarize his reign by completing the following chart.

Government	
Economics	
Religion	

Terms To Know

Define or describe the following key term from this lesson.

absolutism _____

_____

Academic Vocabulary

Write the letter of the correct definition next to each of these academic vocabulary words from this lesson.

____ **1.** sole

____ **2.** deviated

a. to depart from a course

b. being the only one

c. to go away

Terms To Review

Write the definition of each of the following terms that you studied earlier.

maintaining
(Chapter 2, Section 2)

_____

_____

aware
(Chapter 3, Section 1)

_____

_____

Copyright © by The McGraw-Hill Companies, Inc.

Absolutism in Central and Eastern Europe *(pages 226–227)*

Analyzing

Why was the Austrian monarchy unable to create a highly centralized, absolutist state? Summarize your answer on the lines below.

_____

_____

_____

_____

_____

Terms To Review

Write the definition of the following term that you studied in an earlier chapter.

significant
(Chapter 1 Section 2)

_____

_____

Russia Under Peter The Great *(pages 227–229)*

Monitoring Comprehension

As you read, write down one question for each subhead for a partner to answer. Exchange questions and see if you can answer your partner's questions.

Military and Governmental Changes

_____

_____

Cultural Change

_____

_____

St. Petersburg

_____

_____

Copyright © by The McGraw-Hill Companies, Inc.

Terms To Know

Define or describe the following key terms from this lesson.

czar

_____

_____

boyar

_____

_____

Academic Vocabulary

Use each of the following academic vocabulary words from this lesson in a sentence that shows you understand the word's meaning.

drafted

_____

_____

credit

_____

_____

Section Wrap-up

Now that you have read the section, answer these questions from Setting a Purpose for Reading *at the beginning of the section.*

What is absolutism?

_____

_____

_____

_____

Besides France, what other European states practiced absolutism?

_____

_____

_____

_____

Copyright © by The McGraw-Hill Companies, Inc.

Chapter 7, Section 4
The World of European Culture

(Pages 230–233)

Reason To Read

Setting a Purpose for Reading Think about these questions as you read:

- What two new art movements emerged in the 1500s?
- Why are Shakespeare's works considered those of a genius?

Main Idea

As you read pages 230–233 in your textbook, complete the chart below by summarizing the political thoughts of Thomas Hobbes and John Locke.

Thomas Hobbes	John Locke

Sequencing Events

As you read, place the following events on the time line below.

- **Shakespeare appears in London**
- **Cervantes completes *Don Quixote***
- **Baroque movement begins in Italy**
- ***Leviathan* by Hobbes is published**

◆1575　　　◆1600　　　◆1625　　　◆1650

Copyright © by The McGraw-Hill Companies, Inc.

Mannerism (pages 230–231)

Clarifying

As you read the lesson, focus on the descriptions of Mannerism. Use the lines below to compare and contrast the art of the Renaissance period and the emerging style of Mannerism.

_____

_____

_____

_____

_____

Terms To Know

Define or describe the following key term from this lesson.

Mannerism

_____

_____

Academic Vocabulary

Use each of the following academic vocabulary words in a sentence that shows you understand the word's meaning.

proportion

_____

_____

decline

_____

_____

Terms To Review

Write the definition of the following term that you studied earlier.

principles
(Chapter 1, Section 2)

_____

_____

Copyright © by The McGraw-Hill Companies, Inc.

The Baroque Period (page 231)

Analyzing

As you read this lesson, focus on how the art of a certain time reflects the ideas and interests of the whole society. How did Baroque art suit the ideas of powerful kings and princes? Write your answer on the lines below.

_____

_____

_____

Terms To Know

Define or describe the following key term from this lesson.

baroque >

_____

_____

A Golden Age of Literature (pages 231–232)

Connecting

As you read this lesson, think about how popular Shakespeare's plays were at the Globe Theater in London. Today, movies are the popular form of entertainment. Think of a few films that are well-liked today. What qualities make them popular? Do you think people in the 1600s found the same qualities in Shakespeare? Why or why not? Summarize your ideas in a short paragraph.

_____

_____

_____

_____

Academic Vocabulary

Define the following academic vocabulary word from this lesson.

psychology >

_____

_____

Copyright © by The McGraw-Hill Companies, Inc.

Terms To Review

Define each of the following terms that you studied earlier.

varied
(Chapter 3, Section 2)

_____
_____
_____

structure
(Chapter 4, Section 1)

_____
_____

Political Thought (page 233)

Evaluating

As you read, think about what was happening in England when Thomas Hobbes was alive—between 1588 and 1679. Why do you think Hobbes was more concerned with order than liberty? Write a short response to this question below.

_____
_____
_____
_____

Terms To Know

Define or describe the following key term from this lesson.

natural rights

_____
_____

Academic Vocabulary

Use the following academic vocabulary word from this lesson in a sentence.

advocate

_____
_____

Copyright © by The McGraw-Hill Companies, Inc.

 **Key Points**

 **Notes**

Copyright © by The McGraw-Hill Companies, Inc.

Terms To Review

Write the definition of the following terms that you studied earlier.

contract
(Chapter 1, Section 2)

_____
_____
_____

revolutions
(Chapter 1, Section 1)

_____
_____
_____

Section Wrap-up

Now that you have read the section, answer these questions from Setting a Purpose for Reading *at the beginning of the section.*

What two new art movements emerged in the 1500s?

_____
_____
_____
_____
_____

Why are Shakespeare's works considered those of a genius?

_____
_____
_____
_____
_____

Chapter 8, Section 1
The Ottoman Empire

(Pages 239–245)

Reason To Read

Setting a Purpose for Reading Think about these questions as you read:
- What were the major events in the growth of the Ottoman Empire?
- What role did religion play in the Ottoman Empire?

Main Idea

As you read pages 239–245 in your textbook, complete the graphic organizer below by listing the structure of Ottoman society in order of importance.

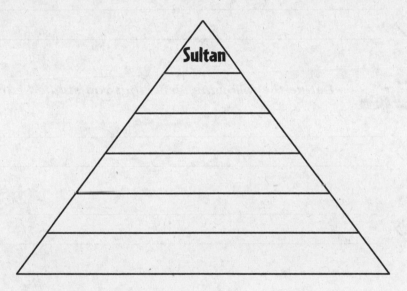

Sultan

Sequencing Events

As you read, write the correct date next to each event on the time line below.

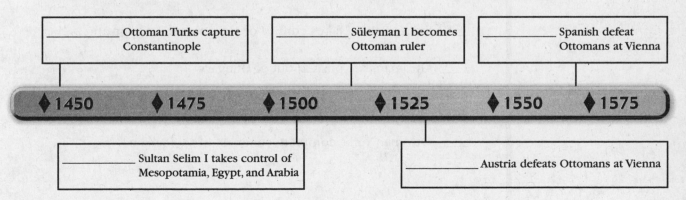

_____ Ottoman Turks capture Constantinople

_____ Süleyman I becomes Ottoman ruler

_____ Spanish defeat Ottomans at Vienna

♦ 1450   ♦ 1475   ♦ 1500   ♦ 1525   ♦ 1550   ♦ 1575

_____ Sultan Selim I takes control of Mesopotamia, Egypt, and Arabia

_____ Austria defeats Ottomans at Vienna

Copyright © by The McGraw-Hill Companies, Inc.

Key Points

Notes

Rise of the Ottoman Turks *(pages 239–240)*

Skimming

Read the title and quickly look over the lesson to get a general idea of its content. Then write a sentence or two below explaining what the lesson is about.

_____

_____

_____

Terms To Know

Define or describe the following key term from this lesson.

janissaries

_____

_____

Terms To Review

Define the following terms that you studied earlier.

converted
(Chapter 3, Section 1)

_____

_____

technology
(Chapter 4, Section 1)

_____

_____

Expansion of the Empire *(pages 240–242)*

Sequencing

As you read, number the following events in the order in which they occurred.

_____ Sultan Selim I takes control of Mesopotamia, Egypt, and Arabia

_____ Ottomans are pushed out of Hungary

_____ Ottomans began their attack on Constantinople

_____ Ottoman Turks complete conquest of the Balkans

Copyright © by The McGraw-Hill Companies, Inc.

Key Points

Notes

Terms To Know

Define or describe the following key term from this lesson.

pashas >
_____
_____

Academic Vocabulary

Define the following academic vocabulary word from this lesson.

approximately >
_____
_____

The Nature of Ottoman Rule (pages 242–243)

Analyzing

What was the role of the sultan in the Ottoman Empire?

_____
_____
_____

Terms To Know

Write the letter of the correct definition next to each of these terms from this lesson.

____ **1.** gunpowder empire

____ **2.** sultan

____ **3.** harem

____ **4.** grand vizier

a. private domain of the sultan
b. the supreme political and military authority in Ottoman rule
c. chief minister who led meetings of Ottoman imperial council
d. appointed officials who maintained law and order in the Ottoman Empire
e. formed by outside conquerors who unified the regions that they conquered

Academic Vocabulary

Define the following academic vocabulary word from this lesson.

label >
_____
_____

Copyright © by The McGraw-Hill Companies, Inc.

 Key Points

 Notes

Terms To Review

Write the definition of each of the following terms that you studied earlier.

individual
(Chapter 5, Section 1)

_____

_____

resided
(Chapter 2, Section 2)

_____

_____

Religion in the Ottoman World (pages 243–244)

Questioning

As you read, write down two questions about the main ideas presented in this lesson. After you have finished reading, write the answers to these questions.

_____

_____

_____

_____

Terms To Know

Define or describe the following key term from this lesson.

ulema

_____

_____

Terms To Review

Write the definition of each of the following terms that you studied earlier.

areas
(Chapter 6, Section 3)

_____

_____

legal
(Chapter 3, Section 4)

_____

_____

Copyright © by The McGraw-Hill Companies, Inc.

Key Points

Notes

Ottoman Society (page 244)

Evaluating

After you read the lesson, evaluate the position of women in the Ottoman Empire with that of women in other Muslim societies. Summarize your thoughts in a short paragraph below.

_____

_____

_____

Terms To Review

Use the following term, which you studied earlier, in a sentence.

seek
(Chapter 13, Section 1)

_____

_____

Problems in the Ottoman Empire (pages 244–245)

Identifying Cause and Effect

As you read this lesson, focus on the causes that led to the disintegration of the Ottoman Empire. Record your findings in a short paragraph below.

_____

_____

_____

_____

Academic Vocabulary

Define the following academic vocabulary word from this lesson.

assigned

_____

_____

Copyright © by The McGraw-Hill Companies, Inc.

Key Points

Notes

Terms To Review

Write the definition of the following term that you studied in an earlier chapter.

links
(Chapter 4, Section 2)

_____

_____

Ottoman Art (page 245)

Visualizing

To help you understand and remember what you have read, try to visualize what you are reading about. As you read, ask yourself, "What would this look like?" Then write a description on the lines below.

_____

_____

_____

_____

Academic Vocabulary

Define the following academic vocabulary word from this lesson.

schemes

_____

_____

Section Wrap-up

Now that you have read the section, answer these questions from Setting a Purpose for Reading *at the beginning of the section.*

What were the major events in the growth of the Ottoman Empire?

_____

_____

_____

What role did religion play in the Ottoman Empire?

_____

_____

Copyright © by The McGraw-Hill Companies, Inc.

Chapter 8, Section 2
The Rule of the Safavids

(Pages 250–253)

Reason To Read

Setting a Purpose for Reading Think about these questions as you read:
- What events led to the creation and growth of the Safavid dynasty?
- What cultural contributions were made by the Safavid dynasty?

Main Idea

As you read pages 250–253 in your textbook, complete the chart below by listing the key features of the Ottoman and Safavid Empires.

Ottoman Empire	Safavid Empire

Sequencing Events

As you read, place the following events on the time line below.
- **Shah Abbas dies**
- **Azerbaijan is returned to Safavids**
- **Ismail captures Iran and Iraq**
- **Shah Abbas becomes the Safavid ruler**
- **Ottomans place Azerbaijan under Ottoman rule**

♦1500　　♦1535　　♦1570　　♦1605　　♦1640　　♦1675

Copyright © by The McGraw-Hill Companies, Inc.

Rise of the Safavid Dynasty *(pages 250–251)*

Previewing

Preview the lesson to get an idea of what is ahead. First, skim the lesson. Then write a sentence or two explaining what you expect to learn. After you have finished reading, revise your statements as needed.

_____

_____

_____

Terms To Know

Define or describe the following key term from this lesson.

shah

_____

_____

Academic Vocabulary

Use the following academic vocabulary word from this lesson in a sentence that shows you understand the word's meaning.

integrate

_____

_____

Terms To Review

Write the definition of each of the following terms that you studied earlier.

sultan
(Chapter 3, Section 1)

_____

_____

major
(Chapter 2, Section 2)

_____

_____

decades
(Chapter 2, Section 2)

_____

_____

Copyright © by The McGraw-Hill Companies, Inc.

Key Points

Notes

Glory and Decline (pages 251–252)

Summarizing

After you have read the lesson, write a brief paragraph summarizing what caused the Safavid Empire to decline after the death of Shah Abbas.

_____

_____

_____

Terms To Know

Define or describe the following key terms from this lesson.

orthodoxy

_____

_____

anarchy

_____

_____

Academic Vocabulary

Write the definition of the following academic vocabulary word from this lesson.

initial

_____

_____

Political and Social Structures (pages 252–253)

Outlining

As you read this lesson, fill in the outline below.

I. The Role of the Shah

   A. _____

   B. _____

II. Economy and Trade

   A. _____

   B. _____

Copyright © by The McGraw-Hill Companies, Inc.

Key Points

Notes

Terms To Review

Use the following term, which you studied in an earlier chapter, in a sentence that reflects the term's meaning in this lesson.

elements
(Chapter 1, Section 3)

_____
_____

Safavid Culture (page 253)

Responding

As you read, think about what captures your attention. Use the lines below to write down facts you find interesting or surprising.

_____
_____
_____
_____

Section Wrap-up

Now that you have read the section, answer these questions from Setting a Purpose for Reading at the beginning of the section.

What events led to the creation and growth of the Safavid dynasty?

_____
_____
_____
_____

What cultural contributions were made by the Safavid dynasty?

_____
_____
_____
_____

Copyright © by The McGraw-Hill Companies, Inc.

Chapter 8, Section 3
The Grandeur of the Moguls
(Pages 255–260)

Reason To Read

Setting a Purpose for Reading Think about these questions as you read:
- How did Mogul rulers develop the empire's culture?
- What were the chief characteristics of Mogul society?

Main Idea

As you read pages 255–260 in your textbook, complete the chart below by listing the accomplishments and weaknesses of the Mogul rulers.

Ruler	Accomplishments	Weaknesses

Sequencing Events

As you read, number the following events in the order in which they occurred.

_____ **British trading forts are established at Surat, Fort Williams, and Chennai**

_____ **Akbar becomes Mogul ruler**

_____ **Moguls rule most of India**

_____ **Aurangzeb is crowned emperor**

Copyright © by The McGraw-Hill Companies, Inc.

Key Points

Notes

The Mogul Dynasty (pages 255–256)

Clarifying

As you read this lesson, think about Babur, the founder of the Mogul dynasty. How was he able to establish the Mogul dynasty in India?

_____

_____

_____

_____

The Reign of Akbar (pages 256–257)

Questioning

As you read, write two questions about the main ideas presented in the text. After you have finished reading, write the answers to these questions.

_____

_____

_____

_____

Terms To Know

Define or describe the following key term from this lesson.

zamindar

_____

_____

Academic Vocabulary

Define the following academic vocabulary words from this lesson.

domain

_____

_____

annual

_____

Copyright © by The McGraw-Hill Companies, Inc.

Decline of the Moguls (page 257)

Summarizing   *As you read, complete the following sentences to help you summarize the lesson.*

1. Akbar was succeeded by his son _____ , who continued to strengthen the central _____ .

2. Aurangzeb was a very _____ ruler. He had high _____ , but was also _____ .

Terms To Know   *Define or describe the following key term from this lesson.*

suttee   _____

_____

Academic Vocabulary   *Use the following academic vocabulary word from this lesson in a sentence.*

eliminate   _____

_____

Terms To Review   *Write the definition of each of the following terms that you studied earlier.*

ultimate
(Chapter 1, Section 3)   _____

_____

expanded
(Chapter 1, Section 2)   _____

_____

Copyright © by The McGraw-Hill Companies, Inc.

Key Points

Notes

The British in India (pages 257–258)

Determining the Main Idea

As you read, write down the main idea of the passage. Review your statement when you have finished reading and revise as needed.

_____

_____

_____

_____

Academic Vocabulary

Define each of the following academic vocabulary words from this lesson.

restricted

_____

_____

constant

_____

_____

Terms To Review

Write the definition of the following term that you studied earlier.

brief
(Chapter 3, Section 3)

_____

_____

Society and Daily Life in Mogul India (page 259)

Evaluating

In your opinion, did the lives of women improve under Mogul rule? Explain.

_____

_____

_____

_____

Copyright © by The McGraw-Hill Companies, Inc.

Terms To Review

Use the following term, which you studied earlier, in a sentence that reflects the term's meaning in this lesson.

attitudes
(Chapter 5, Section 1)

_____

_____

Mogul Culture (pages 259–260)

Visualizing

Imagine that you are a painter during the Mogul period. Use the lines below to explain how your art is influenced by the Persian and Indian cultures.

_____

_____

_____

_____

Terms To Review

Write the definition of the following term that you studied in an earlier chapter.

goal
(Chapter 1, Section 3)

_____

_____

Section Wrap-up

Now that you have read the section, answer these questions from Setting a Purpose for Reading at the beginning of the section.

How did Mogul rulers develop the empire's culture?

_____

_____

_____

What were the chief characteristics of Mogul society?

_____

_____

_____

Copyright © by The McGraw-Hill Companies, Inc.

Chapter 9, Section 1
China at Its Height

(Pages 267–272)

Reason To Read

Setting a Purpose for Reading Think about these questions as you read:
- What was remarkable about the naval voyages under Emperor Yong Le?
- How did the Manchus gain the support of the Chinese?

Main Idea

As you read pages 267–272 in your textbook, complete the graphic organizer below by comparing and contrasting the achievements of the Ming and Qing dynasties.

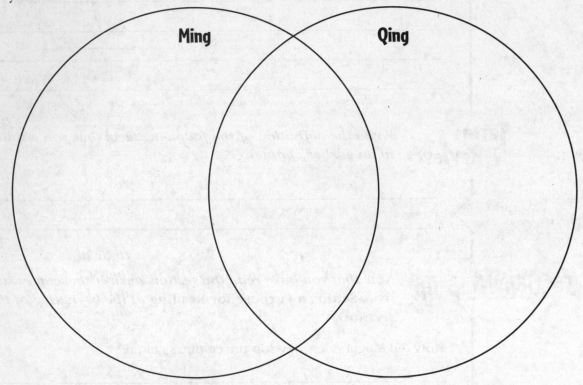

Ming   Qing

Sequencing Events

As you read, number the following events in the order in which they occurred.

_____ **Major epidemic reduces the population in many areas**

_____ **Emperor Qianlong begins reign**

_____ **China allows Portuguese to occupy Macao**

_____ **Ming dynasty ends**

Copyright © by The McGraw-Hill Companies, Inc.

The Ming Dynasty (pages 267–270)

Connecting

Modern politicians often talk about rebuilding the infrastructure, such as bridges and roads, to improve the American economy. Use the lines below to describe how Ming emperors improved China's infrastructure during their rule of China.

_____

_____

_____

Terms To Review

Define or describe each of the following terms that you studied earlier.

items
(Chapter 3, Section 3)

_____

_____

perspective
(Chapter 5, Section 2)

_____

_____

The Qing Dynasty (pages 270–272)

Monitoring Comprehension

As you read the lesson, think about ethnic differences between the new Manchu rulers and their Chinese subjects. Why do you think the new Manchu rulers, known as the Qing dynasty, were eventually accepted?

_____

_____

_____

Terms To Know

Define or describe each of the following key terms from this lesson.

queue

_____

_____

Copyright © by The McGraw-Hill Companies, Inc.

Key Points

Notes

banners

Academic Vocabulary

Define the following academic vocabulary words from this lesson.

accommodating

facilitate

Terms To Review

Use the following term, which you studied earlier, in a sentence that reflects the term's meaning in this lesson.

revenues
(Chapter 2, Section 2)

Section Wrap-up

Now that you have read the section, answer these questions from Setting a Purpose for Reading *at the beginning of the section.*

What was remarkable about the naval voyages under Emperor Yong Le?

How did the Manchus gain the support of the Chinese?

Copyright © by The McGraw-Hill Companies, Inc.

Chapter 9, Section 2
Chinese Society and Culture
(Pages 273–276)

Reason To Read

Setting a Purpose for Reading Think about these questions as you read:
- Why did the population increase between 1500 and 1800?
- Why did commercial capitalism not develop in China during this period?

Main Idea

As you read pages 273–276 in your textbook, complete the graphic organizer below by showing the organization of the Chinese family.

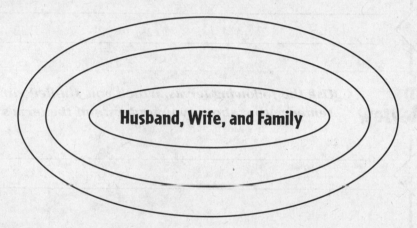

Husband, Wife, and Family

Sequencing Events

As you read, place the following events on the time line below.

- **Popular novel, *The Dream of the Red Chamber,* is published**
- **Ming dynasty begins a new era of greatness in China**
- **Chinese population is less than 80 million**
- **Renovations are begun on the Imperial City**

♦1300   ♦1400   ♦1500   ♦1600   ♦1700   ♦1800

Copyright © by The McGraw-Hill Companies, Inc.

Economic Changes (pages 273–274)

Determining the Main Idea

As you read, write down the main idea of the passage. Review your statement when you have finished reading and revise as needed.

_____

_____

_____

Terms To Know

Define or describe the following key term from this lesson.

commercial capitalism

_____

_____

Terms To Review

Use the following terms, which you studied earlier, in a sentence that shows you understand the term's meaning.

percent
(Chapter 4, Section 1)

_____

_____

available
(Chapter 3, Section 1)

_____

_____

Daily Life (pages 274–275)

Visualizing

As you read the descriptions of the Chinese family, try to imagine what it would be like to live with your entire extended family. What would be the advantages and disadvantages of this arrangement? Summarize your thoughts in a paragraph.

_____

_____

_____

_____

Copyright © by The McGraw-Hill Companies, Inc.

Terms To Know

Define or describe the following key term from this lesson.

clan 〉 _____
_____

Academic Vocabulary

Define the following academic vocabulary word from this lesson.

incentive 〉 _____
_____

Terms To Review

Use each of the following terms, which you studied earlier, in a sentence.

contrast
(Chapter 2, Section 2) 〉 _____
_____

subordinate
(Chapter 1, Section 3) 〉 _____
_____

Cultural Developments (page 276)

Synthesizing

As you read this lesson, recall from Chapter 8 the type of literature that Chinese writers created earlier. What was it? What new form of literature arose during the Ming dynasty?

_____
_____
_____

Terms To Know

Define or describe the following key term from this lesson.

porcelain 〉 _____

Copyright © by The McGraw-Hill Companies, Inc.

Key Points

Notes

Academic Vocabulary

Use each of the following academic vocabulary words from this lesson in a sentence.

manipulate

_____

_____

_____

compound

_____

_____

_____

Terms To Review

Use the following term, which you studied earlier, in a sentence that reflects the term's meaning.

individuals
(Chapter 5, Section 1)

_____

_____

Section Wrap-up

Now that you have read the section, answer these questions from Setting a Purpose for Reading *at the beginning of the section.*

Why did the population increase between 1500 and 1800?

_____

_____

_____

_____

Why did commercial capitalism not develop in China during this period?

_____

_____

_____

_____

_____

Copyright © by The McGraw-Hill Companies, Inc.

Chapter 9, Section 3
Tokugawa Japan and Korea
(Pages 278–282)

Reason To Read

Setting a Purpose for Reading Think about these questions as you read:
• What economic changes took place under the Tokugawa shoguns?
• How did Japanese culture change during the Tokugawa Era?

Main Idea

As you read pages 278–282 in your textbook, complete the graphic organizer below by categorizing the different elements of Japanese culture.

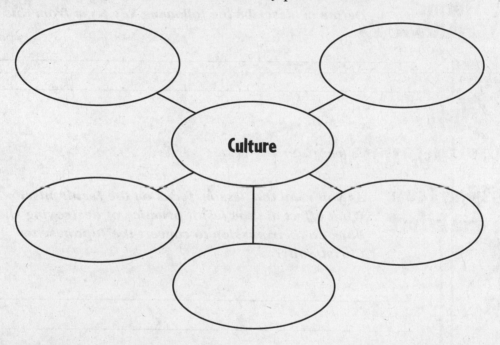

Culture

Sequencing Events

As you read, write the correct date next to each event on the time line below.

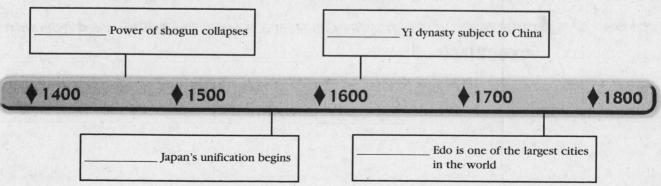

_____ Power of shogun collapses

_____ Yi dynasty subject to China

♦ 1400   ♦ 1500   ♦ 1600   ♦ 1700   ♦ 1800

_____ Japan's unification begins

_____ Edo is one of the largest cities in the world

Copyright © by The McGraw-Hill Companies, Inc.

Key Points

Notes

The Three Great Unifiers (pages 278–279)

Visualizing

As you read this lesson, imagine you are a poor Japanese farmer caught between warlords fighting for power. Write a brief paragraph explaining why you might be glad that Tokugawa Ieyasu attained control of Japan by about 1600.

_____

_____

_____

_____

Terms To Know

Define or describe the following key term from this lesson.

daimyo

_____

_____

Europeans in Japan (page 279)

Identifying Cause and Effect

As you read this lesson, focus on the Jesuit missionaries. What effect did the Jesuit practice of destroying shrines have on their mission to convert the Japanese to Christianity?

_____

_____

_____

_____

Academic Vocabulary

Define the following academic vocabulary word from this lesson.

prohibiting

_____

_____

Copyright © by The McGraw-Hill Companies, Inc.

 Key Points

 Notes

Terms To Review

Use each of the following terms, which you studied earlier, in a sentence that reflects the term's meaning.

converted
(Chapter 3, Section 1)

_____

_____

community
(Chapter 3, Section 2)

_____

_____

_____

Tokugawa Rule *(pages 279–280)*

Determining the Main Idea

As you read this lesson, describe the important changes that came about in the status of the daimyo, or Japanese feudal lords, during the rule of the Tokugawa.

_____

_____

_____

Terms To Know

Define or describe each of the following key terms from this lesson.

hans

_____

_____

hostage system

_____

_____

Academic Vocabulary

Use the following academic vocabulary word from this lesson in a sentence.

ceased

_____

_____

Copyright © by The McGraw-Hill Companies, Inc.

Economic and Social Changes (pages 280–281)

Reviewing

As you read, focus on the social classes during Tokugawa rule. In the space below, draw a diagram that illustrates the classes in order, from top to bottom.

Terms To Know

Define or describe the following key term from this lesson.

eta _____

Copyright © by The McGraw-Hill Companies, Inc.

 **Key Points**

 **Notes**

Academic Vocabulary

Define the following academic vocabulary words from this lesson.

exploiting

_____

_____

hierarchy

_____

_____

Terms To Review

Write the letter of the correct definition next to each of these terms that you studied earlier.

_____ **1.** rigid
(Chapter 3, Section 2)

_____ **2.** declining
(Chapter 7, Section 4)

a. an extreme measure

b. very closely enforced

c. drawing to a close

Tokugawa Culture *(pages 281–282)*

Analyzing

As you read, notice that there was an increase in building in the cities during the Tokugawa period. What policy of the shogun was responsible for this growth?

_____

_____

_____

Academic Vocabulary

Define the following academic vocabulary word from this lesson.

dramas

_____

_____

Copyright © by The McGraw-Hill Companies, Inc.

Korea: The Hermit Kingdom (page 282)

Questioning

As you read, write two questions about the main ideas in the passage. After you have finished, write the answers to these questions.

_____

_____

_____

_____

Terms To Review

Define the following term that you studied in an earlier chapter.

isolated
(Chapter 2, Section 1)

_____

_____

Section Wrap-up

Now that you have read the section, answer these questions from Setting a Purpose for Reading *at the beginning of the section.*

What economic changes took place under the Tokugawa shoguns?

_____

_____

_____

_____

How did Japanese culture change during the Tokugawa Era?

_____

_____

_____

_____

Copyright © by The McGraw-Hill Companies, Inc.

Chapter 10, Section 1
The Scientific Revolution
(Pages 293–299)

Reason To Read

Setting a Purpose for Reading Think about these questions as you read:
• How did the Scientific Revolution begin?
• What is the scientific method?

Main Idea

As you read pages 293–299 in your textbook, complete the table below by identifying the contributions of Copernicus, Kepler, Galileo, and Newton to a new concept of the universe.

Copernicus	
Kepler	
Galileo	
Newton	

Sequencing Events

As you read, place the following events on the time line below.
• **Harvey publishes *On the Motion of the Heart and Blood***
• **Galileo's *Starry Messenger* is published**
• **Galileo faces the Inquisition**
• **Copernicus publishes *On the Revolutions of the Heavenly Spheres***

♦1545   ♦1560   ♦1575   ♦1590   ♦1605   ♦1620   ♦1635

Copyright © by The McGraw-Hill Companies, Inc.

Key Points

Notes

Background to the Revolution (pages 293–294)

Previewing

Preview the section to get an idea of what's ahead. Write a sentence or two below explaining what you expect to learn. After you have finished reading, revise your statements as needed.

_____

_____

_____

_____

Academic Vocabulary

Define the each of following academic vocabulary words from this lesson.

obvious

_____

_____

technical

_____

_____

Terms To Review

Write the definition of the following term that you studied earlier.

intense
(Chapter 4, Section 1)

_____

_____

A Revolution in Astronomy (pages 294–297)

Summarizing

As you read, think about the discoveries in astronomy. Then write a paragraph summarizing the work of the four mathematicians that had an impact on astronomy.

_____

_____

_____

Copyright © by The McGraw-Hill Companies, Inc.

Terms To Know

Write the letter of the correct definition next to each of these terms from this lesson.

_____ **1.** geocentric

_____ **2.** Ptolemaic system

_____ **3.** heliocentric

_____ **4.** universal law of gravitation

a. geocentric model of the universe named after astronomer Ptolemy

b. explains why the planetary bodies continue in elliptical orbits about the Sun

c. earth-centered

d. the belief that reason is the chief source of knowledge

e. sun-centered

Breakthroughs in Medicine and Chemistry *(page 297)*

Evaluating

As you read this lesson, think about a recent medical breakthrough you might have heard about in the news. How do you think it compares to the breakthroughs of Vesalius and Harvey?

_____

_____

_____

_____

Academic Vocabulary

Use the following academic vocabulary word from this lesson in a sentence.

instances

_____

_____

Terms To Review

Write the definition of the following term that you studied in an earlier chapter.

conduct
(Chapter 7, Section 2)

_____

_____

Copyright © by The McGraw-Hill Companies, Inc.

Key Points | Notes

Women and the Origins of Modern Science (pages 297–298)

Connecting

As you read, compare the role of women scientists during the Scientific Revolution with the role of women scientists today. Summarize your thoughts in a paragraph.

_____

_____

_____

_____

Academic Vocabulary

Define the following academic vocabulary word from this lesson.

denied >

_____

_____

Descartes and Reason (pages 298–299)

Skimming

Read the title and quickly look over the lesson to get a general idea of its content. Then write a sentence or two explaining what the lesson is about.

_____

_____

_____

_____

Terms To Know

Define or describe the following key term from this lesson.

rationalism >

_____

_____

Copyright © by The McGraw-Hill Companies, Inc.

The Scientific Method (page 299)

Monitoring Comprehension

As you read the lesson, write down any questions you may have below. When you have finished reading, answer your questions.

_____

_____

_____

_____

Terms To Know

Define or describe the following key terms from this lesson.

scientific method >

_____

_____

inductive reasoning >

_____

_____

Section Wrap-up

Now that you have read the section, answer these questions from Setting a Purpose for Reading *at the beginning of the section.*

How did the Scientific Revolution begin?

_____

_____

_____

What is the scientific method?

_____

_____

_____

Copyright © by The McGraw-Hill Companies, Inc.

Chapter 10, Section 2
The Enlightenment
(Pages 300–307)

Reason To Read

Setting a Purpose for Reading Think about these questions as you read:
- What was the Enlightenment?
- What role did religion play during the Enlightenment?

Main Idea

As you read pages 300–307 in your textbook, complete the graphic organizer below by listing some of the main ideas introduced during the Enlightenment.

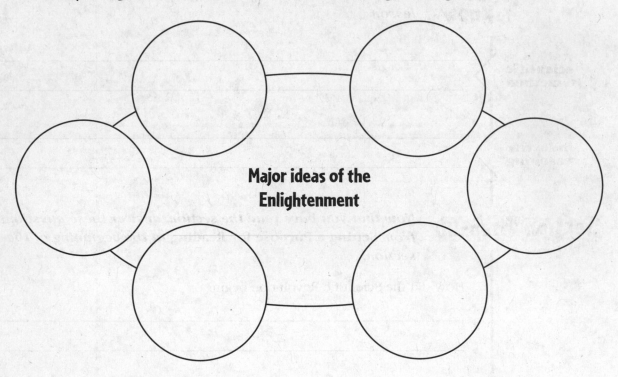

Major ideas of the Enlightenment

Sequencing Events

As you read, number the following events in the order in which they occurred.

_____ Baron de Montesquieu publishes *The Spirit of the Laws*

_____ Adam Smith publishes *The Wealth of Nations*

_____ Rousseau publishes *The Social Contract*

_____ Cesare Beccaria publishes *On Crimes and Punishments*

Copyright © by The McGraw-Hill Companies, Inc.

 **Key Points**

 **Notes**

Path to the Enlightenment (pages 300–301)

Summarizing

As you read, complete the following sentences to help you summarize the lesson.

1. John Locke believed that people were _____ by the experiences that came through their _____ .

2. Isaac Newton believed that _____ laws existed and that _____ could follow these laws to produce the _____ society.

Academic Vocabulary

Use the following academic vocabulary word from this lesson in a sentence.

> **affected** ⟩ _____

_____

Philosophes and Their Ideas (pages 301–303)

Reviewing

As you read this lesson, describe the contributions made by the following philosophes: Montesquieu, Voltaire, Diderot.

_____

_____

_____

Terms To Know

Define or describe each of the following key terms from this lesson.

> **philosophe** ⟩ _____

_____

> **separation of powers** ⟩ _____

_____

Copyright © by The McGraw-Hill Companies, Inc.

Key Points / Notes

deism ⟩ _____

_____

Toward a New Social Science (pages 303–304)

Clarifying

As you read, think about the Physiocrats and Adam Smith. Then describe their views on natural economic laws and the doctrine of laissez-faire. What did Adam Smith believe were the three basic roles of the government?

_____

_____

_____

_____

Terms To Know

Define or describe the following key term from this lesson.

laissez-faire ⟩ _____

_____

The Later Enlightenment (page 304)

Evaluating

As you read, form an opinion about Rousseau's view of education as stated in Emile. *Summarize your opinion in a paragraph.*

_____

_____

_____

Terms To Know

Define or describe the following key term from this lesson.

social contract ⟩ _____

_____

Copyright © by The McGraw-Hill Companies, Inc.

Rights of Women *(page 305)*

Connecting

As you read, think about the issues women sometimes face today. How do these issues compare with what women faced during the Enlightenment? Summarize your thoughts in a paragraph.

_____

_____

_____

_____

Terms To Review

Use the following term, which you studied earlier, in a sentence that reflects the term's meaning in this lesson.

arbitrary
(Chapter 2, Section 2)

_____

_____

Social World of the Enlightenment *(pages 305–307)*

Monitoring Comprehension

As you read, write down one question from each subhead for a partner to answer. Exchange questions and see if you can answer your partner's questions.

The Growth of Reading

_____

_____

The Salon

_____

_____

Terms To Know

Define or describe the following key term from this lesson.

salon

_____

_____

Copyright © by The McGraw-Hill Companies, Inc.

Religion in the Enlightenment (page 307)

Determining the Main Idea

As you read, write down the main idea of the passage on the lines below. Review your statement when you have finished reading and revise as needed.

_____

_____

_____

_____

_____

Terms To Review

Write the definition of each of the following terms that you studied earlier.

assured
(Chapter 5, Section 3)

_____

_____

initial
(Chapter 8, Section 2)

_____

_____

Section Wrap-up

Now that you have read the section, answer these questions from Setting a Purpose for Reading *at the beginning of the section.*

What was the Enlightenment?

_____

_____

_____

What role did religion play during the Enlightenment?

_____

_____

_____

Copyright © by The McGraw-Hill Companies, Inc.

Chapter 10, Section 3
The Impact of the Enlightenment
(Pages 308–316)

Reason To Read

Setting a Purpose for Reading Think about these questions as you read:

• What innovation in the arts occurred during the 1700s?

• What were the causes and results of the Seven Years' War?

Main Idea

As you read pages 308–316 in your textbook, complete the chart below by listing the conflicts of the Seven Years' War. Include the countries involved and where the conflicts were fought.

Conflicts of the Seven Years' War

Sequencing Events

As you read, write the correct date next to each event on the time line below.

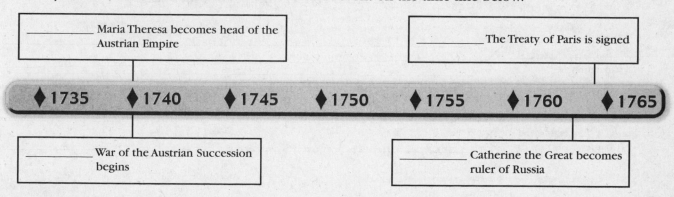

_____ Maria Theresa becomes head of the Austrian Empire

_____ The Treaty of Paris is signed

♦1735   ♦1740   ♦1745   ♦1750   ♦1755   ♦1760   ♦1765

_____ War of the Austrian Succession begins

_____ Catherine the Great becomes ruler of Russia

Copyright © by The McGraw-Hill Companies, Inc.

The Arts (pages 308–310)

Outlining

As you read this lesson, fill in the outline below.

I. Architecture and Art

    A. _____

    B. _____

II. Music

    A. _____

    B. _____

III. Literature

    A. _____

    B. _____

Terms To Know

Define or describe the following key term from this lesson.

rococo

_____

_____

Academic Vocabulary

Define the academic vocabulary word from this lesson.

style

_____

_____

Terms To Review

Use each of these terms, which you studied earlier, in a sentence that reflects the term's meaning.

enormous
(Chapter 4, Section 2)

_____

_____

unique
(Chapter 1, Section 2)

_____

_____

Copyright © by The McGraw-Hill Companies, Inc.

---

design
(Chapter 5, Section 2)

_____

_____

Enlightenment and Enlightened Absolutism (pages 310–313)

Clarifying

As you read this lesson, choose one term or concept you find unfamiliar, research it, and write an explanation of it. Share your explanation with other students.

_____

_____

_____

_____

Terms To Know

Define or describe the following key term from this lesson.

enlightened absolutism

_____

_____

Academic Vocabulary

Use each of the following academic vocabulary words from this lesson in a sentence.

priority

_____

_____

assumed

_____

_____

Terms To Review

Use this term, which you studied earlier, in a sentence that reflects the term's meaning in this lesson.

pursue
(Chapter 3, Section 4)

_____

_____

Copyright © by The McGraw-Hill Companies, Inc.

Notes

War of the Austrian Succession (pages 313–314)

Identifying Cause and Effect

As you read this lesson, focus on the effects of the War of the Austrian Succession. Write your findings below.

_____

_____

_____

_____

Terms To Review

Write the definition of each of the following terms that you studied earlier.

occupied
(Chapter 3, Section 1)

_____

_____

traditional
(Chapter 1, Section 2)

_____

_____

The Seven Years' War (pages 314–316)

Responding

As you read this lesson, notice how often France and Britain were fighting one another in the 1700s. Besides North America, where else in the world were these two nations at war?

_____

_____

_____

_____

Academic Vocabulary

Define the following academic vocabulary words from this lesson.

transferred

_____

Copyright © by The McGraw-Hill Companies, Inc.

persistent >

_____
_____
_____

focused >

_____
_____
_____

Terms To Review

Use each of the following terms, which you studied earlier, in a sentence.

labeled
(Chapter 8, Section 1) >

_____
_____
_____

ultimately
(Chapter 1, Section 3) >

_____
_____
_____

Section Wrap-up

Now that you have read the section, answer these questions from Setting a Purpose for Reading *at the beginning of the section.*

What innovation in the arts occurred during the 1700s?

_____
_____
_____
_____

What were the causes and results of the Seven Years' War?

_____
_____
_____
_____

Copyright © by The McGraw-Hill Companies, Inc.

Chapter 10, Section 4
Colonial Empires and the American Revolution

(Pages 318–322)

Reason To Read

Setting a Purpose for Reading Think about these questions as you read:

• What were the chief characteristics of Latin American society?
• What caused the American Revolution, and what did it accomplish?

Main Idea

As you read pages 318–322 in your textbook, complete the graphic organizer below by identifying key aspects of the government the American colonists created.

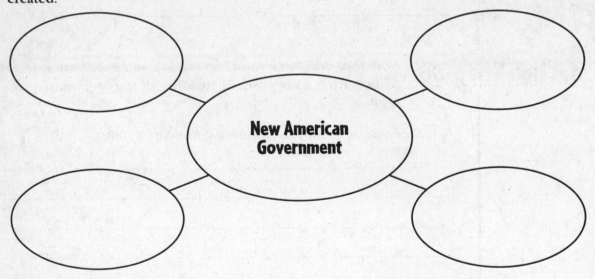

New American Government

Sequencing Events

As you read, number the following events in the order in which they occurred.

_____ American Revolution begins

_____ Hanoverian dynasty is established

_____ Treaty of Paris recognizes American independence

_____ Population of British colonies in North America is estimated at more than one million

Copyright © by The McGraw-Hill Companies, Inc.

Colonial Empires in Latin America (pages 318–320)

Copyright © by The McGraw-Hill Companies, Inc.

Analyzing

As you read, think about the economic activities in Latin American colonies. Then write a paragraph explaining how the Portuguese and the Spanish profited from their colonies in Latin America.

_____

_____

_____

_____

Terms To Know

Define or describe each of the following key terms from this lesson.

mestizo

_____

_____

mulatto

_____

_____

Academic Vocabulary

Use the following academic vocabulary words from this lesson in a sentence.

regulated

_____

_____

virtually

_____

_____

Terms To Review

Use the following term, which you studied earlier, in a sentence that reflects the term's meaning.

feature
(Chapter 1, Section 2)

_____

_____

Chapter 10, Section 4

Britain and British North America (page 320)

Summarizing

After you read this lesson, list the countries below that made up Great Britain in the 1700s.

_____

_____

Academic Vocabulary

Define the following academic vocabulary word from this lesson.

levy

_____

_____

The American Revolution (page 321)

Sequencing

As you read, number the following events in the order in which they occurred.

_____ Second Continental Congress meets

_____ Parliament imposes the Stamp Act on the colonies

_____ Fighting starts at Lexington and Concord

_____ First Continental Congress meets

Academic Vocabulary

Use the following academic vocabulary word from this lesson in a sentence.

resolved

_____

_____

Copyright © by The McGraw-Hill Companies, Inc.

Terms To Review

Use each of these terms, which you studied in an earlier chapter, in a sentence that reflects the term's meaning in this lesson.

impose
(Chapter 6, Section 3)

_____

_____

widespread
(Chapter 5, Section 3)

_____

_____

The Birth of a New Nation (pages 321–322)

Drawing Conclusions

As you read, write down three details about the Constitution and the Bill of Rights. Then write a conclusion based on these details.

_____

_____

_____

_____

_____

Terms To Know

Define or describe the following key term from this lesson.

federal system

_____

_____

Academic Vocabulary

Define the following academic vocabulary word from this lesson.

currency

_____

_____

Copyright © by The McGraw-Hill Companies, Inc.

Terms To Review

Use each of the following terms, which you studied earlier, in a sentence that reflects the term's meaning in this lesson.

concentrated
(Chapter 1, Section 1)

_____

_____

derived
(Chapter 2, Section 1)

_____

_____

Section Wrap-up

Now that you have read the section, answer these questions from Setting a Purpose for Reading *at the beginning of the section.*

What were the chief characteristics of Latin American society?

_____

_____

_____

_____

_____

What caused the American Revolution, and what did it accomplish?

_____

_____

_____

_____

_____

Copyright © by The McGraw-Hill Companies, Inc.

Chapter 11, Section 1
The French Revolution Begins

(Pages 329–335)

Reason To Read

Setting a Purpose for Reading Think about these questions as you read:
• What groups made up the three estates of France?
• How did the fall of the Bastille save the National Assembly?

Main Idea

As you read pages 329–335 in your textbook, complete the graphic organizer below by listing the factors that contributed to the French Revolution.

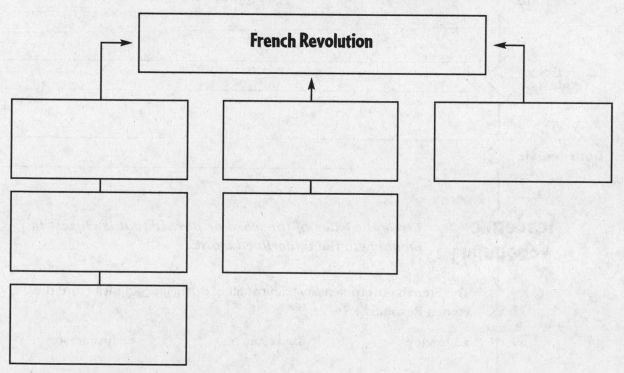

Sequencing Events

As you read, number the following events in the order in which they occurred.

_____ **National Assembly completes new constitution**

_____ **National Assembly adopts Declaration of the Rights of Man**

_____ **Bad harvests lead to food shortages**

_____ **Estates-General meets at Versailles**

Copyright © by The McGraw-Hill Companies, Inc.

Notes

Background to the Revolution (pages 329–331)

Skimming

Skim this lesson before you begin reading it, looking at headings and words in color or boldface type. Write a sentence explaining what you expect to learn. After reading, revise your sentence if needed.

_____

_____

_____

Terms To Know

Define or describe the following key terms from this lesson.

estate

_____

_____

relics of feudalism

_____

_____

_____

bourgeoisie

_____

_____

Academic Vocabulary

Circle the letter of the word or phrase that is closest in meaning to the underlined word.

finances

The French government lost almost all of its <u>finances</u> right before the French Revolution.

a. money   **b.** resources   **c.** businesses

sums

Even though the French government had economic problems, it still spent enormous <u>sums</u> of money.

a. average   **b.** amounts   **c.** extremely small

Copyright © by The McGraw-Hill Companies, Inc.

Key Points

Notes

 **Terms To Review**

Write the definition of each of the following terms that you studied earlier.

crucial
(Chapter 1, Section 1)

_____

_____

proportions
(Chapter 7, Section 4)

_____

_____

From Estates-General to National Assembly (pages 331–332)

Evaluating

As you read, think about whether the Third Estate was justified in its decision to call itself a National Assembly and draft a constitution. How else might the issue of voting among the three estates have been resolved?

_____

_____

_____

Academic Vocabulary

Define the following academic vocabulary words from this lesson.

fees

_____

_____

abandoned

_____

_____

Terms To Review

Use the following term, which you studied earlier, in a sentence that reflects the term's meaning.

authority
(Chapter 4, Section 1)

_____

_____

Copyright © by The McGraw-Hill Companies, Inc.

The Destruction of the Old Regime *(pages 332–335)*

Outlining   *As you read this lesson, fill in the outline below.*

I. Declaration of the Rights of Man

   A. _____

   B. _____

   C. _____

II. The King Concedes

   A. _____

   B. _____

III. Church Reforms

   A. _____

   B. _____

IV. A New Constitution and New Fears

   A. _____

   B. _____

   C. _____

V. War with Austria

   A. _____

   B. _____

VI. Rise of the Paris Commune

   A. _____

   B. _____

   C. _____

Terms To Know   *Define or describe the following key term from this lesson.*

sans-culottes ⟩ _____

_____

Copyright © by The McGraw-Hill Companies, Inc.

 **Key Points**

 **Notes**

Academic Vocabulary

Define the following academic vocabulary words from this lesson.

issue

_____

_____

_____

radical

_____

_____

_____

Terms To Review

Use the following term, which you studied earlier, in a sentence.

functions
(Chapter 5, Section 4)

_____

_____

Section Wrap-up

Now that you have read the section, answer these questions from Setting a Purpose for Reading *at the beginning of the section.*

What groups made up the three estates of France?

_____

_____

_____

_____

_____

How did the fall of the Bastille save the National Assembly?

_____

_____

_____

_____

_____

Copyright © by The McGraw-Hill Companies, Inc.

Chapter 11, Section 2
Radical Revolution and Reaction

(Pages 337–343)

Reason To Read

Setting a Purpose for Reading Think about these questions as you read:
• Why did a coalition of European countries take up arms against France?
• Why did the Reign of Terror occur?

Main Idea

As you read pages 337–343 in your textbook, complete the chart below by listing the actions taken by the National Convention.

Actions Taken by the National Convention
1.
2.
3.
4.

Sequencing Events

As you read, write the correct date next to each event on the time line below.

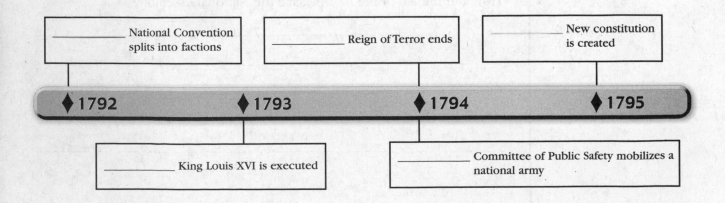

_____ National Convention splits into factions

_____ Reign of Terror ends

_____ New constitution is created

♦1792   ♦1793   ♦1794   ♦1795

_____ King Louis XVI is executed

_____ Committee of Public Safety mobilizes a national army

Copyright © by The McGraw-Hill Companies, Inc.

The Move to Radicalism (pages 337–339)

Analyzing

As you read, think about the move to radicalism in France. Then write a paragraph describing the two major aspects of the domestic crisis after the National Convention was established.

_____

_____

_____

_____

Terms To Know

Define or describe the following key term from this lesson.

faction

_____

_____

Academic Vocabulary

Define the following academic vocabulary word from this lesson.

aspect

_____

_____

Terms To Review

Use each of the following terms, which you studied earlier, in a sentence that reflects the term's meaning.

draft
(Chapter 7, Section 3)

_____

_____

convinced
(Chapter 3, Section 1)

_____

_____

Copyright © by The McGraw-Hill Companies, Inc.

The Reign of Terror (pages 339–342)

Monitoring Comprehension

As you read, write down one question for each subhead for a partner to answer. Exchange questions and see if you can answer your partner's questions.

Crushing Rebellion
_____
_____

The Republic of Virtue
_____
_____

Academic Vocabulary

Circle the letter of the word or phrase that is closest in meaning to the underlined word.

temporary

The Committee of Public Safety claimed the massive executions were <u>temporary</u>.

a. lasting only for a time   **b.** lasting permanently   **c.** ending

enforce

One of the failures of the Committee of Public Safety was its inability to <u>enforce</u> the controls it set up.

a. undo   **b.** explain   **c.** put in force

Terms To Review

Define each of the following terms that you studied earlier.

participate
(Chapter 2, Section 1)
_____
_____

military
(Chapter 1, Section 2)
_____
_____

founded
(Chapter 2, Section 2)
_____
_____

Copyright © by The McGraw-Hill Companies, Inc.

A Nation in Arms *(page 342)*

Drawing Conclusions

As you read, write down three details about the French revolutionary army. Then write a conclusion based on these details.

_____

_____

_____

_____

Academic Vocabulary

Define the following academic vocabulary words from this lesson.

external

_____

_____

nonetheless

_____

The Directory *(pages 342–343)*

Summarizing

As you read, complete the following sentences to help you summarize the lesson.

1. As a reaction to the Reign of Terror, the Constitution of 1795 divided power between a legislative assembly with a lower house called the

   _____ and an upper house called the

   _____ .

2. Five directors made up the executive committee known

   as the _____ , which ruled with the legislature to restore stability after the Reign of Terror.

Copyright © by The McGraw-Hill Companies, Inc.

 Key Points

 Notes

Terms To Know

Define or describe the following key terms from this lesson.

electors >

_____

_____

coup d'état >

_____

_____

Academic Vocabulary

Write the letter of the correct definition next to each of these academic vocabulary words from this lesson.

____ **1.** initiated

____ **2.** stability

a. set in motion

b. halted

c. firmly established

Section Wrap-up

Now that you have read the section, answer these questions from Setting a Purpose for Reading *at the beginning of the section.*

Why did a coalition of European countries take up arms against France?

_____

_____

_____

_____

Why did the Reign of Terror occur?

_____

_____

_____

_____

_____

Copyright © by The McGraw-Hill Companies, Inc.

Chapter 11, Section 3
The Age of Napoleon

(Pages 345–351)

Reason To Read

Setting a Purpose for Reading Think about these questions as you read:
- Why did Napoleon want to stop British goods from reaching Europe?
- What were two reasons for the collapse of Napoleon's empire?

Main Idea

As you read pages 345–351 in your textbook, complete the graphic organizer below by listing the achievements of Napoleon's rule.

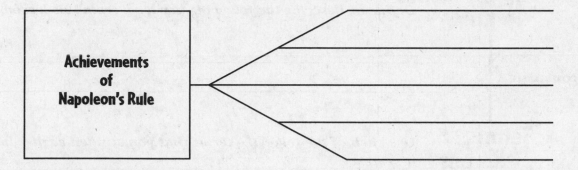

Achievements of Napoleon's Rule

Sequencing Events

As you read, place the following events on the time line below.
- **Napoleon is crowned emperor**
- **Napoleon's Grand Army invades Russia**
- **Napoleon takes part in coup d'état**
- **Napoleon is defeated at Waterloo**
- **French are defeated at Trafalgar**

♦ 1790   ♦ 1800   ♦ 1810   ♦ 1820

Copyright © by The McGraw-Hill Companies, Inc.

The Rise of Napoleon *(pages 345–346)*

Analyzing

As you read, think about Napoleon's invasion of Egypt, a British colony. Besides striking at British power there, what else might have motivated Napoleon to invade Egypt?

_____

_____

_____

_____

_____

Terms To Know

Define or describe the following key term from this lesson.

consulate

_____

_____

Terms To Review

Use each of the following terms that you studied earlier in a sentence.

intelligence
(Chapter 3, Section 4)

_____

_____

ceased
(Chapter 9, Section 3)

_____

_____

philosophes
(Chapter 10, Section 2)

_____

_____

Copyright © by The McGraw-Hill Companies, Inc.

Napoleon's Domestic Policies (pages 347–348)

Questioning

As you read, think about Napoleon having himself crowned emperor and then his creation of the Napoleonic Code. Write a paragraph explaining the apparent contradiction between these two actions.

_____

_____

_____

_____

_____

Academic Vocabulary

Circle the letter of the word or phrase that is closest in meaning to the underlined word.

published

Napoleon insisted that all manuscripts be reviewed by the government before they were allowed to be <u>published</u>.

a. read   **b.** distributed   **c.** printed

code

The Napoleonic <u>Code</u> guaranteed certain rights for French citizens.

a. set of symbols   **b.** set of laws   **c.** military rank

Terms To Review

Use each of the following terms, which you studied earlier, in a sentence that reflects the term's meaning.

hierarchy
(Chapter 9, Section 3)

_____

_____

obtain
(Chapter 1, Section 3)

_____

_____

Copyright © by The McGraw-Hill Companies, Inc.

Key Points

Notes

Napoleon's Empire (pages 348–349)

Previewing

Preview the section to get an idea of what's ahead. First, skim the section. Then write a sentence or two explaining what you think you will be learning. After you have finished reading, revise your statements as needed.

_____

_____

_____

_____

Academic Vocabulary

Use each of the following academic vocabulary words in a sentence.

core

_____

_____

factor

_____

_____

The European Response (pages 349–350)

Responding

As you read about how European nations reacted to Napoleon, imagine you live in a small German state. Write a short paragraph explaining how you feel about Napoleon's armies bringing French revolutionary ideas to your region.

_____

_____

_____

_____

_____

Copyright © by The McGraw-Hill Companies, Inc.

Terms To Know

Define or describe the following key term from this lesson.

nationalism >

_____

_____

Academic Vocabulary

Define the following academic vocabulary words from this lesson.

collapsed >

_____

_____

exports >

_____

_____

The Fall of Napoleon *(pages 350–351)*

Clarifying

As you read this lesson, write down terms or concepts you find confusing. Then read the lesson again, and write an explanation of those confusing parts. If you are still confused, write your questions down and ask your teacher to clarify.

_____

_____

_____

Terms To Review

Use the following term, which you studied earlier, in a sentence that shows you understand the word's meaning.

challenge
(Chapter 3, Section 3) >

_____

_____

Copyright © by The McGraw-Hill Companies, Inc.

 **Key Points**

 **Notes**

Now that you have read the section, answer these questions from Setting a Purpose for Reading *at the beginning of the section.*

Why did Napoleon want to stop British goods from reaching Europe?

_____

_____

_____

_____

_____

What were two reasons for the collapse of Napoleon's empire?

_____

_____

_____

_____

_____

Copyright © by The McGraw-Hill Companies, Inc.

Chapter 12, Section 1
The Industrial Revolution
(Pages 363–370)

Reason To Read

Setting a Purpose for Reading Think about these questions as you read:
- What technological changes led to industrialization?
- What was the social impact of the Industrial Revolution in Europe, especially on women and children?

Main Idea

As you read pages 363–370 in your textbook, complete the chart below by identifying the inventors and their inventions mentioned in this section.

Inventors	Inventions

Sequencing Events

As you read, number the following events in the order in which they occurred.

_____ **James Watt builds a steam engine that can drive machinery**

_____ **Factory Act reduces child labor in Britain**

_____ **James Hargreaves invents spinning jenny**

_____ **Steamships begin to cross the Atlantic**

_____ **Edmund Cartwright invents water-powered loom**

Copyright © by The McGraw-Hill Companies, Inc.

The Industrial Revolution in Great Britain *(pages 363–365)*

Outlining   *As you read this lesson, fill in the outline below.*

I. Contributing Factors

   A. _____

   B. _____

II. Changes in Cotton Production

   A. _____

   B. _____

III. The Coal and Iron Industries

   A. _____

   B. _____

IV. Railroads

   A. _____

   B. _____

V. The New Factories

   A. _____

   B. _____

Terms To Know   *Write the letter of the correct definition next to each of these terms from this lesson.*

____ **1.** capital

____ **2.** entrepreneur

____ **3.** cottage industry

____ **4.** puddling

a. process in which coke is used to burn away impurities in crude iron to produce high quality iron

b. people interested in finding new business opportunities and new ways to make profits

c. system in which the government owns and controls the means of production

d. method of production in which tasks are done by individuals in their rural homes

e. ready supply of money

Copyright © by The McGraw-Hill Companies, Inc.

 **Key Points**

 **Notes**

Academic Vocabulary

Define the following academic vocabulary word from this lesson.

invest

_____

_____

Terms To Review

Define each of the following terms that you studied earlier.

dramatic
(Chapter 9, Section 3)

_____

_____

transporting
(Chapter 1, Section 3)

_____

_____

The Spread of Industrialization (page 366)

Connecting

As you read, think about the time it took for the Industrial Revolution to spread to other nations in Europe and to the United States. How long do you think it took for the com puter revolution to spread from the United States to the rest of the world? Do you think it was faster or slower than the spread of the Industrial Revolution? Write your thoughts on the lines below.

_____

_____

_____

_____

Academic Vocabulary

Define the following academic vocabulary word from this lesson.

occurred

_____

_____

Copyright © by The McGraw-Hill Companies, Inc.

Key Points

Notes

Terms To Review

Use each of the following terms, which you studied earlier, in a sentence that reflects its meaning in this lesson.

network
(Chapter 1, Section 3)

_____

_____

sought
(Chapter 6, Section 1)

_____

_____

Social Impact in Europe (pages 367–370)

Identifying Cause and Effect

As you read, make a list of the effects the Industrial Revolution had on Europe. After you have finished reading, use the lines below to summarize your notes.

_____

_____

_____

_____

_____

Terms To Know

Define or describe the following key terms from this lesson.

industrial capitalism

_____

_____

socialism

_____

_____

Academic Vocabulary

Use each of the following academic vocabulary words from this lesson in a sentence.

minimum

_____

_____

Copyright © by The McGraw-Hill Companies, Inc.

 transformed

_____

_____

Section Wrap-up *Now that you have read the section, answer these questions from* Setting a Purpose for Reading *at the beginning of the section.*

What technological changes led to industrialization?

_____

_____

_____

_____

_____

What was the social impact of the Industrial Revolution in Europe, especially on women and children?

_____

_____

_____

_____

_____

Copyright © by The McGraw-Hill Companies, Inc.

Chapter 12, Section 2
Reaction and Revolution
(Pages 371–376)

Reason To Read

Setting a Purpose for Reading Think about these questions as you read:
- What did the Congress of Vienna try to accomplish?
- Why did revolutions occur in 1848?

Main Idea

As you read pages 371–376 in your textbook, complete the graphic organizer below by identifying the causes of the revolutions in France in 1830 and 1848.

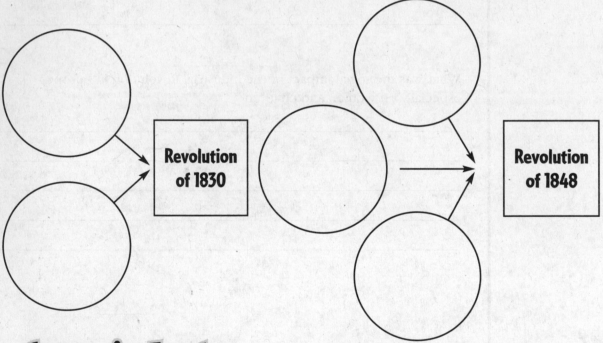

Sequencing Events

As you read, number the following events in the order in which they occurred.

_____ Austria reestablishes control over Lombardy

_____ Liberals overthrow Charles X and establish a constitutional monarchy in France

_____ Congress of Vienna meets to create balance of power

_____ Revolutions sweep through Europe

_____ Russians crush revolution in Poland

Copyright © by The McGraw-Hill Companies, Inc.

 **Key Points**

 **Notes**

The Congress of Vienna (pages 371–372)

Previewing

Preview the section to get an idea of what's ahead. First, skim the section. Then write a sentence or two explaining what you expect to learn. After you have finished reading, revise your statements as needed.

_____

_____

_____

_____

Terms To Review

Define the following term that you studied earlier.

restore
(Chapter 5, Section 4)

_____

_____

The Conservative Order (pages 372–373)

Summarizing

In a brief paragraph, summarize the lesson by describing the conservative point of view. How did they attempt to maintain the balance of power in Europe?

_____

_____

_____

_____

Terms To Know

Define or describe each of the following key terms from this lesson.

conservatism

_____

_____

principle of intervention

_____

_____

Copyright © by The McGraw-Hill Companies, Inc.

Key Points

Notes

Terms To Review

Use each of these terms, which you studied earlier, in a sentence that reflects the term's meaning in this lesson.

philosophy
(Chapter 5, Section 2)

_____
_____

internal
(Chapter 1, Section 2)

_____
_____

maintain
(Chapter 2, Section 2)

_____
_____

Forces of Change (pages 373–374)

Monitoring Comprehension

As you read, write down one question for each subhead for a partner to answer. Exchange questions and see if you can answer your partner's questions.

Liberalism

_____
_____

Nationalism

_____
_____

Revolutionary Outbursts

_____
_____

Terms To Know

Define or describe the following key term from this lesson.

liberalism

_____
_____

Copyright © by The McGraw-Hill Companies, Inc.

Academic Vocabulary

Use the following academic vocabulary word from this lesson in a sentence.

guaranteed >

_____

_____

Terms To Review

Define each of the following terms that you studied earlier.

regulated
(Chapter 10, Section 4) >

_____

_____

democracy
(Chapter 2, Section 1) >

_____

_____

The Revolutions of 1848 (pages 374–376)

Reviewing

After you have read this lesson, write a paragraph describing the revolutions that took place in Europe in 1848.

_____

_____

_____

_____

_____

Terms To Know

Define or describe the following key term from this lesson.

universal male suffrage >

_____

_____

Copyright © by The McGraw-Hill Companies, Inc.

Academic Vocabulary

Use the following academic vocabulary word from this lesson in a sentence that shows you understand the word's meaning.

 bond

_____

_____

Terms To Review

Write the letter of the correct definition next to each of these terms that you studied earlier.

____ **1.** drafted
(Chapter 7, Section 3)

____ **2.** unified
(Chapter 1, Section 2)

a. consistent in conduct

b. a coherent whole

c. selected for a required service, particularly military

Section Wrap-up

Now that you have read the section, answer these questions from Setting a Purpose for Reading *at the beginning of the section.*

What did the Congress of Vienna try to accomplish?

_____

_____

_____

_____

_____

Why did revolutions occur in 1848?

_____

_____

_____

_____

_____

Copyright © by The McGraw-Hill Companies, Inc.

Chapter 12, Section 3
National Unification and the National State

(Pages 378–385)

Reason To Read

Setting a Purpose for Reading Think about these questions as you read:
- What were the roles of Camillo di Cavour and Otto von Bismarck in the unification of their countries?
- What caused the American Civil War?

Main Idea

As you read pages 378–385 in your textbook, complete the chart below by listing the changes that took place in the countries indicated during the nineteenth century.

Great Britain	France	Austrian Empire	Russia

Sequencing Events

As you read, write the correct date next to each event on the time line below.

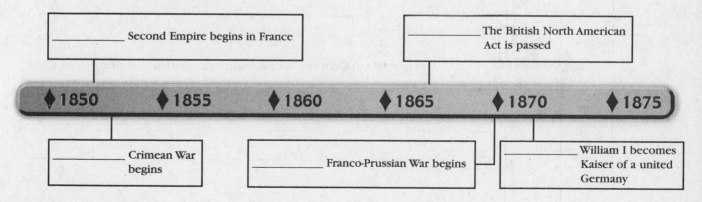

_____ Second Empire begins in France

_____ The British North American Act is passed

♦1850   ♦1855   ♦1860   ♦1865   ♦1870   ♦1875

_____ Crimean War begins

_____ Franco-Prussian War begins

_____ William I becomes Kaiser of a united Germany

Copyright © by The McGraw-Hill Companies, Inc.

Breakdown of the Concert of Europe (pages 378–379)

Skimming

Skim this lesson before you begin reading, looking at the title and quickly glancing over the first and last paragraphs to get an idea of its content. Write a sentence or two below explaining what the section is about.

_____

_____

_____

Academic Vocabulary

Define or describe the following academic vocabulary word from this lesson

access

_____

_____

Italian Unification (pages 379–380)

Connecting

As you read, think about what motivated Giuseppe Garibaldi to raise an army in southern Italy. Use your knowledge and compare Garibaldi's motivations to a prominent figure in American history, such as George Washington or Paul Revere. Write a sentence or two below comparing their goals.

_____

_____

_____

_____

Academic Vocabulary

Define the following academic vocabulary word from this lesson.

equip

_____

_____

Copyright © by The McGraw-Hill Companies, Inc.

German Unification (pages 380–381)

Sequencing

As you read, number the following events in the order in which they occurred.

_____ Bismarck defeats Austria

_____ Otto von Bismarck becomes prime minister

_____ Franco-Prussian War starts

_____ Bismarck defeats Denmark

Terms To Know

Define or describe the following key terms from this lesson.

militarism _____
_____
_____

kaiser _____
_____

Terms To Review

Define the following term that you studied in an earlier chapter.

levy
(Chapter 10, Section 4) _____
_____

Nationalism and Reform in Europe (pages 382–384)

Outlining

As you read this lesson, fill in the outline below.

I. Great Britain

   A. _____

   B. _____

II. France

   A. _____

   B. _____

Copyright © by The McGraw-Hill Companies, Inc.

III. The Austrian Empire

    A. _____

    B. _____

IV. Russia

    A. _____

    B. _____

Terms To Know

Define or describe the following key terms from this lesson.

plebiscite

_____

_____

_____

emancipation

_____

_____

Academic Vocabulary

Define the following academic vocabulary word from this lesson.

components

_____

_____

Terms To Review

Use each of the following terms, which you studied earlier, in a sentence that reflects the term's meaning in this lesson.

attitudes
(Chapter 5, Section 1)

_____

_____

focused
(Chapter 10, Section 3)

_____

_____

Copyright © by The McGraw-Hill Companies, Inc.

Nationalism in the United States (pages 384–385)

Connecting

As you read about the issues facing the United States in the 1800s, think about the issues facing the United States today. Which issue do you think is most important? Summarize your thoughts in a paragraph below.

_____

_____

_____

_____

Terms To Know

Define or describe the following key terms from this lesson.

abolitionism

_____

_____

_____

secede

_____

_____

Terms To Review

Choose one of these two terms, which you studied earlier, to fill in each blank.

subordinate
(Chapter 1, Section 3)

1. The Republicans in the first half of the nineteenth century wanted the federal government to be _____ to the state governments.

issue
(Chapter 11, Section 1)

2. By the mid-nineteenth century the _____ of slavery became a threat to national unity.

3. The _____ of secession was the topic of a South Carolina convention in 1860.

Copyright © by The McGraw-Hill Companies, Inc.

The Emergence of a Canadian Nation (page 385)

Reviewing

As you read, think about the British North America Act and its effects on Canada. Then write a paragraph explaining how the Act changed the government of Canada.

_____

_____

_____

Academic Vocabulary

Use the following academic vocabulary word from this lesson in a sentence.

whereas

_____

_____

Terms To Review

Define the following term that you studied earlier.

designs
(Chapter 5, Section 2)

_____

_____

Section Wrap-up

Now that you have read the section, answer these questions from Setting a Purpose for Reading *at the beginning of the section.*

What were the roles of Camillo di Cavour and Otto von Bismarck in the unification of their countries?

_____

_____

_____

What caused the American Civil War?

_____

_____

_____

Copyright © by The McGraw-Hill Companies, Inc.

Chapter 12, Section 4
Culture: Romanticism and Realism

(Pages 387–391)

Reason To Read

Setting a Purpose for Reading Think about these questions as you read:
- What were the major features of romanticism and realism?
- How did the Scientific Revolution lead to secularization?

Main Idea

As you read pages 387–391 in your textbook, complete the table below by listing popular literature from the romantic and realist movements.

Romanticism	Realism

Sequencing Events

As you read, place the following events on the time line below.
- **Courbet paints *The Stonebreakers***
- **Walter Scott writes *Ivanhoe***
- **Charles Dickens writes *The Old Curiosity Shop***
- **Mendeleyev presents classification of material elements**

♦ 1820　　♦ 1840　　♦ 1860　　♦ 1880

Copyright © by The McGraw-Hill Companies, Inc.

Romanticism (pages 387–389)

Interpreting

As you read, focus on how the artists and writers of the Romantic period related to society. List some popular modern-day artists and musicians below. Can you determine how they relate to society by listening to their music, looking at their art, or observing their behavior? Do they want to fit in, rebel, or be left alone?

_____

_____

_____

_____

Terms To Know

Define or describe the following key term from this lesson.

romanticism

_____

_____

Academic Vocabulary

Use the following academic vocabulary word from this lesson in a sentence.

altered

_____

_____

A New Age of Science (pages 389–390)

Analyzing

How did Darwin's theory of natural selection influence the way in which people viewed the world?

_____

_____

_____

_____

_____

Copyright © by The McGraw-Hill Companies, Inc.

Terms To Know

Write the letter of the correct definition next to each of these terms from this lesson.

_____ **1.** secularization

_____ **2.** organic evolution

_____ **3.** natural selection

a. a movement in the literary and visual arts

b. the idea that each kind of plant and animal evolved over a long period of time from earlier and simpler forms of life

c. indifference to religion or rejection of religion

d. Darwin's principle that some organisms are more adaptable to the environment than others

Academic Vocabulary

Define the following academic vocabulary words from this lesson.

rational

_____

_____

evolved

_____

_____

Terms To Review

Define the following term that you studied earlier.

foundation
(Chapter 2, Section 1)

_____

_____

Realism (pages 390–391)

Responding

As you read, think about the kind of literature you enjoy. Would you prefer the literature of the realists or that of the romanticists? Why? Summarize your thoughts in a paragraph below.

_____

_____

_____

_____

Copyright © by The McGraw-Hill Companies, Inc.

Key Points

Notes

Terms To Know

Define or describe the following key term from this lesson.

realism >

_____

_____

Terms To Review

Use each of the following terms, which you studied earlier, in a sentence.

rejected >
(Chapter 3, Section 1)

_____

_____

precise >
(Chapter 5, Section 3)

_____

_____

Section Wrap-up

Now that you have read the section, answer these questions from Setting a Purpose for Reading *at the beginning of the section*

What were the major features of romanticism and realism?

_____

_____

_____

_____

How did the Scientific Revolution lead to secularization?

_____

_____

_____

_____

Copyright © by The McGraw-Hill Companies, Inc.

Chapter 13, Section 1
The Growth of Industrial Prosperity

(Pages 397–401)

Reason To Read

Setting a Purpose for Reading Think about these questions as you read:
- What was the Second Industrial Revolution?
- What were the chief ideas of Karl Marx?

Main Idea

As you read pages 397–401 in your textbook, complete the graphic organizer below by identifying the cause-and-effect relationship between economic resources and the products produced.

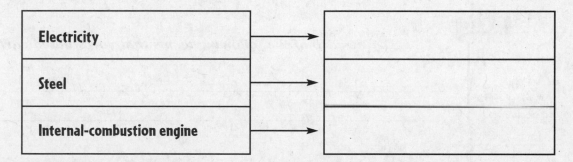

Electricity	→	
Steel	→	
Internal-combustion engine	→	

Sequencing Events

As you read, place the following events on the time line below.

- **Second International socialist association forms**
- **Thomas Edison invents the light bulb**
- **Wright brothers make first flight**
- **Marx and Engels publish *The Communist Manifesto***
- **Alexander Graham Bell invents the telephone**

| ◆ 1845 | ◆ 1865 | ◆ 1885 | ◆ 1905 |

Copyright © by The McGraw-Hill Companies, Inc.

The Second Industrial Revolution (pages 397–400)

Outlining   *As you read this lesson, fill in the outline below.*

I. New Products

   A. _____

   B. _____

II. New Patterns

   A. _____

   B. _____

III. Toward a World Economy

   A. _____

   B. _____

Terms To Review   *Define each of the following terms that you studied earlier.*

enabled
(Chapter 1, Section 2)

_____

_____

series
(Chapter 2, Section 2)

_____

_____

Organizing the Working Classes (pages 400–401)

Responding   *As you read, think about Marx's Theory, which was based on economic changes that began in England in the 1780s. Such changes included the shift of weavers and spinners from producing items in the home to manufacturing the items in factories. On the the lines below, explain why workers felt that their status had been lowered as a result of this shift.*

_____

_____

_____

Copyright © by The McGraw-Hill Companies, Inc.

Key Points

Notes

Copyright © by The McGraw-Hill Companies, Inc.

Terms To Know

Write the letter of the correct definition next to each of these terms from this lesson.

_____ **1.** bourgeoisie

_____ **2.** proletariat

_____ **3.** dictatorship

_____ **4.** revisionists

a. the working class

b. the middle class

c. Marxists who rejected the revolutionary approach, believing instead in evolution by democratic means to achieve the goal of socialism

d. government in which a person or group has absolute power

e. indifference or rejection of religion or religious consideration

Academic Vocabulary

Define the following academic vocabulary word from this lesson.

predicted >

_____

_____

Terms To Review

Use each of the following terms, which you studied earlier, in a sentence that reflects the term's meaning.

advocated
(Chapter 7, Section 4) >

_____

_____

approach
(Chapter 5, Section 2) >

_____

_____

considerable
(Chapter 2, Section 2) >

_____

_____

Now that you have read the section, answer these questions from Setting a Purpose for Reading *at the beginning of the section.*

What was the Second Industrial Revolution?

_____

_____

_____

_____

_____

What were the chief ideas of Karl Marx?

_____

_____

_____

_____

_____

Copyright © by The McGraw-Hill Companies, Inc.

Chapter 13, Section 2
The Emergence of Mass Society

(Pages 403–410)

Reason To Read

Setting a Purpose for Reading Think about these questions as you read:
- What were the chief characteristics of the middle class in the nineteenth century?
- How did the position of women change between 1870 and 1914?

Main Idea

As you read pages 403–410 in your textbook, complete the chart below by summarizing the divisions among the social classes.

Social Classes		
Working	**Middle**	**Wealthy**

Sequencing Events

As you read, write the correct date next to each event on the time line below.

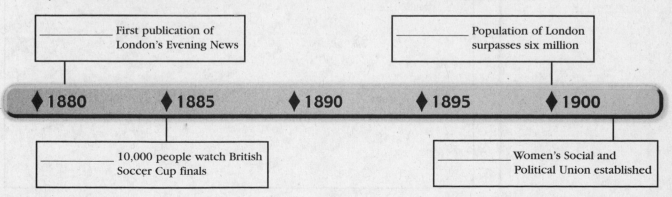

_____ First publication of London's Evening News

_____ Population of London surpasses six million

♦1880   ♦1885   ♦1890   ♦1895   ♦1900

_____ 10,000 people watch British Soccer Cup finals

_____ Women's Social and Political Union established

Copyright © by The McGraw-Hill Companies, Inc.

 **Key Points**　　　　　　　 **Notes**

The New Urban Environment (pages 403–404)

Identifying Cause and Effect

As you read this lesson, concentrate on the reasons for the increase in population in the cities during the nineteenth century. List these causes on the lines provided below.

_____

_____

_____

_____

Terms To Review

Define each of the following terms that you studied earlier.

percent
(Chapter 4, Section 1)

_____

_____

migration
(Chapter 1, Section 2)

_____

_____

Social Structure of Mass Society (pages 404–406)

Reviewing

After you read the lesson, create a diagram below that shows who belonged to the three major social classes in Europe in the nineteenth century.

Copyright © by The McGraw-Hill Companies, Inc.

Terms To Review

Use each of the following terms, which you studied earlier, in a sentence that reflects the term's meaning in this lesson.

sources
(Chapter 1, Section 3)

_____

_____

conduct
(Chapter 7, Section 2)

_____

_____

The Experiences of Women *(pages 406–408)*

Evaluating

After you have read the lesson, review the quotation by Lord Tennyson on page 624. What were Tennyson's beliefs about the roles of men and women? How were the women of the nineteenth century challenging this viewpoint? Write your thoughts on the lines below.

_____

_____

_____

_____

Terms To Know

Define or describe the following key term from this lesson.

feminism

_____

_____

Academic Vocabulary

Use each of the following academic vocabulary words from this lesson in a sentence.

ensure

_____

_____

income

_____

_____

Copyright © by The McGraw-Hill Companies, Inc.

 **Key Points**

 **Notes**

Universal Education (pages 408–409)

Determining the Main Idea

As you read, write down the main idea of the passage. Review your statement when you have finished reading and revise as needed.

_____

_____

_____

_____

Terms To Know

Define or describe the following key term from this lesson.

> **literacy**

_____

_____

Terms To Review

Write the letter of the correct definition next to each of these terms that you studied earlier.

____ **1.** motive
(Chapter 6, Section 1)

____ **2.** incentive
(Chapter 9, Section 2)

a. something that urges a person to do something

b. a reason for someone to act

c. a hindrance

New Form of Leisure (page 410)

Connecting

As you read, compare the leisure activities of people in the nineteenth century with those of people today. Summarize your thoughts in a paragraph below.

_____

_____

_____

_____

Copyright © by The McGraw-Hill Companies, Inc.

Academic Vocabulary

Define the academic vocabulary word from this lesson.

> **passive**

_____

_____

Terms To Review

Use each of the following terms, which you studied earlier, in a sentence that shows you understand the term's meaning.

> **pursue**
> (Chapter 3, Section 4)

_____

_____

> **technology**
> (Chapter 4, Section 1)

_____

_____

Section Wrap-up

Now that you have read the section, answer these questions from Setting a Purpose for Reading *at the beginning of the section.*

What were the chief characteristics of the middle class in the nineteenth century?

_____

_____

_____

_____

How did the position of women change between 1870 and 1914?

_____

_____

_____

_____

Copyright © by The McGraw-Hill Companies, Inc.

Chapter 13, Section 3
The National State and Democracy

(Pages 411–416)

Reason To Read

Setting a Purpose for Reading Think about these questions as you read:
- What domestic problems did the United States and Canada face?
- What issues sparked the crises in the Balkans?

Main Idea

As you read pages 411–416 in your textbook, complete the graphic organizer below by listing the countries in each alliance.

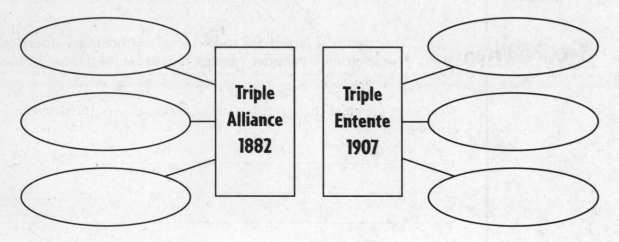

Sequencing Events

As you read, number the following events in the order in which they occurred.

_____ Triple Alliance created

_____ Thirteenth Amendment passed in the United States

_____ Triple Entente formed

_____ Dual monarchy of Austria-Hungary created

_____ Hawaii annexed by the United States

Copyright © by The McGraw-Hill Companies, Inc.

Western Europe and Political Democracy (pages 411–413)

Skimming

Skim this lesson before you begin reading it, looking at headings and words in boldface or colored type. Write a sentence below describing what you expect to learn. After reading, revise your sentence as needed.

_____

_____

_____

Terms To Know

Define or describe the following key term from this lesson.

ministerial responsibility

_____

_____

Academic Vocabulary

Define the following academic vocabulary words from this lesson.

intervals

_____

_____

injured

_____

_____

Terms To Review

Use each of the following terms, which you studied earlier, in a sentence.

benefits
(Chapter 3, Section 4)

_____

_____

retain
(Chapter 3, Section 3)

_____

_____

nevertheless
(Chapter 3, Section 3)

_____

Copyright © by The McGraw-Hill Companies, Inc.

Central and Eastern Europe: The Old Order (pages 413–414)

Analyzing

What are the major political differences between western and central Europe?

_____

_____

_____

_____

Terms To Know

Define or describe the following key term from this lesson.

Duma

_____

_____

Terms To Review

Define the following terms that you studied earlier.

conflicts
(Chapter 1, Section 2)

_____

_____

_____

grant
(Chapter 1, Section 2)

_____

_____

The United States and Canada (page 415)

Interpreting

As you read, think about the increase in population in the cities between 1860 and 1914 in the United States. Use the lines below to suggest reasons, other than immigration from Europe, for this urban growth.

_____

_____

_____

_____

Copyright © by The McGraw-Hill Companies, Inc.

Key Points

Academic Vocabulary

Use the following academic vocabulary word from this lesson in a sentence.

acquired

_____
_____

Terms To Review

Use each of the following terms, which you studied earlier, in a sentence that reflects the term's meaning in this lesson.

cycles
(Chapter 4, Section 2)

_____
_____
_____

labor
(Chapter 1, Section 2)

_____
_____

International Rivalries *(pages 415–416)*

Drawing Conclusions

After you have read this lesson, refer to the map on page 630. Where was Germany located in relation to Russia and France? Why would an alliance between Russia and France be a problem for Germany? Write your answer on the lines provided below.

_____
_____
_____

Terms To Review

Define each of the following terms that you studied earlier.

policy
(Chapter 5, Section 4)

_____
_____

enhancing
(Chapter 3, Section 1)

_____
_____

Copyright © by The McGraw-Hill Companies, Inc.

Crises in the Balkans (page 416)

Reviewing

As you read this lesson, refer to an earlier map in your textbook on page 590. What empire controlled the territory of the Balkans in the early 1800s? Why do you think Balkan countries were able to gradually break free of that empire?

_____

_____

_____

_____

Terms To Review

Use the following term, which you studied earlier, in a sentence that reflects the term's meaning.

creating
(Chapter 2, Section 2)

_____

_____

Section Wrap-up

Now that you have read the section, answer these questions from Setting a Purpose for Reading at the beginning of the section.

What domestic problems did the United States and Canada face?

_____

_____

_____

_____

What issues sparked the crises in the Balkans?

_____

_____

_____

_____

Copyright © by The McGraw-Hill Companies, Inc.

Chapter 13, Section 4
Toward the Modern Consciousness

(Pages 418–423)

Reason To Read

Setting a Purpose for Reading Think about these questions as you read:
- How did Einstein and Freud challenge people's views of the world?
- How did modernism revolutionize architecture?

Main Idea

As you read pages 418–423 in your textbook, complete the chart below by listing an artist and a characteristic of the art movement indicated.

	Artist	**Characteristic**
Impressionism		
Post-Impressionism		
Cubism		
Abstract Expressionism		

Sequencing Events

As you read, write the correct date next to each event on the time line below.

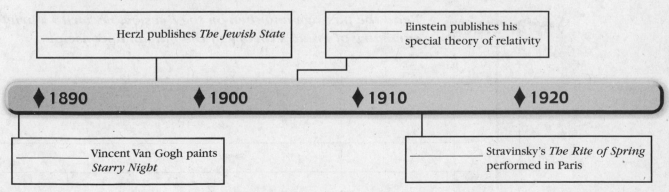

_____ Herzl publishes *The Jewish State*

_____ Einstein publishes his special theory of relativity

♦ 1890   ♦ 1900   ♦ 1910   ♦ 1920

_____ Vincent Van Gogh paints *Starry Night*

_____ Stravinsky's *The Rite of Spring* performed in Paris

Copyright © by The McGraw-Hill Companies, Inc.

A New Physics (pages 418–419)

Monitoring Comprehension

As you read the lesson, write down questions you have about the passage. When you have finished reading, answer your questions.

_____

_____

_____

_____

Academic Vocabulary

Use each of the following academic vocabulary words from this lesson in a sentence.

accurate

_____

_____

physical

_____

_____

Terms To Review

Write the definition of the following term that you studied earlier.

element
(Chapter 1, Section 3)

_____

_____

Freud and Psychoanalysis (page 419)

Summarizing

Read the passage and then on the lines below, write a brief summary of Freud's theory of the human unconscious.

_____

_____

_____

_____

Copyright © by The McGraw-Hill Companies, Inc.

Terms To Know

Define or describe the following key term from this lesson.

psychoanalysis

_____

_____

Terms To Review

Write the definition of the following term that you studied in an earlier chapter.

theories
(Chapter 1, Section 1)

_____

_____

Social Darwinism *(page 420)*

Determining the Main Idea

As you read, write down the main idea of the passage. Review your statement when you have finished reading and revise as needed.

_____

_____

_____

Academic Vocabulary

Define the following academic vocabulary word from this lesson.

method

_____

_____

Terms To Review

Use each of the following terms, which you studied earlier, in a sentence that reflects the term's meaning.

declined
(Chapter 7, Section 4)

_____

_____

radical
(Chapter 11, Section 1)

_____

_____

Copyright © by The McGraw-Hill Companies, Inc.

Anti-Semitism and Zionism (pages 420–421)

Drawing Conclusions

As you read, write down three details about anti-Semitism and Zionism. Then write a conclusion you draw based on these details.

_____

_____

_____

_____

Terms To Know

Define or describe the following key term from this lesson.

pogroms >

_____

_____

Terms To Review

Write the definition of the following terms that you studied earlier.

widespread
(Chapter 5, Section 3) >

_____

_____

evident
(Chapter 2, Section 1) >

_____

_____

The Culture of Modernity (pages 421–423)

Connecting

As you read this lesson, think about how today's artists express themselves in their work. Do they depict similar subjects, or use similar techniques and styles as those described in the lesson? Write your thoughts on the lines below.

_____

_____

_____

_____

Copyright © by The McGraw-Hill Companies, Inc.

 Key Points

 Notes

Terms To Know

Define or describe the following key term from this lesson.

> modernism

_____

_____

Academic Vocabulary

Define the following academic vocabulary words from this lesson.

> visual

_____

_____

> paralleled

_____

_____

Terms To Review

Use the following term, which you studied earlier, in a sentence that reflects the term's meaning in this lesson.

> external
> (Chapter 11, Section 2)

_____

_____

Section Wrap-up

Now that you have read the section, answer these questions from Setting a Purpose for Reading *at the beginning of the section.*

How did Einstein and Freud challenge people's views of the world?

_____

_____

_____

How did modernism revolutionize architecture?

_____

_____

_____

Copyright © by The McGraw-Hill Companies, Inc.

Chapter 14, Section 1
Colonial Rule in Southeast Asia

(Pages 429–434)

Reason To Read

Setting a Purpose for Reading Think about these questions as you read:
- Why were Westerners so determined to colonize Southeast Asia?
- What was the chief goal of the Western nations?

Main Idea

As you read pages 429–434 in your textbook, complete the chart below by indicating which countries controlled what parts of Southeast Asia.

Spain (until 1898)	
Netherlands	
United States (after 1898)	
France	
Great Britian	

Sequencing Events

As you read, place the following events on the time line below.

- **France and Great Britain agree to maintain Thailand as a buffer state**
- **Saya San leads Burma uprising**
- **France seizes Hanoi**

◆ 1880   ◆ 1900   ◆ 1920   ◆ 1940

Copyright © by The McGraw-Hill Companies, Inc.

The New Imperialism *(pages 429–430)*

Summarizing

As you read, write a brief paragraph below summarizing four motivations for the "new imperialism."

_____

_____

_____

_____

Terms To Know

Define or describe the following key term from this lesson.

imperialism

_____

_____

Academic Vocabulary

Define the following academic vocabulary word from this lesson.

phase

_____

_____

Terms To Review

Write the definition of the following terms that you studied earlier.

intense
(Chapter 4, Section 1)

_____

_____

issue
(Chapter 11, Section 1)

_____

_____

participate
(Chapter 2, Section 1)

_____

_____

Copyright © by The McGraw-Hill Companies, Inc.

Key Points

Notes

Colonial Takeover in Southeast Asia (pages 431–432)

Identifying Cause and Effect

As you read this lesson, focus on the rivalry between Great Britain and France over trade opportunities. What region did the British take over? Use the lines below to describe France's reaction to Britain's advances.

_____

_____

_____

Terms To Know

Define or describe the following key term from this lesson.

protectorate

_____

_____

Terms To Review

Use each of the following terms, which you studied earlier, in a sentence.

decades
(Chapter 2, Section 2)

_____

_____

occurred
(Chapter 12, Section 1)

_____

_____

Colonial Regimes in Southeast Asia (pages 432–433)

Drawing Conclusions

As you read, write three details about the colonial regimes in Southeast Asia. Then write a conclusion you draw based on these details.

_____

_____

_____

_____

Copyright © by The McGraw-Hill Companies, Inc.

Terms To Know

Define or describe the following key terms from this lesson.

indirect rule

_____

_____

direct rule

_____

_____

Terms To Review

Write the definition of the following terms that you studied earlier.

imposed
(Chapter 6, Section 3)

_____

_____

entrepreneur
(Chapter 12, Section 1)

_____

_____

Resistance to Colonial Rule *(pages 433–434)*

Determining the Main Idea

As you read, write down the main idea of the passage. Review your statement when you have finished reading and revise as needed.

_____

_____

_____

Terms To Review

Use the following term, which you studied earlier, in a sentence.

contrast
(Chapter 2, Section 2)

_____

_____

Copyright © by The McGraw-Hill Companies, Inc.

Now that you have read the section, answer these questions from Setting a Purpose for Reading *at the beginning of the section.*

Why were Westerners so determined to colonize Southeast Asia?

_____

_____

_____

_____

_____

What was the chief goal of the Western nations?

_____

_____

_____

_____

_____

Copyright © by The McGraw-Hill Companies, Inc.

Chapter 14, Section 2
Empire Building in Africa
(Pages 436–442)

Reason To Read

Setting a Purpose for Reading Think about these questions as you read:
- What new class of Africans developed in many African nations?
- What was the relationship between the Boers and the Zulu?

Main Idea

As you read pages 436–442 in your textbook, complete the chart below by showing what countries controlled what parts of Africa.

Controlling Country	Part of Africa
	West Africa
	North Africa (including Egypt)
	Central Africa
	East Africa
	South Africa

Sequencing Events

As you read, number the following events in the order in which they occurred.

_____ **Ethiopia defeats Italian forces**

_____ **Berlin Conference divides Africa among Europeans**

_____ **Egypt becomes British protectorate**

_____ **Suez Canal is completed**

_____ **British troops seize the Sudan**

Copyright © by The McGraw-Hill Companies, Inc.

West Africa (pages 436–437)

Previewing

Preview the lesson to get an idea of what's ahead. First, skim the lesson. Then write a sentence or two explaining what you expect to learn. After you have finished reading, revise your statements as needed.

_____

_____

_____

Terms To Know

Define or describe the following key term from this lesson.

annexed

_____

_____

Terms To Review

Use each of the following terms, which you studied earlier, in a sentence that reflects the term's meaning in this lesson.

virtually
(Chapter 10, Section 4)

_____

_____

eventually
(Chapter 3, Section 4)

_____

_____

North Africa (page 438)

Summarizing

As you read, complete the following sentences to help you summarize the lesson.

1. In 1805, _____ seized power and established a separate

   Egyptian state. He introduced a series of _____ to bring

   Egypt into the _____ .

2. The growing economic importance of the _____ in

   Egypt gave Europeans the desire to build a canal to connect the

   _____ Sea and the _____ Sea.

Copyright © by The McGraw-Hill Companies, Inc.

3. After the Suez Canal opened, the _____ took an

interest in it, believing that it was the _____ to India.

4. The _____ and the _____ also had

colonies in North Africa.

Central Africa *(pages 438–439)*

Reviewing

After you have read this lesson, write a paragraph describing King Leopold's effect on the colonization of Central Africa.

_____

_____

_____

_____

Terms To Review

Use the following term, which you studied earlier, in a sentence that reflects the term's meaning.

empire
(Chapter 1, Section 2)

_____

_____

East Africa *(pages 439–440)*

Evaluating

Read the passage and write a brief summary of what was significant about the Berlin Conference.

_____

_____

_____

Terms To Review

Define the following term that you studied earlier.

area
(Chapter 6, Section 3)

_____

_____

Copyright © by The McGraw-Hill Companies, Inc.

 **Key Points**

 **Notes**

South Africa *(pages 440–441)*

Connecting

After you read the section, write a sentence or two comparing the situation in South Africa in the early 1900s with the situation in South Africa today.

_____

_____

_____

Terms To Know

Define or describe the following key term from this lesson.

indigenous >

_____

_____

Terms To Review

Use the following term, which you studied earlier, in a sentence that shows you understand the term's meaning.

linked
(Chapter 4, Section 2) >

_____

_____

Colonial Rule in Africa *(pages 441–442)*

Determining the Main Idea

As you read, pay attention to how indirect rule worked in African colonies. Why was indirect rule destined to fail in the long run?

_____

_____

_____

Terms To Review

Use the following term, which you studied in an earlier chapter, in a sentence.

feature
(Chapter 1, Section 2) >

_____

_____

Copyright © by The McGraw-Hill Companies, Inc.

Rise of African Nationalism (page 442)

Skimming

Before you read, skim the passage, quickly looking over the lesson to get an idea of its content. Then write a sentence or two explaining what you expect to learn.

_____

_____

_____

Academic Vocabulary

Define the following academic vocabulary word from this lesson.

adult

_____

_____

Terms To Review

Use the following term, which you studied earlier, in a sentence.

bureaucracy
(Chapter 6, Section 3)

_____

_____

Section Wrap-up

Now that you have read the section, answer these questions from Setting a Purpose for Reading at the beginning of the section.

What new class of Africans developed in many African nations?

_____

_____

_____

What was the relationship between the Boers and the Zulu?

_____

_____

_____

Copyright © by The McGraw-Hill Companies, Inc.

Chapter 14, Section 3
British Rule in India

(Pages 448–452)

Reason To Read

Setting a Purpose for Reading Think about these questions as you read:
- What was the goal of the Indian National Congress?
- Why was India called the "Jewel in the Crown" of the British monarch?

Main Idea

As you read pages 448–452 in your textbook, complete the chart below by identifying some causes and effects of British influence on India.

Cause	Effects
1. British textiles	
2. cotton crops	
3. school system	
4. railroad, telegraph, telephone services	

Sequencing Events

As you read, place the following events on the time line.
- **Queen Victoria is named "Empress of India"**
- **Sepoy Mutiny fails**
- **Indian National Congress forms**
- **Mohandas Gandhi born in Gujarat**

◆1850 ◆1860 ◆1870 ◆1880 ◆1890

Copyright © by The McGraw-Hill Companies, Inc.

The Sepoy Mutiny (pages 448–449)

Identifying Cause and Effect

As you read, focus on the Sepoy Mutiny. Use the lines below to describe the effects it had on government and on Indians.

_____

_____

_____

_____

Terms To Know

Define or describe the following key term from this lesson.

sepoys

_____

_____

Terms To Review

Write the definition of each of the following terms that you studied earlier.

declined
(Chapter 7, Section 4)

_____

_____

transferred
(Chapter 10, Section 3)

_____

_____

Colonial Rule (pages 449–451)

Visualizing

As you read the lesson, list the costs and benefits of British rule in India. Then imagine you are an Indian nationalist. What would your opinion be of British rule in India? Write your answer below.

_____

_____

_____

_____

Copyright © by The McGraw-Hill Companies, Inc.

Key Points

Notes

Terms To Know

Define or describe the following key term from this lesson.

viceroy

_____

_____

Academic Vocabulary

Use the following academic vocabulary word from this lesson in a sentence.

despite

_____

_____

Terms To Review

Write the definition of each of the following terms that you studied earlier.

civil
(Chapter 2, Section 2)

_____

_____

goal
(Chapter 1, Section 3)

_____

_____

An Indian Nationalist Movement (pages 451–452)

Evaluating

As you read, think about the Muslim League. Then write a paragraph describing the advantages and disadvantages of its formation.

_____

_____

_____

_____

Terms To Review

Use the following term, which you studied earlier, in a sentence that reflects the term's meaning.

aware
(Chapter 3, Section 1)

_____

_____

Copyright © by The McGraw-Hill Companies, Inc.

Colonial Indian Culture (page 452)

Responding   *As you read, think about what captures your attention.*
Write down two facts you find interesting or surprising.

_____

_____

_____

Academic Vocabulary   *Use the following academic vocabulary words in a sentence*
that shows you understand the word's meaning.

promote >   _____

_____

mutual >   _____

_____

Section Wrap-up   *Now that you have read the section, answer these questions*
from Setting a Purpose for Reading *at the beginning of the*
section.

What was the goal of the Indian National Congress?

_____

_____

_____

_____

Why was India called the "Jewel in the Crown" of the British monarch?

_____

_____

_____

_____

Copyright © by The McGraw-Hill Companies, Inc.

Chapter 14, Section 4
Nation Building in Latin America

(Pages 453–459)

Reason To Read

Setting a Purpose for Reading Think about this question as you read:
- How did the American Revolution inspire political changes in Latin America?

Main Idea

As you read pages 453–459 in your textbook, complete the graphic organizer below by comparing and contrasting colonial rule in Africa and in Latin America.

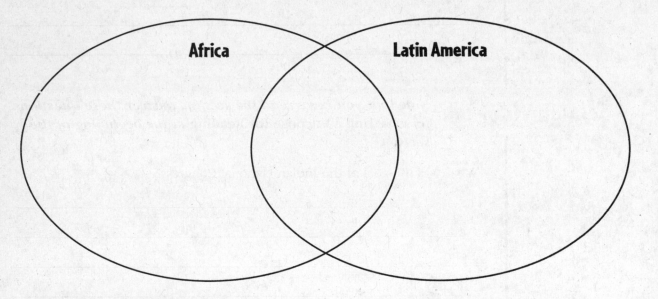

Africa   Latin America

Sequencing Events

As you read, write the correct date next to each event on the time line below.

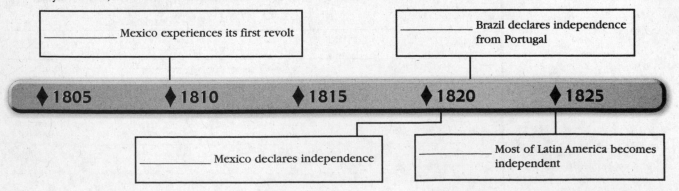

_____ Mexico experiences its first revolt

_____ Brazil declares independence from Portugal

1805   1810   1815   1820   1825

_____ Mexico declares independence

_____ Most of Latin America becomes independent

Copyright © by The McGraw-Hill Companies, Inc.

Nationalist Revolts (pages 453–455)

 **Outlining**   *As you read this lesson, fill in the outline below.*

I. Prelude to Revolution

A. _____

B. _____

II. Revolt in Mexico

A. _____

B. _____

III. Revolts in South America

A. _____

B. _____

Terms To Know   *Write the letter of the correct definition next to each of these terms from this lesson.*

____ **1.** Creole

____ **2.** *peninsulare*

____ **3.** mestizo

____ **4.** Monroe Doctrine

a. Spanish and Portuguese residing in Latin America for political and economic gain who later returned to Spain or Portugal

b. governors who ruled as representatives of a monarch

c. descendants of Europeans born in Latin America who lived there permanently

d. people of European and Indian descent

e. U.S. policy that warned against any European intervention in the Americas

Terms To Review   *Use each of the following terms, which you studied earlier, in a sentence that reflects the term's meaning.*

resided
(Chapter 2, Section 2)
_____
_____

enabled
(Chapter 1, Section 2)
_____
_____

Copyright © by The McGraw-Hill Companies, Inc.

 **Notes**

Difficulties of Nation Building (pages 455–458)

Reviewing

As you read, think about the difficulties faced by the new Latin American republics. Then write a paragraph summarizing these difficulties.

_____

_____

_____

_____

_____

Terms To Know

Define or describe the following key term from this lesson.

caudillos

_____

_____

Academic Vocabulary

Define the following academic vocabulary words from this lesson.

ongoing

_____

_____

underlying

_____

_____

Terms To Review

Use each of the following terms that you studied earlier in a sentence.

emphasis
(Chapter 5, Section 4)

_____

_____

estates
(Chapter 2, Section 2)

_____

_____

Copyright © by The McGraw-Hill Companies, Inc.

 Notes

Political Change in Latin America (page 458)

Evaluating

By the early 1900s, Latin Americans referred to the United States as the "big bully" to the north. Do you think they were justified in their feelings? Why or why not? Summarize your opinion in a paragraph below.

_____

_____

_____

_____

Academic Vocabulary

Define the following academic vocabulary word from this lesson.

intervene

_____

_____

Terms To Review

Define each of the following terms that you studied earlier.

similar
(Chapter 3, Section 1)

_____

_____

revolution
(Chapter 1, Section 1)

_____

_____

Economic Change in Latin America (page 459)

Drawing Conclusions

As you read, think about the various classes in most Latin American nations. What size was the middle class, and how did they vote in most cases? How do you think this social structure affected poorer groups in these nations?

_____

_____

_____

_____

Copyright © by The McGraw-Hill Companies, Inc.

Key Points

Notes

Academic Vocabulary

Define the following academic vocabulary word from this lesson.

sectors

_____

_____

Terms To Review

Use each of these terms, which you studied earlier, in a sentence.

items
(Chapter 3, Section 3)

_____

_____

nevertheless
(Chapter 3, Section 3)

_____

_____

Section Wrap-up

Now that you have read the section, answer this question from Setting a Purpose for Reading *at the beginning of the section.*

How did the American Revolution inspire political changes in Latin America?

_____

_____

_____

_____

Copyright © by The McGraw-Hill Companies, Inc.

Chapter 15, Section 1
The Decline of the Qing Dynasty

(Pages 465–471)

Reason To Read

Setting a Purpose for Reading Think about these questions as you read:
• What internal problems led to the decline of the Qing dynasty?
• What role did Western nations play in the Qing dynasty's decline?

Main Idea

As you read pages 465–471 in your textbook, complete the chart below by comparing and contrasting the Tai Ping and Boxer Rebellions.

	Tai Ping	Boxer
Reforms Demanded		
Methods Used to Obtain Reforms		
Outcomes		

Sequencing Events

As you read, place the following events on the time line below.
• **Tai Ping Rebellion begins**
• **Boxer Rebellion defeated**
• **Rebels seize Nanjing and massacre 25,000 men, women, and children**
• **Treaty of Nanjing signed**
• **Ci Xi opposes reforms**

◆1840   ◆1860   ◆1880   ◆1900

Copyright © by The McGraw-Hill Companies, Inc.

Key Points

Notes

Causes of Decline *(pages 465–466)*

Identifying Cause and Effect

Briefly summarize the causes of the decline of the Qing dynasty on the lines below.

_____

_____

_____

_____

Terms To Review

Use the following term, which you studied in an earlier chapter, in a sentence.

external
(Chapter 11, Section 2)

_____

_____

The Opium War *(pages 466–467)*

Questioning

As you read, ask yourself questions about the text to help you understand it better. In addition to the questions below, you may develop your own questions. Write your answers on the lines below.

1. What is the main idea of the passage? _____

_____

2. Are there any parts of the passage I do not understand? What are they?

_____

_____

3. How can I go about clarifying the information I do not understand?

_____

_____

Copyright © by The McGraw-Hill Companies, Inc.

Key Points

Notes

Terms To Know

Define or describe the following key term from this lesson.

extra-territoriality >

_____

_____

Academic Vocabulary

Use the following academic vocabulary words from this lesson in a sentence.

appealed >

_____

_____

contact >

_____

_____

The Tai Ping Rebellion (pages 467–468)

Drawing Conclusions

As you read, write down three details about the Tai Ping Rebellion. Then write a conclusion you draw based on these details.

_____

_____

_____

_____

_____

Terms To Review

Define the following term that you studied in an earlier chapter.

convince
(Chapter 3, Section 1) >

_____

_____

Copyright © by The McGraw-Hill Companies, Inc.

 **Key Points**

 **Notes**

Efforts at Reform (pages 468–469)

Analyzing

After you read this lesson, analyze China's self-strengthening policy. Do you think it was an effective reform? Why? Write your thoughts below.

_____

_____

_____

Terms To Know

Define or describe the following key term from this lesson.

self-strengthening

_____

_____

Terms To Review

Choose one of these two terms, which you studied earlier, to fill in each blank.

finance
(Chapter 11, Section 1)

1. During the Tai Ping Rebellion, warlords collected taxes from local

   people to _____ their private armies.

domestic
(Chapter 2, Section 2)

2. "Self-strengthening" guided Chinese _____ policy
   for years.

3. After the rebellion, some warlords continued to collect money to

   _____ their own activities.

The Advance of Imperialism (pages 469–470)

Monitoring Comprehension

As you read, write down one question from each subhead for a partner to answer. Exchange questions and see if you can answer your partner's questions.

_____

_____

_____

_____

Copyright © by The McGraw-Hill Companies, Inc.

 **Key Points**

 **Notes**

Terms To Know

Define or describe the following key term from this lesson.

spheres of influence

_____

_____

Academic Vocabulary

Use the following academic vocabulary word from this lesson in a sentence.

aid

_____

_____

Opening the Door to China *(pages 470–471)*

Summarizing

After you read the lesson, write a sentence or two describing why the United States favored an Open Door policy.

_____

_____

_____

Terms To Review

Circle the letter of the word or phrase that is closest in meaning to the underlined word that you studied earlier.

access
(Chapter 12, Section 3)

1. The Open Door policy ensured equal <u>access</u> to the Chinese market for all nations.

   a. an increase or addition

   b. freedom to enter, obtain, or make use of

   c. a fit of intense feeling

dominate
(Chapter 2, Section 1)

2. The Open Door policy reduced the fears of Britain, France, Germany, and Russia that other powers would attempt to <u>dominate</u> the Chinese market.

   a. control

   b. overlook from above

   c. take away from

Copyright © by The McGraw-Hill Companies, Inc.

The Boxer Rebellion (page 471)

Evaluating

As you read, think about whether the Boxers were justified in their fight against foreign takeover of Chinese lands. How else might the matter have been resolved?

_____

_____

_____

Terms To Know

Define or describe the following key term from this lesson.

indemnity

_____

_____

Terms To Review

Use the following term, which you studied earlier, in a sentence that shows you understand the term's meaning.

restored
(Chapter 5, Section 4)

_____

_____

Section Wrap-up

Now that you have read the section, answer these questions from Setting a Purpose for Reading *at the beginning of the section.*

What internal problems led to the decline of the Qing dynasty?

_____

_____

_____

What role did Western nations play in the Qing dynasty's decline?

_____

_____

_____

Copyright © by The McGraw-Hill Companies, Inc.

Chapter 15, Section 2
Revolution in China

(Pages 473–478)

Reason To Read

Setting a Purpose for Reading Think about these questions as you read:
- What was Sun Yat-sen's role in the collapse of the Qing dynasty?
- How did Western influence affect the Chinese economy and culture?

Main Idea

As you read pages 473–478 in your textbook, complete the chart below by listing the reforms requested by Sun Yat-sen and those implemented by Empress Dowager Ci Xi.

Sun Yat-sen's Proposals	Empress Dowager Ci Xi's Reforms

Sequencing Events

As you read, number the following events in the order in which they occurred.

_____ Followers of Sun Yat-sen launch uprising in central China

_____ Sun Yat-sen issues reform program

_____ Qing dynasty collapses

_____ General Yuan Shigai dies

_____ Emperor Guang Xu and Empress Dowager Ci Xi die

Copyright © by The McGraw-Hill Companies, Inc.

The Fall of the Qing *(pages 473–475)*

Previewing

Before you begin reading, preview the lesson. Use the lines below to write down the topics you expect to learn more about, based on headings and terms in color or boldface.

_____

_____

_____

_____

_____

Terms To Know

Define or describe the following key term from this lesson.

provincial

_____

_____

Academic Vocabulary

Use the following academic vocabulary word from this lesson in a sentence that shows you understand the word's meaning.

generated

_____

_____

Terms To Review

Write the letter of the correct definition next to each of these terms that you studied earlier.

_____ **1.** legal
(Chapter 3, Section 4)

_____ **2.** democracy
(Chapter 2, Section 1)

_____ **3.** abandoned
(Chapter 11, Section 1)

a. government by the people

b. give up support of

c. government by a sovereign ruler

d. founded on law

Copyright © by The McGraw-Hill Companies, Inc.

An Era of Civil War (pages 475–476)

Inferring

As you read, think about General Yuan Shigai's dictatorial way of ruling. What can you infer about how China's history would be different if Yuan had understood the new ideas that were coming into China from the West?

_____

_____

_____

Terms To Review

Define the following terms that you studied earlier.

motives
(Chapter 6, Section 1)

_____

_____

challenge
(Chapter 3, Section 3)

_____

_____

Chinese Society in Transition (pages 476–477)

Evaluating

Imagine that you are a newspaper editor reporting on China in the middle to late 1800s. Write an editorial explaining whether the arrival of Westerners in China has had a positive or negative effect on Chinese society. Be sure to include reasons for your opinion.

_____

_____

_____

_____

Terms To Know

Define or describe the following key term from this lesson.

commodities

_____

_____

Copyright © by The McGraw-Hill Companies, Inc.

Key Points

Notes

Terms To Review

Choose one of these two terms, which you studied earlier, to fill in each blank.

export
(Chapter 11, Section 3)

process
(Chapter 5, Section 3)

1. Changes to the Chinese economy quickened the _____ of change that had already begun in Chinese society.

2. The arrival of Westerners to China effected the Chinese economy one way by creating a(n) _____ market.

3. After World War I, the _____ of economic development changed as Chinese businesspeople began to pursue new ventures.

China's Changing Culture *(pages 477–478)*

Connecting

After you read the lesson, write a brief paragraph about art and literature in the United States today. What trends do you see?

_____

_____

_____

_____

Academic Vocabulary

Circle the letter of the word or phrase that is closest in meaning to the underlined word.

submit

1. In China in the 1800s, wives were supposed to <u>submit</u> to their husbands.

   a. refuse   **b.** oppose   **c.** give in

trends

2. Some artists in China followed foreign <u>trends</u> in their artwork.

   a. styles   **b.** subjects   **c.** artists

Copyright © by The McGraw-Hill Companies, Inc.

Terms To Review

Write the definition of each of the following terms that you studied earlier.

cycle
(Chapter 4, Section 2)

_____
_____

visible
(Chapter 5, Section 1)

_____
_____

Section Wrap-up

Now that you have read the section, answer these questions from Setting a Purpose for Reading *at the beginning of the section.*

What was Sun Yat-sen's role in the collapse of the Qing dynasty?

_____
_____
_____
_____
_____

How did Western influence affect the Chinese economy and culture?

_____
_____
_____
_____
_____

Copyright © by The McGraw-Hill Companies, Inc.

Chapter 15, Section 3
Rise of Modern Japan

(Pages 479–486)

Reason To Read

Setting a Purpose for Reading Think about these questions as you read:
- What effect did the Meiji Restoration have on Japan?
- What steps did Japan take to become an imperialist nation?

Main Idea

As you read pages 479–486 in your textbook, complete the chart below by listing the promises contained in the Charter Oath of 1868 and the provisions of the Meiji constitution of 1890.

Charter Oath	Constitution

Sequencing Events

As you read, place the following events on the time line below.

- **Japan pursues imperialist policy**
- **Commodore Perry arrives in Japan**
- **Japan defeats Russia**
- **United States signs a treaty that opens several ports to U.S. trade**

♦1850	♦1870	♦1890	♦1910

Copyright © by The McGraw-Hill Companies, Inc.

Key Points **Notes**

An End to Isolation *(pages 479–480)*

Responding   *Complete the following sentences. Then write a brief paragraph supporting your position.*

1. The greatest impact of the Treaty of Kanagawa on Japan was

   _____ .

2. The greatest impact of the Treaty of Kanagawa on the United States was _____ .

   _____

   _____

   _____

   _____

Terms To Know   *Define or describe the following key term from this lesson.*

concessions   _____

   _____

Terms To Review   *Use the following term, which you studied earlier, in a sentence that reflects the term's meaning in this lesson.*

isolated
(Chapter 2, Section 1)   _____

   _____

Resistance to the New Order *(page 480)*

Identifying Cause and Effect   *After you have read this lesson, write a brief paragraph summarizing the causes of the collapse of the shogunate system in Japan.*

   _____

   _____

   _____

   _____

Copyright © by The McGraw-Hill Companies, Inc.

 **Key Points**

 **Notes**

Academic Vocabulary

Define the following academic vocabulary word from this lesson.

exposed ⟩ _____

_____

Terms To Review

Write the letter of the correct definition next to each of these terms that you studied earlier.

_____ **1.** traditions
(Chapter 1, Section 2)

_____ **2.** collapsed
(Chapter 11, Section 3)

a. an organized set of ideas

b. characteristics, manner, method, or style

c. broke down completely

The Meiji Restoration (pages 480–484)

Outlining

As you read this lesson, fill in the outline below.

I. Transformation of Japanese Politics

A. _____

B. _____

II. Meiji Economics

A. _____

B. _____

III. Building a Modern Social Structure

A. _____

B. _____

IV. Daily Life and Women's Rights

A. _____

B. _____

Copyright © by The McGraw-Hill Companies, Inc.

Terms To Know

Define or describe the following key term from this lesson.

prefectures

_____

_____

Academic Vocabulary

Define the following academic vocabulary word from this lesson.

context

_____

_____

Joining the Imperialist Nations (pages 484–485)

Monitoring Comprehension

As you read, write down one question you have about the passage for a partner to answer. Exchange questions and see if you can answer your partner's question.

_____

_____

_____

_____

Terms To Review

Circle the letter of the word or phrase that is closest in meaning to the underlined word that you studied earlier.

expand
(Chapter 1, Section 2)

1. Japan began to <u>expand</u> its territory by claiming control of the Ryukyu Islands.

   a. increase the scope of

   b. express in greater detail

   c. feel optimistic about

restrict
(Chapter 8, Section 3)

2. The Japanese resented efforts by the United States to <u>restrict</u> Japanese immigration.

   a. stop   **b.** limit   **c.** increase

Copyright © by The McGraw-Hill Companies, Inc.

Key Points

 Notes

Culture in an Era of Transition (pages 485–486)

Evaluating As you read, think about the effects that Japanese culture had on other nations. Summarize your thoughts in a paragraph.

_____

_____

_____

_____

Terms To Review Choose one of these terms, which you studied earlier, to fill in each blank.

techniques
(Chapter 3, Section 3)

1. Japanese buildings adopted Western _____

architecture, using reinforced concrete.

style
(Chapter 10, Section 3)

2. Many Japanese artists returned to older _____ .

3. The Japanese copied Western artisitic _____ and

styles.

Section Wrap-up Now that you have read the section, answer these questions from **Setting a Purpose for Reading** _at the beginning of the section._

What effect did the Meiji Restoration have on Japan?

_____

_____

_____

What steps did Japan take to become an imperialist nation?

_____

_____

_____

Copyright © by The McGraw-Hill Companies, Inc.

Chapter 16, Section 1
The Road to World War I
(Pages 499–502)

Reason To Read

Setting a Purpose for Reading Think about these questions as you read:
- How did the assassination of Archduke Francis Ferdinand lead to World War I?
- How did the system of alliances help cause the war?

Main Idea

As you read pages 499–502 in your textbook, complete the graphic organizer below by identifying the factors that led to World War I.

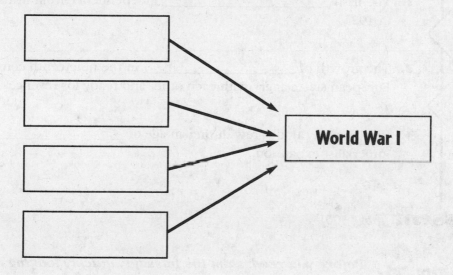

World War I

Sequencing Events

As you read, place the following events on the time line below.
- **Archduke Francis Ferdinand is assassinated**
- **Triple Entente forms**
- **World War I begins**
- **Triple Alliance forms**

◆ 1880   ◆ 1890   ◆ 1900   ◆ 1910   ◆ 1920

Copyright © by The McGraw-Hill Companies, Inc.

Key Points / Notes

Nationalism and the System of Alliances (pages 499–500)

Reviewing

After you read the lesson and study the map on page 718, use the space below to list the countries that belonged to the Triple Alliance and those that belonged to the Triple Entente.

_____

_____

_____

Terms To Review

Choose one of these two terms, which you studied in an earlier chapter, to fill in each blank.

nationalism
(Chapter 11, Section 3)

achieved
(Chapter 1, Section 3)

1. The Irish _____ independence from British rule in 1921.

2. The growth of _____ in the nineteenth century left European states angry with each other and ready for revenge.

3. Rivalries over trade grew during an age of _____ and imperialist expansion.

Internal Dissent (page 500)

Skimming

Before you read, skim the passage, quickly looking over the lesson to get an idea of its content. Then write a sentence or two explaining what you expect the lesson to be about.

_____

_____

_____

Terms To Review

Use the following term, which you studied earlier, in a sentence that reflects the term's meaning.

revolution
(Chapter 1, Section 1)

_____

_____

Copyright © by The McGraw-Hill Companies, Inc.

Key Points

Notes

Militarism *(pages 500–501)*

Connecting

Conscription, or the draft, was established in several countries before 1914. Would you support conscription in the United States today? Why or why not?

_____

_____

_____

_____

Terms To Know

Use the following key term from this lesson in a sentence.

conscription

_____

_____

Terms To Review

Write the letter of the correct definition next to each of these terms that you studied earlier.

_____ **1.** obvious (Chapter 10, Section 1)

_____ **2.** militarism (Chapter 1, Section 2)

a. aggressive preparation for war

b. a payment for damages

c. evident

The Outbreak of War: Summer 1914 *(pages 501–502)*

Monitoring Comprehension

As you read, write down two questions from the lesson for a partner to answer. Exchange questions and see if you can answer your partner's questions.

_____

_____

_____

_____

_____

_____

Copyright © by The McGraw-Hill Companies, Inc.

Key Points / Notes

Terms To Know

Define or describe the following key term from this lesson.

mobilization ⟩

_____

_____

Academic Vocabulary

Define the following academic vocabulary word from this lesson.

furthermore ⟩

_____

_____

Terms To Review

Circle the letter of the word or phrase that is closest in meaning to the underlined word you studied earlier.

rely
(Chapter 2, Section 2) ⟩

1. After the assassination of Archduke Francis Ferdinand, Emperor William II of Germany responded by saying that Austria-Hungary could <u>rely</u> on Germany's full support.

   a. refuse   **b.** have confidence in   **c.** not expect

maintaining
(Chapter 2, Section 2) ⟩

2. Concerned about <u>maintaining</u> its own world power, Great Britain declared war on Germany.

   a. preserving   **b.** losing   **c.** finding

Section Wrap-up

Now that you have read the section, answer these questions from Setting a Purpose for Reading *at the beginning of the section.*

How did the assassination of Archduke Francis Ferdinand lead to World War I?

_____

_____

_____

How did the system of alliances help cause the war?

_____

_____

_____

Copyright © by The McGraw-Hill Companies, Inc.

Chapter 16, Section 2
The War

(Pages 503–509)

Reason To Read

Setting a Purpose for Reading Think about these questions as you read:
- How did trench warfare lead to a stalemate?
- Why did the United States enter the war?

Main Idea

As you read pages 503–509 in your textbook, complete the graphic organizer below by identifying which countries belonged to the Allies and the Central Powers, and which countries changed allegiance or withdrew from the war.

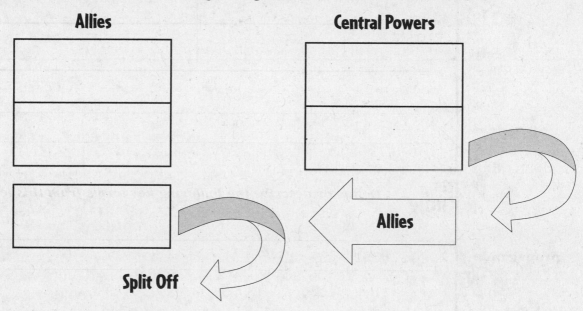

Allies

Central Powers

Allies

Split Off

Sequencing Events

As you read, number the following events in the order in which they occurred.

_____ **United States enters the war**

_____ *Lusitania* **sunk by German forces**

_____ **Battle of Verdun**

_____ **Most British women gain the right to vote**

_____ **Allied forces withdraw from Gallipoli**

Copyright © by The McGraw-Hill Companies, Inc.

1914 to 1915: Illusions and Stalemate (pages 503–505)

Reviewing

As you read the lesson, fill in the chart below by listing the conditions and events on each front of the war. Then write a statement comparing and contrasting the Western Front and the Eastern Front.

The Western Front	The Eastern Front

Statement

_____

_____

Terms To Know

Define or describe the following key terms from this lesson.

propaganda

_____

_____

trench warfare

_____

_____

Academic Vocabulary

Use the following academic vocabulary word from this lesson in a sentence.

involved

_____

_____

Copyright © by The McGraw-Hill Companies, Inc.

1916 to 1917: The Great Slaughter (pages 505–506)

Skimming

Skim this lesson before you begin reading it, looking at headings and words in boldface or colored type. Write a sentence below describing what you expect to learn in this lesson. After reading, revise your sentence if needed.

_____

_____

_____

Terms To Know

Define or describe the following key term from this lesson.

> **war of attrition**

_____

_____

Terms To Review

Circle the letter of the word or phrase that is closest in meaning to the underlined word that you studied earlier.

> **constant**
> (Chapter 8, Section 3)

1. World War I turned into a war based on wearing the other side down by <u>constant</u> attacks and heavy losses.

   a. continual **b.** sporadic **c.** heavy

> **occurred**
> (Chapter 12, Section 1)

2. The use of airplanes on the battlefront <u>occurred</u> for the first time during World War I.

   a. ran **b.** happened **c.** worked

Widening of the War (page 506)

Identifying Cause and Effect

Read the passage and write a brief summary of what caused the widening of World War I.

_____

_____

_____

Copyright © by The McGraw-Hill Companies, Inc.

Key Points

Notes

Terms To Review

Write the definition of the following term that you studied in an earlier chapter.

conflict
(Chapter 1, Section 2)

_____

_____

Entry of the United States (pages 507–508)

Evaluating

Imagine that you are living in the United States in 1917. Would you have supported or opposed U.S. entry into the war? Explain your reasons in a paragraph.

_____

_____

_____

Terms To Review

Use each of the following terms, which you studied earlier, in a sentence.

assured
(Chapter 5, Section 3)

_____

_____

intervene
(Chapter 14, Section 4)

_____

_____

The Home Front: The Impact of Total War (pages 508–509)

Synthesizing

Why did the U.S. government use propaganda during World War I? Do you think the government today uses propaganda to gain support for its policies? Explain your position.

_____

_____

_____

_____

Copyright © by The McGraw-Hill Companies, Inc.

Terms To Know

Define or describe each of the following key terms from this lesson.

total war > _____

_____

planned economies > _____

_____

Terms To Review

Write the letter of the correct definition next to each of these terms that you studied earlier.

____ **1.** available
(Chapter 3, Section 1)

a. obtainable

b. equal

____ **2.** evident
(Chapter 2, Section 1)

c. apparent

Section Wrap-up

Now that you have read the section, answer these questions from Setting a Purpose for Reading *at the beginning of the section.*

How did trench warfare lead to a stalemate?

_____

_____

_____

Why did the United States enter the war?

_____

_____

_____

Copyright © by The McGraw-Hill Companies, Inc.

Chapter 16, Section 3
The Russian Revolution

(Pages 514–519)

Reason To Read

Setting a Purpose for Reading Think about these questions as you read:
- What promises did the Bolsheviks make to the Russian people?
- Why did civil war break out in Russia after the Russian Revolution?

Main Idea

As you read pages 514–519 in your textbook, complete the graphic organizer below by identifying the factors and events that led to Lenin coming to power in 1917.

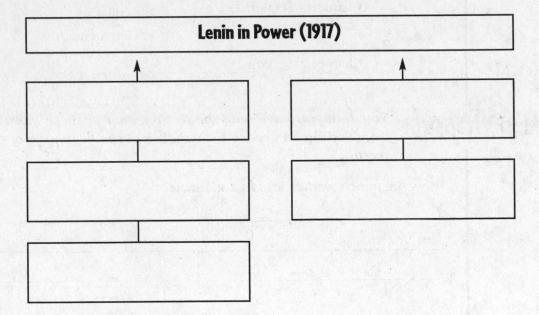

Lenin in Power (1917)

Sequencing Events

As you read, number the following events in the order in which they occurred.

_____ **Lenin signs Treaty of Brest-Litovsk**

_____ **Rasputin assassinated**

_____ **Communists control Russia**

_____ **Local soviets murder Czar Nicholas and his family**

Copyright © by The McGraw-Hill Companies, Inc.

Background to Revolution (pages 514–516)

Inferring

As you read, think about Czar Nicholas II and his method of autocratic rule. How might Russia's history have been different if Czar Nicholas had allowed the Duma, or parliament, to have a real voice in the government?

_____

_____

_____

Terms To Know

Define or describe the following key term from this lesson.

soviets

_____

_____

Academic Vocabulary

Define the following academic vocabulary word from this lesson.

consulting

_____

_____

Terms To Review

Use the following term, which you studied earlier, in a sentence.

crucial
(Chapter 1, Section 1)

_____

_____

The Rise of Lenin (page 517)

Summarizing

As you read, think about the rise of Lenin. Then write a paragraph summarizing Lenin's plan when he arrived in Russia.

_____

_____

_____

Copyright © by The McGraw-Hill Companies, Inc.

Terms To Review

Choose one of these two terms, which you studied earlier, to fill in each blank.

task
(Chapter 2, Section 1)

1. The Bolsheviks promised the _____ of factories and industries from capitalists to committees of workers.

2. Lenin believed that a small party of well-disciplined activists would be needed to accomplish a violent revolution, a _____ intended to destroy the capitalist system.

transfer
(Chapter 10, Section 3)

3. The _____ of government power from the provisional government to the soviets was one of the promises made by the Bolsheviks.

The Bolsheviks Seize Power *(page 518)*

Drawing Conclusions

As you read, write down three details about the Bolsheviks' seizure of power. Then write a conclusion you draw based on these details.

_____

_____

_____

_____

Academic Vocabulary

Define the academic vocabulary word from this lesson.

coincided

_____

_____

Terms To Review

Use the following term, which you studied earlier, in a sentence that reflects the term's meaning.

collapsed
(Chapter 11, Section 3)

_____

_____

Copyright © by The McGraw-Hill Companies, Inc.

Key Points / Notes

Civil War in Russia (page 518)

Reviewing

As you read the lesson, focus on the groups of people who opposed the Bolshevik regime. Identify these people on the lines below.

_____

_____

_____

_____

Terms To Review

Write the letter of the correct definition next to each of these terms that you studied earlier.

_____ **1.** czar
(Chapter 7, Section 3)

_____ **2.** liberals
(Chapter 5, Section 2)

a. people who support civil liberties for the individual, freedom from government restraint, and the vote for those with property

b. title used by Russian emperors

c. people who adhere to traditional ways

Triumph of the Communists (pages 518–519)

Scanning

Before you read, scan the lesson looking for examples of how Lenin and the Communists triumphed in civil war over what seemed to be overwhelming forces. Use the lines below to write down notes.

_____

_____

_____

_____

Terms To Know

Define or describe the following key term from this lesson.

war communism >

_____

_____

Copyright © by The McGraw-Hill Companies, Inc.

 **Key Points**

 **Notes**

Terms To Review

Write the definition of each of the following terms that you studied earlier.

rigid
(Chapter 3 Section 2)

_____

_____

ensure
(Chapter 13, Section 2)

_____

_____

Section Wrap-up

Now that you have read the section, answer these questions from Setting a Purpose for Reading *at the beginning of the section.*

What promises did the Bolsheviks make to the Russian people?

_____

_____

_____

Why did civil war break out in Russia after the Russian Revolution?

_____

_____

_____

Copyright © by The McGraw-Hill Companies, Inc.

Chapter 16, Section 4
End of the War
(Pages 521–526)

Reason To Read

Setting a Purpose for Reading Think about these questions as you read:
- What were the key events in bringing about an end to the war?
- What was the intended purpose of the League of Nations?

Main Idea

As you read pages 521–526 in your textbook, complete the chart below by identifying the goals of each country listed as the peace conference approached.

France	Britain	United States

Sequencing Events

As you read, write the correct date next to each event on the time line below.

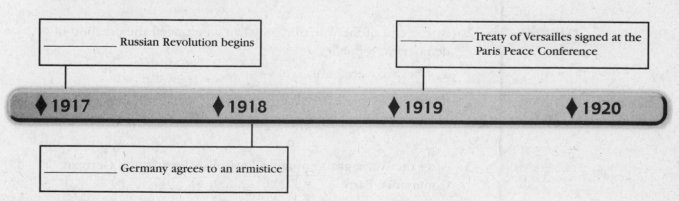

_____ Russian Revolution begins

_____ Treaty of Versailles signed at the Paris Peace Conference

♦1917   ♦1918   ♦1919   ♦1920

_____ Germany agrees to an armistice

Copyright © by The McGraw-Hill Companies, Inc.

The Last Year of the War *(pages 521–523)*

Outlining

As you read this lesson, fill in the outline below.

I. A New German Offensive

   A. _____

   B. _____

II. Collapse and Armistice

   A. _____

   B. _____

III. Revolutionary Forces

   A. _____

   B. _____

Terms To Know

Define or describe the following key term from this lesson.

armistice

_____

_____

Terms To Review

Circle the letter of the word or phrase that is closest in meaning to the underlined word that you studied earlier.

concentrate
(Chapter 1, Section 1)

1. After Russia's withdrawal from the War, Germany could <u>concentrate</u> on the Western Front.

   a. focus   **b.** gather   **c.** accumulate

republic
(Chapter 2, Section 2)

2. By the end of the War, Germany had announced the creation of a democratic <u>republic</u>.

   a. liberal government

   b. government in which the power resides with the people

   c. conservative government

radical
(Chapter 11, Section 1)

3. After the War, a group of <u>radical</u> socialists formed the German Communist Party.

   a. extreme   **b.** moderate   **c.** basic

Copyright © by The McGraw-Hill Companies, Inc.

The Peace Settlements *(pages 523–526)*

Analyzing

If you were a politician in 1919, would you have favored or opposed the provisions of the Treaty of Versailles? Why? Explain your position in a paragraph.

_____

_____

_____

Terms To Know

Define or describe each of the following key terms from this lesson.

reparation

_____

_____

mandate

_____

_____

Section Wrap-up

Now that you have read the section, answer these questions from Setting a Purpose for Reading *at the beginning of the section.*

What were the key events in bringing about an end to the war?

_____

_____

_____

_____

What was the intended purpose of the League of Nations?

_____

_____

_____

_____

Copyright © by The McGraw-Hill Companies, Inc.

Chapter 17, Section 1
The Futile Search for Stability

(Pages 533–538)

Reason To Read

Setting a Purpose for Reading Think about these questions as you read:
- What was the significance of the Dawes Plan and the Treaty of Locarno?
- How was Germany affected by the Great Depression?

Main Idea

As you read pages 533–538 in your textbook, complete the chart below by comparing France's Popular Front with the New Deal in the United States.

Popular Front	New Deal

Sequencing Events

As you read, write the correct date next to each event on the time line below.

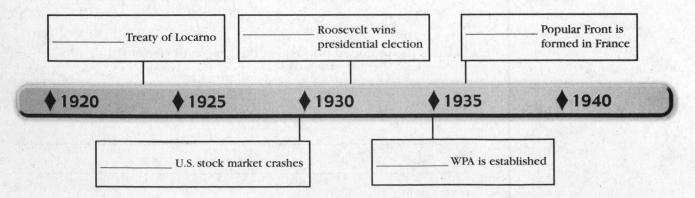

_____ Treaty of Locarno

_____ Roosevelt wins presidential election

_____ Popular Front is formed in France

♦1920   ♦1925   ♦1930   ♦1935   ♦1940

_____ U.S. stock market crashes

_____ WPA is established

Copyright © by The McGraw-Hill Companies, Inc.

Uneasy Peace, Uncertain Security (pages 533–536)

Outlining

As you read this lesson, fill in the outline below.

I. A Weak League of Nations

    A. _____

    B. _____

II. French Demands

    A. _____

    B. _____

III. Inflation in Germany

    A. _____

    B. _____

IV. The Treaty of Locarno

    A. _____

    B. _____

Academic Vocabulary

Circle the letter of the word or phrase that is closest in meaning to the underlined word.

revise

1. Many Germans were upset with the terms of the Treaty of Versailles and wanted to <u>revise</u> them.

    a. keep   **b.** change   **c.** learn

ratio

2. In 1923, the <u>ratio</u> of German marks to U.S. dollars was 4.2 trillion to 1.

    a. relationship in size   **b.** total amount   **c.** the lowest amount

Terms To Review

Use the following term, which you studied earlier, in a sentence that reflects the term's meaning in this lesson.

nationalism
(Chapter 11, Section 3)

_____

_____

Copyright © by The McGraw-Hill Companies, Inc.

The Great Depression (page 536)

Identifying Cause and Effect

Read the passage and write a brief summary of the effects of the Great Depression.

_____

_____

_____

_____

Terms To Know

Define or describe the following key term from this lesson.

depression

_____

_____

Terms To Review

Write the definition of the following term that you studied earlier.

individual
Chapter 5, Section 1)

_____

_____

Democratic States after the War (pages 537–538)

Reviewing

As you read the lesson, focus on the post war conditions of Germany, France, Great Britain, and the United States. Briefly describe them in the chart below.

Country	Conditions
Germany	
France	
Great Britain	
United States	

Copyright © by The McGraw-Hill Companies, Inc.

Terms To Know

Define or describe the following key terms from this lesson.

collective bargaining

_____

_____

_____

deficit spending

_____

_____

_____

Terms To Review

Choose one of these three terms, which you studied earlier, to fill in each blank.

minimum
(Chapter 12, Section 1)

incomes
(Chapter 13, Section 2)

justified
(Chapter 5, Section 3)

1. The New Deal programs provided _____ for many people.

2. In France, workers received a guarantee for a _____ wage.

Section Wrap-up

Now that you have read the section, answer these questions from Setting a Purpose for Reading *at the beginning of the section.*

What was the significance of the Dawes Plan and the Treaty of Locarno?

_____

_____

_____

How was Germany affected by the Great Depression?

_____

_____

_____

Copyright © by The McGraw-Hill Companies, Inc.

Chapter 17, Section 2
The Rise of Dictatorial Regimes

(Pages 540–546)

Reason To Read

Setting a Purpose for Reading Think about these questions as you read:
• To what extent was Fascist Italy a totalitarian state?
• How did Joseph Stalin establish a totalitarian regime in the Soviet Union?

Main Idea

As you read pages 540–546 in your textbook, complete the graphic organizer below by listing the methods Mussolini used to create a Fascist state.

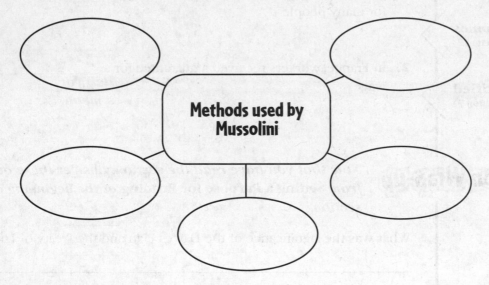

Methods used by Mussolini

Sequencing Events

As you read, number the following events in the order in which they occurred.

_____ **Spanish Civil War begins**

_____ **Lenin dies**

_____ **Mussolini recognizes independence of Vatican City**

_____ **Spanish Civil War ends**

_____ **Stalin launches his first Five-Year Plan**

Copyright © by The McGraw-Hill Companies, Inc.

The Rise of Dictators (pages 540–541)

Reviewing

After you have read the lesson, write a paragraph explaining how totalitarian states achieved their goal of controlling the political, economic, social, intellectual, and cultural lives of citizens.

_____

_____

_____

_____

Terms To Know

Define or describe the following key term from this lesson.

totalitarian state

_____

_____

Terms To Review

Use each of the following terms, which you studied earlier, in a sentence that reflects the term's meaning.

propaganda
(Chapter 16, Section 2)

_____

_____

subordinated
(Chapter 1, Section 3)

_____

_____

Fascism in Italy (pages 541–543)

Summarizing

After reading the lesson, write a paragraph summarizing the steps Mussolini took to gain power in Italy.

_____

_____

_____

_____

Copyright © by The McGraw-Hill Companies, Inc.

Key Points

![key icon] **Key Points**

Terms To Know

fascism

Academic Vocabulary

media

Terms To Review

suspend
(Chapter 7, Section 2)

retained
(Chapter 3, Section 3)

Notes

Terms To Know

Define or describe the following key term from this lesson.

_____

_____

Academic Vocabulary

Define the following academic vocabulary word from this lesson.

_____

_____

Terms To Review

Write the definition of each of the following terms that you studied earlier.

_____

_____

_____

_____

A New Era in the Soviet Union *(pages 543–545)*

Evaluating

After you have read the lesson, write a paragraph evaluating Stalin's Five-Year Plan. Explain whether you think it helped or hurt the Russian people.

_____

_____

_____

_____

_____

_____

Copyright © by The McGraw-Hill Companies, Inc.

Terms To Know

Define or describe each of the following key terms from this lesson.

New Economic Policy

_____
_____
_____

Politburo

_____
_____
_____

collectivization

_____
_____
_____

Academic Vocabulary

Use the following academic vocabulary words from this lesson in a sentence.

modified

_____
_____

version

_____
_____

Terms To Review

Write the definition of each of the following terms that you studied earlier.

overall
(Chapter 2, Section 2)

_____
_____

rejected
(Chapter 3, Section 1)

_____
_____

Copyright © by The McGraw-Hill Companies, Inc.

Authoritarian States in the West (pages 545–546)

Questioning

As you read the lesson, write down two questions about the main ideas presented. After you have finished reading, write the answers to these questions.

_____

_____

_____

_____

Terms To Review

Use each of these terms, which you studied earlier, in a sentence.

aspect
(Chapter 11, Section 2)

_____

_____

dictatorship
(Chapter 13, Section 1)

_____

_____

Section Wrap-up

Now that you have read the section, answer these questions from Setting a Purpose for Reading at the beginning of the section.

To what extent was Fascist Italy a totalitarian state?

_____

_____

_____

How did Joseph Stalin establish a totalitarian regime in the Soviet Union?

_____

_____

_____

Copyright © by The McGraw-Hill Companies, Inc.

Chapter 17, Section 3
Hitler and Nazi Germany

(Pages 548–553)

Reason To Read

Setting a Purpose for Reading Think about these questions as you read:
- How did Adolf Hitler rise to power?
- What were the chief features of the Nazi totalitarian state?
- How did the rise of Nazism affect Germany?

Main Idea

As you read pages 548–553 in your textbook, complete the chart below by listing anti-Semitic policies enforced by the Nazi Party.

Anti-Semitic Policies

Sequencing Events

As you read, place the following events on the time line below.
- **Nazis enact Nuremberg laws**
- **The Kristallnacht occurs**
- **Hitler takes control of the National Socialist German Workers' Party**
- **Enabling Act passes**

♦ 1880   ♦ 1900   ♦ 1920   ♦ 1940

Copyright © by The McGraw-Hill Companies, Inc.

Hitler and His Views (pages 548–549)

Summarizing

After you have read the lesson, write a paragraph summarizing Hitler's views as expressed in Mein Kampf.

_____

_____

_____

_____

Academic Vocabulary

Define the following academic vocabulary word from this lesson.

> **uniforms**

_____

_____

Terms To Review

Use each of the following terms, which you studied earlier, in a sentence.

> **core**
> (Chapter 11, Section 3)

_____

_____

> **eventually**
> (Chapter 3, Section 4)

_____

_____

Rise of Nazism (pages 549–550)

Interpreting

Do you think Hitler gained power legally? Review the previous section in your textbook to see if Mussolini gained power legally in Italy. Are there any differences in the methods they used to obtain their office?

_____

_____

_____

_____

Copyright © by The McGraw-Hill Companies, Inc.

Key Points

Notes

Terms To Know

Define or describe the following key term from this lesson.

Reichstag

_____

_____

Academic Vocabulary

Use the following academic vocabulary word from this lesson in a sentence that shows you understand the word's meaning.

attain

_____

_____

Terms To Review

Write the definition of each of the following terms that you studied earlier.

impact
(Chapter 3, Section 2)

_____

_____

militarism
(Chapter 1, Section 2)

_____

_____

Victory of Nazism (page 550)

Analyzing

Do you think the passage of the Enabling Act made it harder to protect the civil rights of Jews in Germany? Might this have happened anyway, given the level of anti-Semitism in Germany? Write your opinion on the lines below.

_____

_____

_____

_____

Copyright © by The McGraw-Hill Companies, Inc.

Terms To Know

Define or describe the following key term from this lesson.

concentration
camps
_____
_____

Terms To Review

Write the definition of each of the following terms that you studied earlier.

required
(Chapter 4, Section 2)
_____
_____

foundation
(Chapter 2, Section 1)
_____
_____

The Nazi State, 1933–1939 (pages 551–553)

Outlining

As you read this lesson, fill in the outline below.

I. The State and Terror

    A. _____

    B. _____

II. Economic Policies

    A. _____

    B. _____

III. Spectacles and Organizations

    A. _____

    B. _____

IV. Women and Nazism

    A. _____

    B. _____

V. Anti-Semitic Policies

    A. _____

    B. _____

Copyright © by The McGraw-Hill Companies, Inc.

Academic Vocabulary

Use each of the following academic vocabulary words from this lesson in a sentence that reflects the term's meaning.

identify

_____

_____

projects

_____

_____

Section Wrap-up

Now that you have read the section, answer these questions from **Setting a Purpose for Reading** _at the beginning of the section._

How did Adolf Hitler rise to power?

_____

_____

_____

_____

What were the chief features of the Nazi totalitarian state?

_____

_____

_____

_____

How did the rise of Nazism affect Germany?

_____

_____

_____

_____

Copyright © by The McGraw-Hill Companies, Inc.

Chapter 17, Section 4
Cultural and Intellectual Trends

(Pages 554–557)

Reason To Read

Setting a Purpose for Reading Think about these questions as you read:
• What trends dominated the arts and popular culture after 1918?
• How did the new movements in arts and literature reflect the changes after World War I?

Main Idea

As you read pages 554–557 in your textbook, complete the chart below by listing literary works by Hesse and Joyce and describing the techniques used in each work.

Literary Works	Techniques

Sequencing Events

As you read, place the following events on the time line below.

• **Werner Heisenberg explains the uncertainty principle**
• **James Joyce's *Ulysses* is published**
• **First Dada show in Berlin**
• **Great Britain has 2.2 million radios**

◆1915   ◆1920   ◆1925   ◆1930

Copyright © by The McGraw-Hill Companies, Inc.

Mass Culture: Radio and Movies *(pages 554–555)*

Connecting

After you have finished reading the lesson, write a paragraph explaining how popular forms of entertainment are used to spread political messages today. Be sure to include examples in your paragraph.

_____

_____

_____

_____

Academic Vocabulary

Choose one of these three terms from this lesson to fill in each blank.

> **transmitted**

> **potential**

> **opportunity**

1. In the 1920s, the cinema became a popular form of entertainment and

a(n)_____ source of propaganda.

2. People in the 1920s listened to music that was

_____ over radio waves.

More Goods, More Leisure *(page 555)*

Determining the Main Idea

As you read, write down the main idea of the passage. Review your statement when you have finished reading and revise as needed.

_____

_____

_____

Terms To Review

Write the definition of the following term that you studied in an earlier chapter.

> **similar**
> (Chapter 3, Section 1)

_____

_____

Copyright © by The McGraw-Hill Companies, Inc.

Key Points

 **Notes**

Artistic and Literary Trends (pages 556–557)

Visualizing

As you read the lesson, try to visualize the photomontage created by Hannah Höch. Then think about what kinds of photos you would use in a photomontage to portray important aspects of our culture today. In a paragraph, describe the content of your photographs and the message you would want to convey.

_____

_____

_____

_____

_____

Terms To Know

Define or describe each of the following key terms from this lesson.

photomontage

_____

_____

_____

surrealism

_____

_____

Terms To Review

Use each of the following terms, which you studied earlier, in a sentence.

rational
(Chapter 12, Section 4)

_____

_____

contexts
(Chapter 15, Section 3)

_____

_____

Copyright © by The McGraw-Hill Companies, Inc.

The Heroic Age of Physics (page 557)

Monitoring Comprehension

As you read the lesson, write down one question you have about the passage. When you have finished reading, answer your question.

_____

_____

_____

Terms To Know

Define or describe the following key term from this lesson.

uncertainty principle

_____

_____

Academic Vocabulary

Use the following academic vocabulary word from this lesson in a sentence.

implication

_____

_____

Section Wrap-up

Now that you have read the section, answer these questions from Setting a Purpose for Reading *at the beginning of the section.*

What trends dominated the arts and popular culture after 1918?

_____

_____

_____

How did the new movements in arts and literature reflect the changes after World War I?

_____

_____

_____

Copyright © by The McGraw-Hill Companies, Inc.

Chapter 18, Section 1
Nationalism in the Middle East
(Pages 563–567)

Reason To Read

Setting a Purpose for Reading Think about these questions as you read:
- What important force led to the fall of the Ottoman Empire?
- What was the relationship between Arab nationalism and the mandate system?

Main Idea

As you read pages 563–567 in your textbook, complete the graphic organizer below by comparing and contrasting the national policies of Atatürk and Reza Shah Pahlavi.

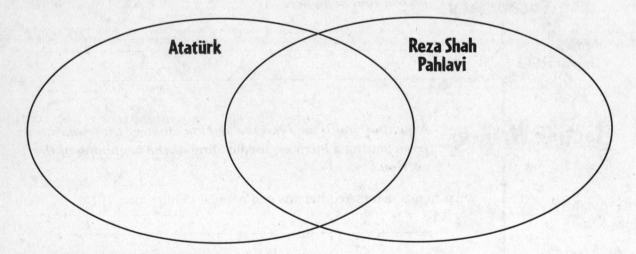

Atatürk   Reza Shah Pahlavi

Sequencing Events

As you read, number the following events in the order in which they occurred.

_____ **Turkish Republic declared**

_____ **Turkish government massacres Armenians**

_____ **Saudi Arabia is established**

_____ **Caliphate formally abolished in Turkey**

Copyright © by The McGraw-Hill Companies, Inc.

Decline and Fall of the Ottoman Empire *(pages 563–565)*

Monitoring Comprehension

As you read, write down one question from each subhead for a partner to answer. Exchange questions and see if you can answer your partner's questions.

_____

_____

_____

_____

Terms To Know

Define or describe each of the following key terms from this lesson.

genocide

_____

_____

_____

ethnic cleansing

_____

_____

Academic Vocabulary

Define the following academic vocabulary words from this lesson.

final

_____

_____

estimated

_____

_____

Terms To Review

Write the definition of the following term that you studied earlier.

estates
(Chapter 2, Section 2)

_____

_____

Copyright © by The McGraw-Hill Companies, Inc.

The Modernization of Turkey *(pages 565–566)*

Responding

As you read, focus on Atatürk's efforts to Westernize the new Turkish Republic. For example, he forbade women to wear the veil. Do you think Atatürk was justified in changing social customs? Why or why not? Explain your answer on the lines below.

_____

_____

_____

_____

Terms To Review

Use each of the following terms, which you studied earlier, in a sentence.

secular
(Chapter 5, Section 1)

_____

_____

transform
(Chapter 12, Section 1)

_____

_____

significant
(Chapter 1, Section 2)

_____

_____

The Beginnings of Modern Iran *(page 566)*

Drawing Conclusions

As you read about Iran in the early twentieth century, focus on how Iran related to foreign countries. When you are finished reading, draw a conclusion about why Iran became close to Nazi Germany in the 1930s.

_____

_____

_____

_____

Copyright © by The McGraw-Hill Companies, Inc.

Terms To Review

Write the letter of the correct definition next to each of these terms that you studied earlier.

_____ **1.** resolving
(Chapter 10, Section 4)

_____ **2.** exports
(Chapter 11, Section 3)

a. becoming part of a process

b. finding a solution

c. goods sent to another country

d. goods brought into a country

Arab Nationalism (pages 566–567)

Analyzing

After you have finished reading the lesson, explain why Arabs were unable to form one nation after the Ottoman Empire ended.

_____

_____

_____

_____

_____

Terms To Review

Use each of the following terms, which you studied earlier, in a sentence that shows you understand the term's meaning.

granted
(Chapter 1, Section 2)

_____

_____

nationalism
(Chapter 11, Section 3)

_____

_____

consisted
(Chapter 1, Section 3)

_____

_____

Copyright © by The McGraw-Hill Companies, Inc.

The Problem of Palestine *(page 567)*

Evaluating

Imagine you are either a Palestinian or a Jew in the 1920s. Write a brief letter to a friend describing two reasons you oppose or support the Balfour Declaration.

_____

_____

_____

_____

_____

_____

Terms To Review

Use the following term, which you studied earlier, in a sentence.

advocated
(Chapter 7, Section 4)

_____

_____

Section Wrap-up

Now that you have read the section, answer these questions from Setting a Purpose for Reading *at the beginning of the section.*

What important force led to the fall of the Ottoman Empire?

_____

_____

_____

What was the relationship between Arab nationalism and the mandate system?

_____

_____

_____

Copyright © by The McGraw-Hill Companies, Inc.

Chapter 18, Section 2
Nationalism in Africa and Asia

(Pages 568–573)

Reason To Read

Setting a Purpose for Reading Think about these questions as you read:
- What different forms did protest against Western rule take?
- How was communism received in Asia?

Main Idea

As you read pages 568–573 in your textbook, complete the chart below by contrasting the backgrounds and values of Gandhi and the younger Nehru.

Mahatma Gandhi	Jawaharlal Nehru

Sequencing Events

As you read, write the correct date next to each event on the time line below.

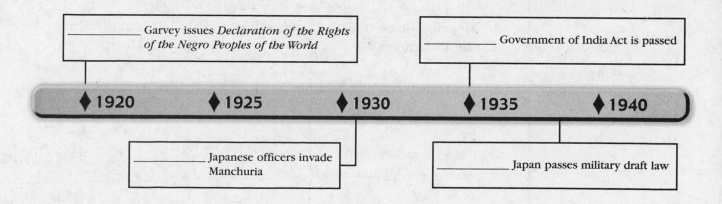

_____ Garvey issues *Declaration of the Rights of the Negro Peoples of the World*

_____ Government of India Act is passed

♦ 1920   ♦ 1925   ♦ 1930   ♦ 1935   ♦ 1940

_____ Japanese officers invade Manchuria

_____ Japan passes military draft law

Copyright © by The McGraw-Hill Companies, Inc.

Movements toward Independence in Africa (pages 568–570)

Reviewing

As you read the lesson, focus on the different paths African leaders followed in their push for independence. Complete the chart below by identifying the leaders and their roles in the independence movements of their countries.

African Leaders	Forms of Protest

Terms To Know

Define or describe the following key term from this lesson.

Pan-Africanism _____

_____

Terms To Review

Choose one of these terms, which you studied earlier, to fill in each blank.

portion
(Chapter 6, Section 2)

1. The peace settlement after World War I gave a vast _____ of Africa to Great Britain and France.

levied
(Chapter 10, Section 4)

2. Africans protested the high taxes _____ against them by European rulers.

3. The French controlled a large _____ of West Africa.

Copyright © by The McGraw-Hill Companies, Inc.

The Movement for Indian Independence (pages 570–571)

Identifying Cause and Effect

As you read, think about the Indian independence movements. Then write a paragraph describing the three non-British conflicts that affected the movements.

_____

_____

_____

_____

Terms To Know

Define or describe each of the following key terms from this lesson.

Mahatma

_____

_____

civil disobedience

_____

_____

Academic Vocabulary

Use the following academic vocabulary word from this lesson in a sentence.

released

_____

_____

Terms To Review

Write the definition of each of the following terms that you studied earlier.

methods
(Chapter 13, Section 4)

_____

_____

provincial
(Chapter 15, Section 2)

_____

_____

approaches
(Chapter 5, Section 2)

_____

Chapter 18, Section 2

Copyright © by The McGraw-Hill Companies, Inc.

The Rise of a Militarist Japan (pages 571–573)

Interpreting

As you read this lesson, think about the different kinds of problems Japan faced in the 1920s and 1930s. Some issues were economic, while others were cultural or political. Complete the chart below by listing one example under each heading.

Economic Issue	Cultural Issue	Political Issue

Terms To Know

Define or describe the following key term from this lesson.

zaibatsu

_____

_____

Academic Vocabulary

Define each of the following academic vocabulary words from this lesson.

integrity

_____

_____

corporation

_____

_____

Terms To Review

Use the following term, which you studied earlier, in a sentence that reflects the term's meaning in this lesson.

oligarchy
(Chapter 2, Section 1)

_____

_____

Copyright © by The McGraw-Hill Companies, Inc.

Nationalism and Revolution in Asia (page 573)

Analyzing

As you read, think about the spread of communism in Asia. Then write a paragraph explaining the relationship between communism and imperialism.

_____

_____

_____

_____

Academic Vocabulary

Use the following academic vocabulary words from this lesson in a sentence.

cooperative

_____

_____

strategies

_____

_____

Section Wrap-up

Now that you have read the section, answer these questions from Setting a Purpose for Reading _at the beginning of the section._

What different forms did protest against Western rule take?

_____

_____

_____

How was communism received in Asia?

_____

_____

_____

Copyright © by The McGraw-Hill Companies, Inc.

Chapter 18, Section 3
Revolutionary Chaos in China

(Pages 575–579)

Reason To Read

Setting a Purpose for Reading Think about these questions as you read:
- Against whom were the Nationalist and Chinese Communist Parties aligned?
- What obstacles did Chiang Kai-shek face in building a new China?

Main Idea

As you read pages 575–579 in your textbook, complete the graphic organizer below by showing the traditional Confucian values Chiang Kai-shek stressed while he was promoting Western industrialization.

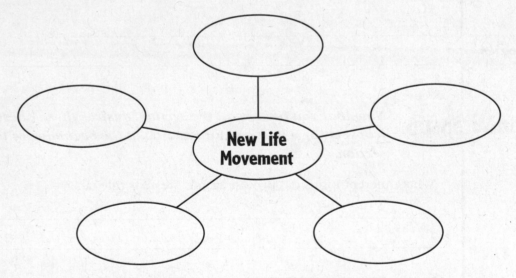

Sequencing Events

As you read, number the following events in the order in which they occurred.

_____ **Nationalists and Communists form an alliance**

_____ **Mao's troops begin the Long March**

_____ **Chinese Communist Party is formed in Shanghai**

_____ **New Chinese Republic is founded at Nanjing**

Copyright © by The McGraw-Hill Companies, Inc.

Nationalists and Communists (pages 575–576)

Skimming

Before you read, skim the passage, quickly looking over the lesson to get an idea of its content. Then write a sentence or two explaining why and how Chiang Kai-shek changed the Communist-Nationalist alliance.

_____

_____

_____

Terms To Review

Use each of the following terms, which you studied earlier, in a sentence.

mutual
(Chapter 14, Section 3)

_____

_____

ceased
(Chapter 9, Section 3)

_____

_____

The Communists in Hiding (pages 576–577)

Monitoring Comprehension

As you read the lesson, write down questions you have about the passage. When you have finished reading, answer your questions.

_____

_____

_____

_____

Terms To Know

Define or describe the following key term from this lesson.

guerrilla tactics

_____

_____

Copyright © by The McGraw-Hill Companies, Inc.

Key Points

Notes

Terms To Review

Write the definition of the following term that you studied in an earlier chapter.

task
(Chapter 2, Section 1)

_____
_____

The Long March (pages 577–578)

Connecting

After you have read the lesson, look at the map on page 795 and trace the route Mao Zedong took to central China. Why was this march important for later Communists? Can you think of a heroic event Americans like to remember? Write your responses on the lines below.

_____
_____
_____
_____

Academic Vocabulary

Use the following academic vocabulary word from this lesson in a sentence.

regime

_____
_____

The New China of Chiang Kai-shek (pages 578–579)

Responding

After you read this lesson, imagine you are a Chinese peasant under Chiang Kai-shek's rule. Write a letter to a family member explaining why you support or oppose Chiang Kai-shek's ideas.

_____
_____
_____
_____

Copyright © by The McGraw-Hill Companies, Inc.

 **Key Points**

 **Notes**

Terms To Know

Define or describe the following key term from this lesson.

redistribution of wealth

_____

_____

Academic Vocabulary

Use the following academic vocabulary word from this lesson in a sentence that shows you understand the word's meaning.

accumulation

_____

_____

Terms To Review

Write the letter of the correct definition next to each of these terms that you studied earlier.

_____ **1.** innovations
(Chapter 4, Section 1)

_____ **2.** undertook
(Chapter 2, Section 1)

a. launched

b. a system of ideas based on the teachings of Laozi

c. new ideas or methods

Section Wrap-up

Now that you have read the section, answer these questions from Setting a Purpose for Reading *at the beginning of the section.*

Against whom were the Nationalist and Chinese Communist Parties aligned?

_____

_____

_____

What obstacles did Chiang Kai-shek face in building a new China?

_____

_____

_____

Copyright © by The McGraw-Hill Companies, Inc.

Chapter 18, Section 4
Nationalism in Latin America

(Pages 581–585)

Reason To Read

Setting a Purpose for Reading Think about these questions as you read:
- What was the Good Neighbor policy?
- How did the Great Depression affect the economies of Latin America?

Main Idea

As you read pages 581–585 in your textbook, complete the chart below by listing the main exports of Latin America.

Country	Exports
Argentina	
Chili	
Brazil	
Peru	

Sequencing Events

As you read, place the following events on the time line below.
- **Getúlio Vargas establishes his New State in Brazil**
- **Good Neighbor policy is announced**
- **Hipólito Irigoyen is elected president of Argentina**

| ♦ 1915 | ♦ 1920 | ♦ 1925 | ♦ 1930 | ♦ 1935 | ♦ 1940 |

Copyright © by The McGraw-Hill Companies, Inc.

The Latin American Economy (pages 581–583)

Analyzing

As you read this lesson, notice that many Latin American countries exported raw materials to the United States and imported manufactured goods. How does this compare to the economic relationship between the American colonies and Great Britain? Write your answer in the space below.

_____

_____

_____

Terms To Review

Write the letter of the correct definition next to each of these terms that you studied earlier.

_____ **1.** economy
(Chapter 3, Section 3)

_____ **2.** revenues
(Chapter 2, Section 2)

a. the structure for producing goods and services in a country or region

b. the act or process of spending

c. the total income a nation collects from taxes and other sources for the public treasury

The Move to Authoritarianism (pages 583–585)

Reviewing

After you have read the lesson, complete the chart below by listing information about the 1930 political coups, or takeovers, which occurred in Argentina and Brazil.

Country	What person or group takes control?	What groups support the coup?	Who overthrows the regime?
Argentina			
Brazil			

Copyright © by The McGraw-Hill Companies, Inc.

Key Points

Notes

Terms To Review

Use each of the following terms, which you studied earlier, in a sentence that reflects the term's meaning in this lesson.

plantations
(Chapter 6, Section 2)

_____
_____
_____

trend
(Chapter 15, Section 2)

_____
_____
_____

features
(Chapter 1, Section 2)

_____
_____
_____

Culture in Latin America (page 585)

Visualizing

Imagine you are an artist in Mexico during the early twentieth century. What kind of images would you portray in your work?

_____
_____
_____
_____

Terms To Review

Write the definition of the following terms that you studied earlier.

techniques
(Chapter 3, Section 3)

_____
_____
_____

adapted
(Chapter 1, Section 1)

_____
_____
_____

Copyright © by The McGraw-Hill Companies, Inc.

Now that you have read the section, answer these questions *from* Setting a Purpose for Reading *at the beginning of the section.*

What was the Good Neighbor policy?

_____

_____

_____

_____

_____

How did the Great Depression affect the economies of Latin America?

_____

_____

_____

_____

_____

Copyright © by The McGraw-Hill Companies, Inc.

Chapter 19, Section 1
Paths to War

(Pages 591–595)

Reason To Read

Setting a Purpose for Reading Think about these questions as you read:
- What agreement was reached at the Munich Conference?
- Why did Germany believe it needed more land?

Main Idea

As you read pages 591–595 in your textbook, complete the chart below by
listing examples of Japanese and German aggression prior to the outbreak of
World War II.

Japanese Aggression	German Aggression

Sequencing Events

As you read, write the correct date next to each event on the time line below.

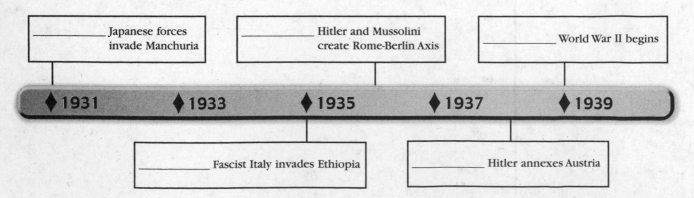

| _____ Japanese forces invade Manchuria | _____ Hitler and Mussolini create Rome-Berlin Axis | _____ World War II begins |

♦ 1931   ♦ 1933   ♦ 1935   ♦ 1937   ♦ 1939

| _____ Fascist Italy invades Ethiopia | _____ Hitler annexes Austria |

Copyright © by The McGraw-Hill Companies, Inc.

Key Points

Notes

The German Path to War (pages 591–594)

Outlining   As you read this lesson, fill in the outline below.

I. The First Steps

A. _____

B. _____

II. New Alliances

A. _____

B. _____

III. Union with Austria

A. _____

B. _____

IV. Demands and Appeasement

A. _____

B. _____

V. Great Britain and France React

A. _____

B. _____

VI. Hitler and the Soviets

A. _____

B. _____

Terms To Know   Define or describe each of the following key terms from this lesson.

demilitarized   _____

_____

appeasement   _____

_____

Copyright © by The McGraw-Hill Companies, Inc.

 **Key Points**

 **Notes**

Academic Vocabulary

Define the following academic vocabulary words from this lesson.

violation

_____
_____
_____

so-called

_____
_____
_____

capable

_____
_____
_____

Terms To Review

Use the following term, which you studied earlier, in a sentence that reflects the term's meaning.

annexed
(Chapter 14, Section 2)

_____
_____

The Japanese Path to War (pages 594–595)

Responding

After you read the lesson, think about the attack of Japanese soldiers on Manchuria. Imagine that you are the Japanese officer who created the idea for carrying out the "Mukden incident." Use the lines below to write a short statement for your commander explaining why this secret mission is necessary.

_____
_____
_____
_____

Terms To Know

Define or describe the following key term from this lesson.

sanctions

_____
_____

Copyright © by The McGraw-Hill Companies, Inc.

Key Points

Notes

Write the definition of each of the following terms that you studied earlier.

major
(Chapter 2, Section 2)

_____

_____

exploiting
(Chapter 9, Section 3)

_____

_____

Section Wrap-up

Now that you have read the section, answer these questions from Setting a Purpose for Reading *at the beginning of the section.*

What agreement was reached at the Munich Conference?

_____

_____

_____

_____

_____

Why did Germany believe it needed more land?

_____

_____

_____

_____

_____

Copyright © by The McGraw-Hill Companies, Inc.

Chapter 19, Section 2
The Course of World War II

(Pages 596–604)

Reason To Read

Setting a Purpose for Reading Think about these questions as you read:
- Why did the United States not enter the war until 1941?
- What major events helped to end the war in Europe and Asia?

Main Idea

As you read pages 596–604 in your textbook, complete the chart below by listing key events during World War II and their effect on the outcome of the war.

Event	Effect

Sequencing Events

As you read, place the following events on the time line below.
- **Allied forces invade France on D-Day**
- **Germans bomb British cities**
- **Germans defeated at Stalingrad**
- **Japan attacks Pearl Harbor**

◆ 1939   ◆ 1941   ◆ 1943   ◆ 1945

Copyright © by The McGraw-Hill Companies, Inc.

Europe at War (pages 596–597)

Skimming

Skim the passage before you begin reading it, looking at headings and words in boldface or colored type. Write a sentence below describing what you expect to learn in this lesson. After reading, revise your sentence if needed.

_____

_____

_____

Terms To Know

Define or describe the following key term from this lesson.

blitzkrieg >

_____

_____

Terms To Review

Write the letter of the correct definition next to each of these terms that you studied earlier.

____ **1.** armistice
(Chapter 16, Section 4)

____ **2.** shift
(Chapter 7, Section 1)

a. an interim period

b. terms of a peace treaty

c. to change place, position, or direction

d. temporary halt in hostilities by agreement between opponents

Japan at War (pages 599–600)

Responding

As you read, imagine you are a Japanese American citizen of the United States living in Hawaii. You have just heard about the Japanese attack on Pearl Harbor. Describe your reaction to the bombings on the lines below.

_____

_____

_____

_____

Copyright © by The McGraw-Hill Companies, Inc.

Academic Vocabulary

Use the following academic vocabulary word from this lesson in a sentence that reflects the term's meaning.

resources

_____

_____

The Allies Advance (pages 600–603)

Questioning

As you read, write two questions about the main ideas presented in the text. After reading, write the answers to these questions.

_____

_____

_____

_____

_____

Terms To Review

Choose one of these terms, which you studied earlier, to fill in each blank.

mutual
(Chapter 7, Section 3)

1. The Allies had a _____ agreement to ignore their differences while fighting together during World War II.

policy
(Chapter 4, Section 3)

2. Hitler and his generals could not reach a _____ agreement about how to proceed on the Eastern Front.

3. The _____ under General MacArthur was to capture some Japanese-held islands.

Copyright © by The McGraw-Hill Companies, Inc.

Last Years of the War (pages 603–604)

Analyzing

After you read the lesson, imagine you must advise President Truman on whether to drop the atomic bomb on Hiroshima, Japan. Use the lines below to list two arguments in support of dropping the bomb or two arguments against dropping the bomb.

_____

_____

_____

Terms To Know

Define or describe the following key term from this lesson.

partisans

_____

_____

Terms To Review

Write the definition of the following term that you studied earlier.

estimates
(Chapter 18, Section 1)

_____

_____

Section Wrap-up

Now that you have read the section, answer these questions from Setting a Purpose for Reading *at the beginning of the section.*

Why did the United States not enter the war until 1941?

_____

_____

_____

What major events helped to end the war in Europe and Asia?

_____

_____

_____

Copyright © by The McGraw-Hill Companies, Inc.

Chapter 19, Section 3
The New Order and the Holocaust

(Pages 606–611)

Reason To Read

Setting a Purpose for Reading Think about these questions as you read:
- How did the Nazis carry out their Final Solution?
- How did the Japanese create a dilemma for nationalists in the lands they occupied?

Main Idea

As you read pages 606–611 in your textbook, complete the graphic organizer below by comparing and contrasting the New Order of Germany with the New Order of Japan.

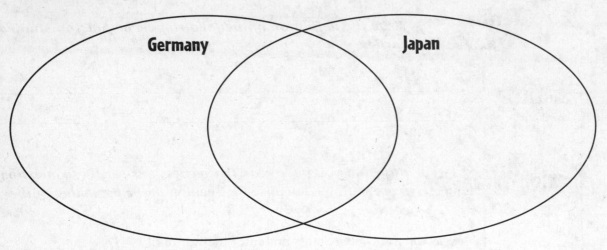

Germany   Japan

Sequencing Events

As you read, number the following events in the order in which they occurred.

_____ **Hitler's death camps in full operation**

_____ ***Einsatzgruppen* ordered to act as mobile killing units**

_____ **Many British children evacuated from cities**

_____ **Thousands of Allied prisoners of war die working on Burma-Thailand railroad**

Copyright © by The McGraw-Hill Companies, Inc.

The New Order in Europe (pages 606–607)

Summarizing

After reading the lesson, write a paragraph summarizing Hitler's plan for the people of eastern Europe.

_____

_____

_____

_____

Academic Vocabulary

Define the following academic vocabulary word from this lesson.

ethnic >

_____

_____

Terms To Review

Use each of the following terms, which you studied earlier, in a sentence that reflects the term's meaning in this lesson.

abandoned
(Chapter 11, Section 1) >

_____

_____

labor
(Chapter 1, Section 2) >

_____

_____

The Holocaust (pages 607–610)

Connecting

After reading the lesson, write a paragraph about the impact of the Holocaust on history. What lessons does the Holocaust have for us today? Has everyone learned from these lessons? Explain.

_____

_____

_____

_____

Copyright © by The McGraw-Hill Companies, Inc.

Key Points

Notes

Terms To Know

Write the letter of the correct definition next to each of these key terms from this lesson.

_____ **1.** genocide

_____ **2.** collaborators

a. an atrocity during wartime

b. the use of biological and chemical weapons in terrorist attacks

c. the deliberate mass murder of a racial, political, or cultural group

d. people who help an enemy

Academic Vocabulary

Define the following academic vocabulary word from this lesson.

mode

_____

_____

Terms To Review

Write the definition of each of the following terms that you studied earlier.

element
(Chapter 1, Section 3)

_____

_____

despite
(Chapter 14, Section 3)

_____

_____

The New Order in Asia (pages 610–611)

Drawing Conclusions

As you read, write down three details about Japanese policies in Asia. Then write a conclusion you draw based on these details.

_____

_____

_____

_____

_____

Copyright © by The McGraw-Hill Companies, Inc.

Terms To Review

Use each of the following terms, which you studied earlier, in a sentence that reflects the term's meaning in this lesson.

areas
(Chapter 6, Section 3)

_____

_____

designed
(Chapter 5, Section 2)

_____

_____

Section Wrap-up

Now that you have read the section, answer these questions from Setting a Purpose for Reading *at the beginning of the section.*

How did the Nazis carry out their Final Solution?

_____

_____

_____

_____

_____

How did the Japanese create a dilemma for nationalists in the lands they occupied?

_____

_____

_____

_____

_____

Copyright © by The McGraw-Hill Companies, Inc.

Chapter 19, Section 4
The Home Front and the Aftermath of the War

(Pages 612–618)

Reason To Read

Setting a Purpose for Reading Think about these questions as you read:
- Why were the Japanese encouraged to serve as kamikaze pilots?
- What was the outcome of the Yalta Conference in 1945?

Main Idea

As you read pages 612–618 in your textbook, complete the chart below by comparing and contrasting how World War II affected the lives of civilians.

Country	Impact on Lives of Civilians
Soviet Union	
United States	
Japan	
Germany	

Sequencing Events

As you read, place the following events on the time line below.

- **Big Three meet at Yalta**
- **Allies bomb Dresden**
- **Churchill first describes the "iron curtain" in Europe**
- **Stalin, Roosevelt, and Churchill hold a war conference in Tehran**

◆1942	◆1943	◆1944	◆1945	◆1946

Copyright © by The McGraw-Hill Companies, Inc.

The Mobilization of Peoples: Four Examples (pages 612–614)

Outlining

As you read the lesson, fill in the outline below.

I. The Soviet Union

   A. _____

   B. _____

II. The United States

   A. _____

   B. _____

III. Germany

   A. _____

   B. _____

IV. Japan

   A. _____

   B. _____

Terms To Know

Define or describe the following key terms from this lesson.

mobilization
_____
_____

kamikaze
_____
_____

Terms To Review

Use each of the following terms, which you studied earlier, in a sentence.

enormous
(Chapter 4, Section 2)
_____
_____

guarantee
(Chapter 12, Section 2)
_____
_____

Copyright © by The McGraw-Hill Companies, Inc.

Key Points  Notes

Frontline Civilians: The Bombing of Cities *(pages 615–616)*

Visualizing

As you read this lesson, look closely at the photos of Dresden and Hiroshima on pages 615–616. Imagine you were a resident of one of these cities. Explain how you would go about rebuilding your city. Where would you turn for help? What services would be needed immediately?

_____

_____

_____

_____

Academic Vocabulary

Define the following academic vocabulary words from this lesson.

sustained ⟩

_____

_____

_____

circumstances ⟩

_____

_____

Peace and a New War *(pages 616–618)*

Reviewing

As you read, complete the chart below by summarizing the outcome of each conference held during and after the war.

Conference	Outcome

Copyright © by The McGraw-Hill Companies, Inc.

 **Key Points**

 **Notes**

Terms To Know

Define or describe the following key term from this lesson.

Cold War

_____

_____

Terms To Review

Use each of the following terms, which you studied earlier, in a sentence that shows you understand the term's meaning.

aid
(Chapter 15, Section 1)

_____

_____

responded
(Chapter 3, Section 4)

_____

_____

Section Wrap-up

Now that you have read the section, answer these questions from Setting a Purpose for Reading *at the beginning of the section.*

Why were the Japanese encouraged to serve as kamikaze pilots?

_____

_____

_____

_____

_____

What was the outcome of the Yalta Conference in 1945?

_____

_____

_____

_____

_____

Copyright © by The McGraw-Hill Companies, Inc.

Chapter 20, Section 1
Development of the Cold War

(Pages 631–636)

Reason To Read

Setting a Purpose for Reading Think about these questions as you read:
• What were the major turning points in the development of the Cold War?
• What was the Cuban missile crisis?

Main Idea

As you read pages 631–636 in your textbook, complete the chart below by listing
the American presidents who held office during the Cold War and major events
related to the Cold War that took place during their administrations.

President	Major Event

Sequencing Events

As you read, write the correct date next to each event on the time line below.

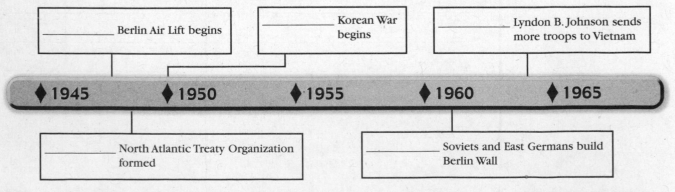

_____ Berlin Air Lift begins

_____ Korean War begins

_____ Lyndon B. Johnson sends more troops to Vietnam

◆ 1945   ◆ 1950   ◆ 1955   ◆ 1960   ◆ 1965

_____ North Atlantic Treaty Organization formed

_____ Soviets and East Germans build Berlin Wall

Copyright © by The McGraw-Hill Companies, Inc.

Confrontation of the Superpowers (pages 631–633)

Outlining

As you read this lesson, fill in the outline below.

I. Rivalry in Europe

   A. _____

   B. _____

II. The Truman Doctrine

   A. _____

   B. _____

III. The Marshall Plan

   A. _____

   B. _____

IV. The Division of Germany

   A. _____

   B. _____

Terms To Know

Define or describe each of the following key terms from this lesson.

satellite state _____
_____

policy of containment _____
_____

Terms To Review

Write the definition of each of the following terms that you studied earlier.

secure
(Chapter 3, Section 2) _____
_____

underlying
(Chapter 14, Section 4) _____
_____

Copyright © by The McGraw-Hill Companies, Inc.

The Spread of the Cold War (pages 633–635)

Connecting

As you read about the Cold War, think about people's fears of a nuclear war. How do you think this compares to the fears of terrorism today? Summarize your thoughts in a paragraph below.

_____

_____

_____

_____

Terms To Know

Define or describe the following key term from this lesson.

arms race >

_____

_____

Academic Vocabulary

Use the following academic vocabulary word from this lesson in a sentence.

confirmed >

_____

_____

The Cuban Missile Crisis (page 635)

Identifying Cause and Effect

After reading this lesson, write a paragraph summarizing the causes and effects of the Cuban missile crisis.

_____

_____

_____

_____

_____

Copyright © by The McGraw-Hill Companies, Inc.

Key Points

Notes

Academic Vocabulary

Define the following academic vocabulary word from this lesson.

option > _____
_____

Terms To Review

Write the definition of each of the following terms that you studied earlier.

approach
(Chapter 5, Section 2) > _____
_____
_____

revealed
(Chapter 7, Section 1) > _____
_____

Vietnam and the Domino Theory (pages 635–636)

Evaluating

Imagine that you lived during the time of the Vietnam War. Would you have supported or opposed the war? Explain your position in a paragraph below.

_____
_____
_____
_____
_____

Terms To Know

Define or describe the following key term from this lesson.

domino theory > _____
_____

Copyright © by The McGraw-Hill Companies, Inc.

Key Points

Notes

Terms To Review

Use each of the following terms, which you studied earlier, in a sentence that reflects the term's meaning in this lesson.

impact
(Chapter 3, Section 2)

_____

_____

draft
(Chapter 7, Section 3)

_____

_____

Section Wrap-up

Now that you have read the section, answer these questions from Setting a Purpose for Reading *at the beginning of the section.*

What were the major turning points in the development of the Cold War?

_____

_____

_____

_____

_____

What was the Cuban missile crisis?

_____

_____

_____

_____

_____

Copyright © by The McGraw-Hill Companies, Inc.

Chapter 20, Section 2
The Soviet Union and Eastern Europe

(Pages 637–640)

Reason To Read

Setting a Purpose for Reading Think about these questions as you read:
- What were Khrushchev's policies of de-Stalinization?
- How did the Soviet Union exert its power over Eastern Europe?

Main Idea

As you read pages 637–640 in your textbook, complete the chart below by identifying how the Soviet Union carried out Communist policies.

Soviet Union's Communist Policies

Sequencing Events

As you read, number the following events in the order in which they occurred.

_____ **Khrushchev is voted out of office**

_____ **The Soviet Army invades Czechoslovakia**

_____ **Khrushchev is named general secretary**

_____ **Protests erupt in Poland**

_____ **Solzhenitsyn's *One Day in the Life of Ivan Denisovich* is published**

Copyright © by The McGraw-Hill Companies, Inc.

Key Points

Notes

The Reign of Stalin *(pages 637–638)*

Identifying Cause and Effect

After you read the lesson, write a paragraph summarizing the effects of Stalin's economic policy on the Russian people.

_____

_____

_____

_____

Terms To Know

Define or describe the following key term from this lesson.

heavy industry

_____

_____

Terms To Review

Write the definition of each of the following terms that you studied earlier.

conform
(Chapter 7, Section 1)

_____

_____

sole
(Chapter 7, Section 3)

_____

_____

The Khrushchev Era *(pages 638–639)*

Analyzing

After you have read this lesson, write a paragraph comparing and contrasting the policies and style of governing of Stalin and Khrushchev.

_____

_____

_____

_____

Copyright © by The McGraw-Hill Companies, Inc.

Terms To Know

Define or describe the following key term from this lesson.

> **de-Stalinization**

_____

_____

Terms To Review

Choose one of these terms, which you studied in an earlier chapter, to fill in each blank.

> **eliminated**
> (Chapter 8, Section 3)

> **identified**
> (Chapter 17, Section 3)

1. Many Russians _____ with Alexander Solzhenitsyn's writings about life in a forced-labor camp.

2. Khrushchev was _____ by Soviet leaders because of his emphasis on increasing the production of consumer goods.

3. Many of Stalin's policies were _____, and the process of de-Stalinization began in the Khrushchev era.

Eastern Europe: Behind the Iron Curtain *(pages 639–640)*

Responding

As you read this lesson, think about what captures your attention. Write down two facts or ideas you find interesting or surprising.

_____

_____

_____

_____

Academic Vocabulary

Define the folling academic vocabulary word from this lesson.

> **forestall**

_____

_____

Copyright © by The McGraw-Hill Companies, Inc.

Key Points

Notes

Terms To Review

Use each of the following terms, which you studied earlier, in a sentence.

occupied
(Chapter 3, Section 1)

_____

_____

democracy
(Chapter 2, Section 1)

_____

_____

pursue
(Chapter 3, Section 4)

_____

_____

Section Wrap-up

Now that you have read the section, answer these questions from Setting a Purpose for Reading *at the beginning of the section.*

What were Khrushchev's policies of de-Stalinization?

_____

_____

_____

_____

How did the Soviet Union exert its power over Eastern Europe?

_____

_____

_____

_____

_____

Copyright © by The McGraw-Hill Companies, Inc.

Chapter 20, Section 3
Western Europe and North America

(Pages 642–650)

Reason To Read

Setting a Purpose for Reading Think about these questions as you read:
- How did the EEC benefit the member nations?
- What were the major social changes in Western society after 1945?

Main Idea

As you read pages 642–650 in your textbook, complete the chart below by listing programs instituted by Great Britain, the United States, and Canada to promote social welfare.

Great Britain	United States	Canada

Sequencing Events

As you read, place the following events on the time line below.
- **The Civil Rights Act is passed**
- **Simone de Beauvoir publishes** *The Second Sex*
- **Student revolts peak**
- **The Rome Treaty establishes the EEC**
- **Charles de Gaulle establishes the Fourth Republic in France**

◆1945   ◆1950   ◆1955   ◆1960   ◆1965   ◆1970

Copyright © by The McGraw-Hill Companies, Inc.

Western Europe: Recovery (pages 642–644)

Outlining — As you read this lesson, fill in the outline below.

I. France and de Gaulle

   A. _____

   B. _____

II. The Economic Miracle of West Germany

   A. _____

   B. _____

III. The Decline of Great Britain

   A. _____

   B. _____

Terms To Know — Define or describe the following key term from this lesson.

welfare state _____

_____

Terms To Review — Define each of the following terms that you studied earlier.

recovery
(Chapter 4, Section 1) _____

_____

colony
(Chapter 6, Section 1) _____

_____

invested
(Chater 12, Section 1) _____

_____

cooperated
(Chapter 18, Section 2) _____

_____

Copyright © by The McGraw-Hill Companies, Inc.

 Key Points

 Notes

Western Europe: The Move toward Unity (pages 644–645)

Analyzing

As you read this lesson, think about the move toward unity in Western Europe. Then write a paragraph explaining why European unity came in the form of an economic alliance.

_____

_____

_____

_____

Terms To Know

Define or describe the following key term from this lesson.

bloc ❯

_____

_____

Terms To Review

Use each of these terms, which you studied earlier, in a sentence that shows you understand the term's meaning.

focused ❯
(Chapter 10, Section 3)

_____

_____

benefited ❯
(Chapter 3, Section 4)

_____

_____

The United States in the 1950s (pages 645–646)

Questioning

As you read, write two questions about the main ideas presented in the passage. After reading, write the answers to these questions.

_____

_____

_____

_____

Copyright © by The McGraw-Hill Companies, Inc.

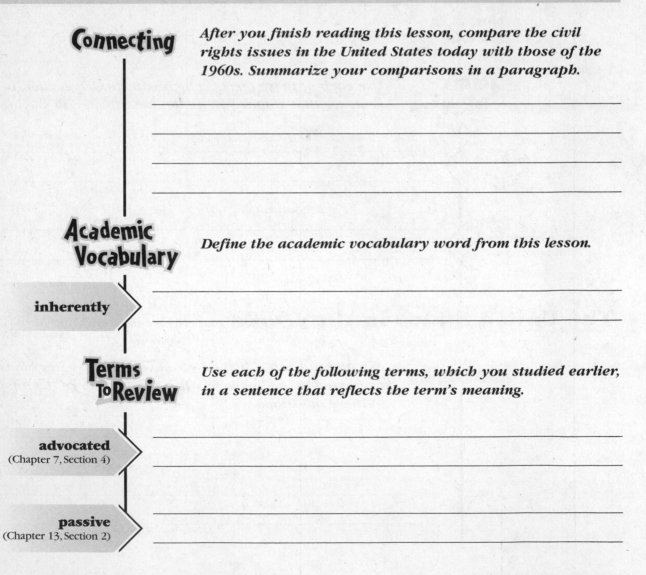

Key Points

Notes

Terms To Know

Define or describe the following key term from this lesson.

real wages >

_____

_____

Terms To Review

Write the definition of the following term that you studied earlier.

domestic >
(Chapter 2, Section 2)

_____

_____

The United States in the 1960s (pages 646–647)

Connecting

After you finish reading this lesson, compare the civil rights issues in the United States today with those of the 1960s. Summarize your comparisons in a paragraph.

_____

_____

_____

_____

Academic Vocabulary

Define the academic vocabulary word from this lesson.

inherently >

_____

_____

Terms To Review

Use each of the following terms, which you studied earlier, in a sentence that reflects the term's meaning.

advocated >
(Chapter 7, Section 4)

_____

_____

passive >
(Chapter 13, Section 2)

_____

_____

Copyright © by The McGraw-Hill Companies, Inc.

The Development of Canada (page 648)

Determining the Main Idea

As you read, write down the main idea of the passage. Review your statement when you have finished reading and revise as needed.

_____

_____

_____

Terms To Review

Write the definition of each of the following terms that you studied earlier.

sought
(Chapter 6, Section 1)

_____

_____

establish
(Chapter 4, Section 2)

_____

_____

The Emergence of a New Society (pages 648–650)

Evaluating

As you read about the revolts of American students in the 1960s, think about a political or social issue you feel strongly about today. Do you think it would be effective to organize a demonstration on this issue? Why or why not?

_____

_____

_____

_____

Academic Vocabulary

Define the following academic vocabulary word from this lesson.

vision

_____

_____

Copyright © by The McGraw-Hill Companies, Inc.

Key Points

Notes

Terms To Review

Use each of the following terms, which you studied earlier, in a sentence.

altered
(Chapter 12, Section 4)

_____
_____

credit
(Chapter 7, Section 3)

_____
_____

defined
(Chapter 3, Section 4)

_____
_____

Section Wrap-up

Now that you have read the section, answer these questions from Setting a Purpose for Reading *at the beginning of the section.*

How did the EEC benefit the member nations?

_____
_____
_____
_____
_____

What were the major social changes in Western society after 1945?

_____
_____
_____
_____
_____

Copyright © by The McGraw-Hill Companies, Inc.

Chapter 21, Section 1
Decline of the Soviet Union

(Pages 657–660)

Reason To Read

Setting a Purpose for Reading Think about these questions as you read:
- How and why did the Cold War end?
- What problems arose when the Soviet Union disintegrated?

Main Idea

As you read pages 657–660 in your textbook, complete the chart below by comparing the policies of Brezhnev and Gorbachev.

	Leonid Brezhnev	**Mikhail Gorbachev**
Foreign Policy		
Economic Policy		
Military Policy		
Personal Policy		

Sequencing Events

As you read, place the following events on the time line below.
- **Ex-KGB agent Vladimir Putin becomes president of Russia.**
- **Boris Yeltsin becomes president of Russia.**
- **Peaceful revolutionary movement sweeps Eastern Europe.**
- **Mikhail Gorbachev assumes leadership of Soviet Union.**

♦1985   ♦1988   ♦1991   ♦1994   ♦1997   ♦2000

Copyright © by The McGraw-Hill Companies, Inc.

Key Points | Notes

From Cold War to Post-Cold War *(pages 657–658)*

Identifying Cause and Effect

After reading this lesson, write a paragraph summarizing the events that led to the end of the Cold War.

_____

_____

_____

_____

Terms To Know

Define or describe the following key term from this lesson.

détente

_____

_____

Academic Vocabulary

Use each of the following academic vocabulary words from this lesson in a sentence.

intermediate

_____

_____

nuclear

_____

_____

Terms To Review

Define the following terms that you studied earlier.

phase
(Chapter 14, Section 1)

_____

_____

arms race
(Chapter 20, Section 1)

_____

_____

Copyright © by The McGraw-Hill Companies, Inc.

Upheaval in the Soviet Union (pages 658–660)

Outlining

As you read this lesson, fill in the outline below.

I. The Brezhnev Era

   A. _____

   B. _____

II. Gorbachev and Perestroika

   A. _____

   B. _____

III. The End of the Soviet Union

   A. _____

   B. _____

IV. The New Russia

   A. _____

   B. _____

Terms To Know

Define or describe the following key terms from this lesson.

dissidents ⟩ _____

_____

perestroika ⟩ _____

_____

Academic Vocabulary

Use the following academic vocabulary word from this lesson in a sentence.

relax ⟩ _____

_____

Copyright © by The McGraw-Hill Companies, Inc.

 **Key Points**

 **Notes**

 **Terms To Review**

Write the letter of the correct definition next to each of these terms that you studied earlier.

_____ **1.** heavy industry
(Chapter 20, Section 2)

_____ **2.** bureaucracy
(Chapter 6, Section 3)

a. administrative organization of nonelected officials and regular procedures

b. upper class whose wealth is based on land

c. the manufacture of machines and equipment for factories and mines

Section Wrap-up

Now that you have read the section, answer these questions from **Setting a Purpose for Reading** at the beginning of the section.

How and why did the Cold War end?

_____

_____

_____

_____

_____

What problems arose when the Soviet Union disintegrated?

_____

_____

_____

_____

_____

Copyright © by The McGraw-Hill Companies, Inc.

Chapter 21, Section 2
Eastern Europe
(Pages 661–664)

Reason To Read

Setting a Purpose for Reading Think about these questions as you read:
- What caused the East German government to open its border in 1989?
- What effect did the 1990 collapse of communism have on Yugoslavia?

Main Idea

As you read pages 661–664 in your textbook, complete the chart below by listing one or two reasons for, and the results of, revolution.

Country	Reasons for Revolution	Results of Revolution
Poland		
Czechoslovakia		
Romania		
East Germany		
Yugoslavia		

Sequencing Events

As you read, number the following events in the order in which they occurred.

_____ **Communism falls in Czechoslovakia and Romania**

_____ **Serbia and Montenegro unite under new charter**

_____ **Milošević's rule of Serbia ends.**

_____ **Poles hold free elections.**

_____ **Serbs carry out ethnic cleansing in Bosnia-Herzegovina**

Copyright © by The McGraw-Hill Companies, Inc.

 Notes

Revolutions in Eastern Europe *(pages 661–663)*

Responding

As you read the lesson, think about the actions of the people in Eastern Europe as they responded to their totalitarian leaders. How would you have reacted to a Communist government if you were living in Eastern Europe at that time?

_____

_____

_____

_____

_____

_____

Academic Vocabulary

Use the following academic vocabulary word from this lesson in a sentence that shows you understand the word's meaning.

incident >

_____

_____

Terms To Review

Choose one of these two terms, which you studied earlier, to fill in each blank.

democracy
(Chapter 2, Section 1)

1. The Berlin Wall, long a symbol of the _____ , fell in November 1989.

2. Václav Havel became a spokesperson for Czech _____ and a new order in Europe.

Cold War
(Chapter 19, Section 4)

3. Countries in Eastern Europe fought against the Communist regimes of

the _____ era.

Copyright © by The McGraw-Hill Companies, Inc.

The Disintegration of Yugoslavia (pages 663–664)

Drawing Conclusions

As you read, write down three details about the disintegration of Yugoslavia. Then write a conclusion you draw based on these details.

_____

_____

_____

_____

Terms To Know

Define or describe the following key terms from this lesson.

ethnic cleansing

_____

_____

autonomous

_____

_____

Academic Vocabulary

Use the following academic vocabulary word from this lesson in a sentence.

monitored

_____

_____

Terms To Review

Define the following terms that you studied earlier.

satellite state
(Chapter 20, Section 1)

_____

_____

aided
(Chapter 15, Section 1)

_____

_____

Copyright © by The McGraw-Hill Companies, Inc.

 Key Points  Notes

Now that you have read the section, answer these questions from Setting a Purpose for Reading *at the beginning of the section.*

What caused the East German government to open its border in 1989?

_____

_____

_____

_____

_____

What effect did the 1990 collapse of communism have on Yugoslavia?

_____

_____

_____

_____

_____

Copyright © by The McGraw-Hill Companies, Inc.

Chapter 21, Section 3
Europe and North America

(Pages 666–670)

Reason To Read

Setting a Purpose for Reading Think about these questions as you read:
• What problems faced Western Europe after 1980?
• What was the focus of U.S. domestic politics in the 1970s?

Main Idea

As you read pages 666–670 in your textbook, complete the graphic organizer below by comparing and contrasting the economic policies of Thatcherism with those of the Reagan Revolution.

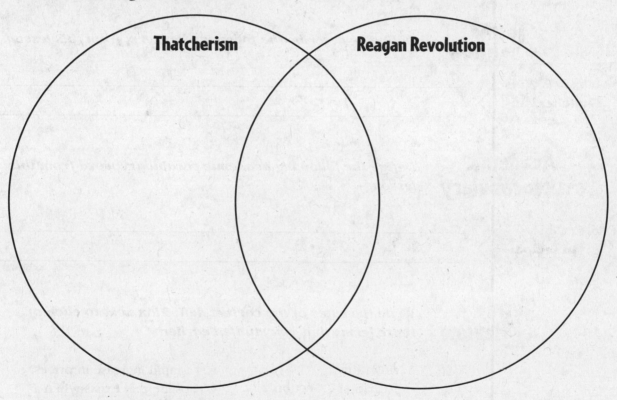

Thatcherism   **Reagan Revolution**

Sequencing Events

As you read, number the following events in the order in which they occurred.

_____ **The two Germanies reunify**

_____ **West German chancellor Willy Brandt wins Nobel Peace Prize**

_____ **Canadian voters reject independence for Quebec**

_____ **Richard Nixon resigns the presidency of the United States**

Copyright © by The McGraw-Hill Companies, Inc.

 **Key Points**

 **Notes**

Winds of Change in Western Europe *(pages 666–668)*

Analyzing

As you read, think about the effects of the reunification of East and West Germany. Do you think the overall effects of this process were more positive or more negative? Explain your answer using examples from the text.

_____

_____

_____

_____

_____

_____

Terms To Know

Define or describe the following key term from this lesson.

Thatcherism

_____

_____

Academic Vocabulary

Define the following academic vocabulary word from this lesson.

principal

_____

_____

Terms To Review

Write the letter of the correct definition next to each of these terms that you studied earlier.

_____ **1.** inflation
(Chapter 7, Section 2)

_____ **2.** bloc
(Chapter 20, Section 3)

a. a rapid increase in prices

b. a state that exists when a government spends more than it collects in revenues

c. a group of nations with a common purpose

Copyright © by The McGraw-Hill Companies, Inc.

The U.S. Domestic Scene (pages 668–669)

Monitoring Comprehension

As you read, write down two questions about the passage for a partner to answer. Exchange questions and see if you can answer your partner's questions.

_____

_____

_____

_____

Terms To Know

Define or describe the following key term from this lesson.

budget deficit

_____

_____

Terms To Review

Use each of the following terms, which you studied earlier, in a sentence that reflects the term's meaning.

methods
(Chapter 13, Section 4)

_____

_____

welfare state
(Chapter 20, Section 3)

_____

_____

Canada (page 670)

Responding

As you read, think about the issue of Quebec's secession. Imagine you are a citizen of Quebec and make a list of pros and cons regarding the province's secession.

_____

_____

_____

_____

Copyright © by The McGraw-Hill Companies, Inc.

Key Points

Notes

Academic Vocabulary

Circle the letter of the word or phrase that is closest in meaning to the underlined word that you studied earlier.

prime

1. Pierre Trudeau became <u>prime</u> minister of Canada in 1968.

   a. chief   **b.** early   **c.** voluntary

guidelines

2. NAFTA established <u>guidelines</u> for trade among Canada, Mexico, and the United States.

   a. cords or ropes   **b.** policies for conduct   **c.** alliances

debate

3. The <u>debate</u> over whether or not Quebec should secede in order to preserve the identity and rights of French speakers still divides Canadians.

   a. agreement   **b.** issue   **c.** argument

Section Wrap-up

Now that you have read the section, answer these questions from Setting a Purpose for Reading *at the beginning of the section.*

What problems faced Western Europe after 1980?

_____

_____

_____

_____

What was the focus of U.S. domestic politics in the 1970s?

_____

_____

_____

_____

Copyright © by The McGraw-Hill Companies, Inc.

Chapter 21, Section 4
Western Society and Culture
(Pages 671–676)

Reason To Read

Setting a Purpose for Reading Think about these questions as you read:
- What have been the major social developments since 1970?
- What have been the major cultural, scientific, and technological developments in the postwar world?

Main Idea

As you read pages 671–676 in your textbook, complete the graphic organizers below by filling in the ways women have been involved with causes related solely to women's issues and to broader, more universal causes.

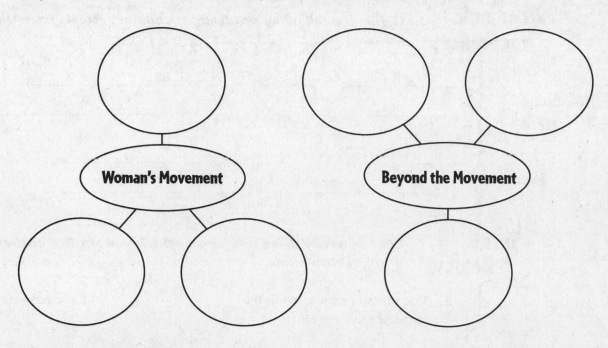

Sequencing Events

As you read, number the following events in the order in which they occurred.

_____ **United States boycotts Moscow Olympics**

_____ **Global opposition to terrorism forms**

_____ **Fighting escalates in Northern Ireland**

_____ **Women protest presence of American nuclear missiles in Britain**

Copyright © by The McGraw-Hill Companies, Inc.

 **Key Points**

 **Notes**

Changes in Women's Lives (pages 671–672)

Reviewing

As you read, make a list of reforms that women worked for, beginning in the 1960s and continuing through the 1990s. Then rank the reforms in order of importance. Explain your rankings.

_____

_____

_____

_____

_____

_____

Academic Vocabulary

Define the following academic vocabulary words from this lesson.

fundamental

_____

_____

gender

_____

_____

Terms To Review

Choose one of these two terms, which you studied earlier, to fill in each blank.

labor
(Chapter 1, Section 2)

legal
(Chapter 3, Section 4)

1. The number of women in the _____ force has increased since 1970.

2. The Equal Pay Act gives _____ support to equal pay for equal work for women.

3. In Great Britain, greater access to universities between 1970 and 1990 enabled women to pursue careers in the _____ and medical fields.

Copyright © by The McGraw-Hill Companies, Inc.

The Growth of Terrorism (pages 672–673)

Evaluating

As you read, write down the reasons that the United States declared war on Iraq. Do you think the United States was justified in declaring this war? Explain your answer.

_____

_____

_____

_____

Academic Vocabulary

Define the following academic vocabulary words from this lesson.

target

_____

_____

inspection

_____

_____

Terms To Review

Use the following term, which you studied earlier, in a sentence that reflects the term's meaning in this lesson.

aspect
(Chapter 11, Section 2)

_____

_____

Science and Technology (page 674)

Summarizing

After you read, write a summary of the lesson by answering the following question: How have technological advances been both positive and negative?

_____

_____

_____

_____

Copyright © by The McGraw-Hill Companies, Inc.

Academic Vocabulary

Define the following academic vocabulary words from this lesson.

research

_____

_____

chemical

_____

_____

Terms To Review

Write the letter of the correct definition next to each of these terms that you studied earlier.

____ **1.** decade
(Chapter 2, Section 2)

____ **2.** revolutionized
(Chapter 1, Section 1)

a. a period of 50 years

b. a period of 10 years

c. to change fundamentally or completely

Religious Revival (page 674)

Previewing

Preview the lesson to get an idea of what is ahead. First, skim the lesson. Then write a sentence or two explaining what you think you will be learning. After you have finished reading, revise your sentences as necessary.

_____

_____

_____

_____

Terms To Review

Use the following term, which you studied earlier, in a sentence that reflects the term's meaning in this lesson.

relevance
(Chapter 2, Section 1)

_____

_____

Copyright © by The McGraw-Hill Companies, Inc.

 **Key Points**

 **Notes**

Trends in Art (page 675)

Visualizing

As you read, visualize how a piece of art from each style described might look. Then write a paragraph comparing and contrasting each style of art discussed in the lesson.

_____

_____

_____

_____

Terms To Know

Define or describe the following key terms from this lesson.

pop art

_____

_____

postmodernism

_____

_____

Academic Vocabulary

Circle the letter of the word or phrase that is closest in meaning to the underlined word.

images

1. Pop art took <u>images</u> of popular culture and transformed them into works of fine art.

   a. titles   **b.** impressions   **c.** descriptions

interactive

2. Some contemporary artists experiment with digital cameras and computer programs to create new <u>interactive</u> art forms.

   a. exchange of information

   b. individual communication

   c. non-verbal communication

Terms To Review

Use the following term, which you studied earlier, in a sentence that reflects the term's meaning in this lesson.

transform
(Chapter 12, Section 1)

_____

_____

Copyright © by The McGraw-Hill Companies, Inc.

Popular Culture *(page 675)*

Connecting

As you read, think about popular culture in the world today. Do you think the United States is trying to Americanize global culture? Is the American culture changing to reflect other cultures? Summarize your thoughts in a paragraph.

_____

_____

_____

_____

_____

_____

Academic Vocabulary

Define the following academic vocabulary word from this lesson.

vehicles

_____

_____

Terms To Review

Choose one of these terms, which you studied earlier, to fill in each blank.

dominate
(Chapter 2, Section 1)

1. Computer _____ has increased consumer access to a variety of artists and music genres.

2. American movies _____ European and American markets.

technology
(Chapter 4, Section 1)

3. Popular music from the United States continues to

_____ the Western world.

Copyright © by The McGraw-Hill Companies, Inc.

Key Points / Notes

Sports, Television, Politics (page 676)

Responding

Do you think politics should be mixed with sports, as has been done with the Olympics in the past? Explain your position on this matter.

_____

_____

_____

Academic Vocabulary

Define the following academic vocabulary word from this lesson.

globe

_____

_____

Terms To Review

Use the following term, which you studied earlier, in a sentence.

trends
(Chapter 15, Section 2)

_____

_____

Section Wrap-up

Now that you have read the section, answer these questions from Setting a Purpose for Reading *at the beginning of the section.*

What have been the major social developments since 1970?

_____

_____

_____

What have been the major cultural, scientific, and technological developments in the postwar world?

_____

_____

_____

Copyright © by The McGraw-Hill Companies, Inc.

Chapter 22, Section 1
General Trends in Latin America

(Pages 683–687)

Reason To Read

Setting a Purpose for Reading Think about these questions as you read:
• What factors undermined the stability of Latin American countries?
• How did the roles of women change in Latin America after 1945?

Main Idea

As you read pages 683–687 in your textbook, complete the graphic organizer
below by identifying social and political challenges in Latin America since 1945.

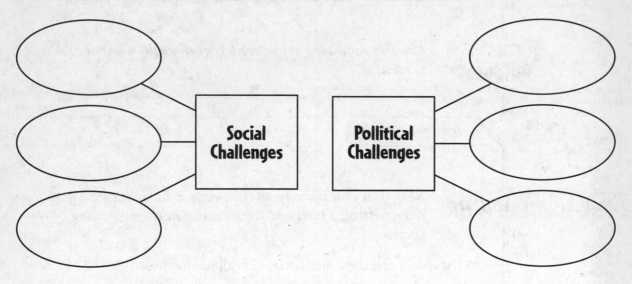

Sequencing Events

As you read, write the correct date next to each event on the time line below.

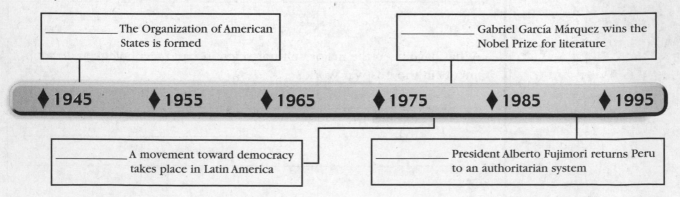

_____ The Organization of American States is formed

_____ Gabriel García Márquez wins the Nobel Prize for literature

♦ 1945   ♦ 1955   ♦ 1965   ♦ 1975   ♦ 1985   ♦ 1995

_____ A movement toward democracy takes place in Latin America

_____ President Alberto Fujimori returns Peru to an authoritarian system

Copyright © by The McGraw-Hill Companies, Inc.

 **Key Points**

 **Notes**

Economic and Political Developments (pages 683–685)

Interpreting

As you read the lesson, think about the debt crisis in Latin America during the 1980s. Write a paragraph explaining why the debt crisis created a movement toward democracy.

_____

_____

_____

_____

_____

_____

Terms To Know

Define or describe the following key term from this lesson.

multinational corporations

_____

_____

Academic Vocabulary

Define the following academic vocabulary word from this lesson.

consent

_____

_____

Terms To Review

Use each of these terms, which you studied earlier, in a sentence that reflects the term's meaning.

financed
(Chapter 11, Section 1)

_____

_____

inflation
(Chapter 7, Section 2)

_____

_____

Copyright © by The McGraw-Hill Companies, Inc.

Key Points

Notes

Latin American Society (page 686)

Analyzing

As you read this lesson, complete the chart below by listing the political and economic effects of Latin America's dramatic increase in population. Then write a statement explaining the steps Latin American countries could take to face the challenge of a growing population.

Economic Effects	Political Effects

Statement

_____

_____

_____

_____

Terms To Review

Write the definition of each of the following terms that you studied earlier.

enormous
(Chapter 4, Section 2)

_____

_____

survive
(Chapter 3, Section 1)

_____

_____

Copyright © by The McGraw-Hill Companies, Inc.

The United States and Latin America (page 687)

Evaluating

As you read this lesson, think about U.S. involvement in Latin America since 1948. Do you think the United States was justified in remaining involved in Latin American affairs even after the Organization of American States was formed? Explain.

_____

_____

_____

_____

Terms To Review

Write the letter of the correct definition next to each of these terms that you studied earlier.

____ **1.** dictators
(Chapter 13, Section 1)

____ **2.** Cold War
(Chapter 19, Section 4)

a. absolute rulers

b. the period of political tension following World War I and ending with the fall of Communism

c. members of the middle class

Latin American Culture (page 687)

Drawing Conclusions

As you read the lesson, think about the use of magic realism in the literature of Latin America. Why do you think magic realism is such a popular form of expression in Latin American literature?

_____

_____

_____

_____

Terms To Know

Define or describe the following key term from this lesson.

magic realism _____

_____

_____

Copyright © by The McGraw-Hill Companies, Inc.

Key Points

Notes

Academic Vocabulary

Use the following academic vocabulary word from this lesson in a sentence.

abstract ⟩

_____

_____

Terms To Review

Choose one of these two terms, which you studied earlier, to fill in each blank.

unique ⟩
(Chapter 1, Section 2)

1. International _____ influenced Latin American art and architecture after World War II.

styles ⟩
(Chapter 10, Section 3)

2. Latin American literature includes a _____ form of expression called magic realism.

3. Abstract _____ in painting were especially important after World War II.

Section Wrap-up

Now that you have read the section, answer these questions from Setting a Purpose for Reading _at the beginning of the section._

What factors undermined the stability of Latin American countries?

_____

_____

_____

_____

How did the roles of women change in Latin America after 1945?

_____

_____

_____

_____

Copyright © by The McGraw-Hill Companies, Inc.

Chapter 22, Section 2
Mexico, Cuba, and Central America

(Pages 688–691)

Reason To Read

Setting a Purpose for Reading Think about these questions as you read:

• What problems did Mexico and the nations of Central America face after 1945?
• What were the chief features and impact of the Cuban Revolution?

Main Idea

As you read pages 688–691 in your textbook, complete the chart below by filling in the political and economic challenges faced by El Salvador, Nicaragua, and Panama after 1945.

El Salvador	Nicaragua	Panama

Sequencing Events

As you read, number the following events in the order in which they occurred.

_____ **The Sandinistas overthrow Somoza rule in Nicaragua**

_____ **Vicente Fox defeats the PRI candidate for the presidency of Mexico**

_____ **Castro's revolutionaries seize Havana**

_____ **José Duarte elected President of El Salvador**

_____ **Manuel Noreiga takes control of Panama**

Copyright © by The McGraw-Hill Companies, Inc.

Key Points

Notes

The Mexican Way (pages 688–689)

Synthesizing

As you read the lesson, look for clues and events that will help you answer the following question: How was Mexico's economy affected by its oil industry?

_____

_____

_____

Terms To Know

Define or describe the following key term from this lesson.

privatization

_____

_____

Terms To Review

Circle the letter of the word or phrase that is closest in meaning to the underlined word that you studied earlier.

stable
(Chapter 11, Section 2)

1. The Mexican Revolution created a <u>stable</u> political order that lasted for many years.

   a. vulnerable   **b.** steady   **c.** large

debate
(Chapter 21, Section 3)

2. In the early 1970s, political reforms in Mexico allowed for greater freedom of <u>debate</u> in the press.

   a. discussion involving different points of view

   b. agreement involving the same points of view

   c. disturbance involving several people

The Cuban Revolution (pages 689–690)

Evaluating

As you read the lesson, make a list of U.S. interactions with Cuba since the 1950s. Then answer the following question: **Do you think the United States should have supported an attempt to overthrow Castro's government in 1961?** *Explain.*

_____

_____

_____

Copyright © by The McGraw-Hill Companies, Inc.

Key Points

Notes

Terms To Know

Define or describe the following key term from this lesson.

trade embargo

_____

_____

Academic Vocabulary

Use the following academic vocabulary word from this lesson in a sentence.

medical

_____

_____

Terms To Review

Write the letter of the correct definition next to each of these terms that you studied earlier.

_____ **1.** collapsed
(Chapter 11, Section 3)

_____ **2.** prohibiting
(Chapter 9, Section 3)

a. blocking

b. allowing

c. toppled

Upheaval in Central America *(pages 690–691)*

Summarizing

After you have read this lesson, write a paragraph summarizing the factors that led to conflicts in Central America from the 1970s to the 1990s.

_____

_____

_____

_____

Terms To Know

Define or describe the following key term from this lesson.

contras

_____

_____

Copyright © by The McGraw-Hill Companies, Inc.

Key Points

Notes

Use each of these terms, which you studied earlier, in a sentence that reflects the term's meaning.

virtual
(Chapter 10, Section 4)

_____

_____

oligarchy
(Chapter 2, Section 1)

_____

_____

Section Wrap-up

Now that you have read the section, answer these questions from Setting a Purpose for Reading *at the beginning of the section.*

What problems did Mexico and the nations of Central America face after 1945?

_____

_____

_____

_____

_____

What were the chief features and impact of the Cuban Revolution?

_____

_____

_____

_____

_____

Copyright © by The McGraw-Hill Companies, Inc.

Chapter 22, Section 3
The Nations of South America

(Pages 693–696)

Reason To Read

Setting a Purpose for Reading Think about these questions as you read:
- What obstacles does the new democratic government in Brazil face?
- What factors have been the greatest causes of South American instability?

Main Idea

As you read pages 693–696 in your textbook, complete the chart below by filling in the factors leading to the change from military rule to civilian rule in Argentina, Brazil, and Chile.

Argentina	Brazil	Chile

Sequencing Events

As you read, place the following events on the time line below.
- **Military forces overthrow Allende presidency in Chile**
- **Juan Perón is elected president of Argentina**
- **Argentina sends troops to the Falkland Islands**
- **Alejandro Toledo is elected president of Peru**
- **Military seizes control of Brazil's government**

♦ 1945   ♦ 1965   ♦ 1985   ♦ 2005

Copyright © by The McGraw-Hill Companies, Inc.

Argentina (pages 693–694)

Analyzing

As you read this lesson, think about Juan Perón's policies. Do you think he improved conditions in Argentina or made them worse? Explain.

_____

_____

_____

_____

Terms To Review

Write the definition of each of the following terms that you studied earlier.

strategy
(Chapter 18, Section 2)

_____

_____

transfer
(Chapter 10, Section 3)

_____

_____

Brazil (pages 694–695)

Inferring

As you read this lesson, look for events that led to the failure of the "economic miracle" in Brazil. Then use the lines below to explain how these events led to the return of democracy in Brazil in 1985.

_____

_____

_____

_____

Terms To Review

Use the following term, which you studied earlier, in a sentence that reflects the term's meaning.

furthermore
(Chapter 16, Section 1)

_____

_____

Copyright © by The McGraw-Hill Companies, Inc.

Chile (page 695)

Evaluating

As you read this lesson, jot down notes about the government of Salvador Allende. Then decide the following: If you had been a citizen of Chile during Allende's presidency, would you have supported or opposed his government? *Explain.*

_____

_____

_____

_____

_____

Terms To Review

Choose one of these terms, which you studied earlier, to fill in each blank.

military
(Chapter 1, Section 2)

dictatorship
(Chapter 13, Section 1)

1. A _____ was established in Chile in 1973.

2. Augusto Pinochet was a general in the Chilean _____ .

3. The _____ seized the presidential palace, which resulted in the death of Allende.

Peru (pages 695–696)

Drawing Conclusions

As you read this lesson, look for information to answer the following question: Did Juan Velasco Alvarado's government help or hurt the peasants of Peru? *Give reasons for your answer.*

_____

_____

_____

_____

_____

Copyright © by The McGraw-Hill Companies, Inc.

 **Key Points**

 **Notes**

Copyright © by The McGraw-Hill Companies, Inc.

Terms To Know

Define or describe the following key terms from this lesson.

cooperatives

_____

_____

_____

Shining Path

_____

_____

Terms To Review

Use the following term, which you studied earlier, in a sentence that reflects the term's meaning in this lesson.

task
(Chapter 2, Section 1)

_____

_____

Colombia (page 696)

Responding

After reading this lesson, do you think the United States should have become involved in the drug issues of Colombia? Why or why not?

_____

_____

_____

Terms To Review

Circle the letter of the word or phrase that is closest in meaning to the underlined word.

responded
(Chapter 3, Section 4)

1. The Colombian government <u>responded</u> violently to the efforts of Marxist guerrilla groups who tried to organize the peasants.

   a. answered   **b.** reacted   **c.** yelled

civil
(Chapter 2, Section 2)

2. In addition to high unemployment, <u>civil</u> war also disrupted the Colombian economy.

   a. polite

   b. involving the general public and their needs

   c. involving one or two individuals and their needs

Section Wrap-up

Now that you have read the section, answer these questions from Setting a Purpose for Reading *at the beginning of the section.*

What obstacles does the new democratic government in Brazil face?

_____

_____

_____

_____

_____

What factors have been the greatest causes of South American instability?

_____

_____

_____

_____

_____

Copyright © by The McGraw-Hill Companies, Inc.

Chapter 23, Section 1
Independence in Africa

(Pages 703–709)

Reason To Read

Setting a Purpose for Reading Think about these questions as you read:
- What economic problems did independent African nations face?
- How have social tensions impacted African culture?

Main Idea

As you read pages 703–709 in your textbook, complete the chart below by identifying the problems in Africa during its first stages of independence.

Africa	
Economic	
Social	
Political	

Sequencing Events

As you read, place the following events on the time line below.
- **Civil war in Nigeria**
- **Organization of African Unity forms**
- **Blacks massacred in Sharpeville**
- **Arrest of ANC leader Nelson Mandela**
- **Ghana gains independence**

◆ 1957   ◆ 1960   ◆ 1963   ◆ 1966   ◆ 1969

Copyright © by The McGraw-Hill Companies, Inc.

The Transition to Independence (pages 703–704)

Identifying Cause and Effect

After you have read the lesson, write a brief paragraph summarizing the effects of European resistance to African independence.

_____

_____

_____

Terms To Know

Define or describe the following key term from this lesson.

apartheid

_____

_____

Terms To Review

Circle the letter of the word or phrase that is closest in meaning to the underlined word.

granted
(Chapter 1, Section 2)

1. France granted full independence to Morocco and Tunisia in 1956.

   a. took over b. gave c. offered

initiated
(Chapter 11, Section 2)

2. Algerian nationalists initiated a guerrilla war to liberate their homeland from France.

   a. started b. supported c. protested

The New Nations (pages 705–707)

Summarizing

As you read, think about the economic problems and political challenges that newly formed African countries faced. Then write a paragraph summarizing why independence did not bring economic prosperity to new nations.

_____

_____

_____

_____

_____

Copyright © by The McGraw-Hill Companies, Inc.

Key Points

Notes

Terms To Know

Define or describe the following key term from this lesson.

Pan-Africanism

_____

_____

Terms To Review

Use the following term, which you studied earlier, in a sentence.

resource
(Chapter 19, Section 2)

_____

_____

New Hopes (pages 707–708)

Connecting

As you read this lesson, think about Mandela's statement, "We shall build a society in which all South Africans, both black and white, will be able to walk tall, without fear in their hearts, assured of their inalienable right to human dignity. . . ." Have we achieved this goal in the United States? Explain.

_____

_____

_____

_____

_____

Terms To Review

Write the definition of the following term that you studied earlier.

secure
(Chapter 3, Section 2)

_____

_____

Copyright © by The McGraw-Hill Companies, Inc.

Society and Culture in Modern Africa *(pages 708–709)*

Synthesizing

As you read the lesson, think about society and culture in modern African states. Can you think of ways that religion or other customs in African states might conflict with modernization? Write your answer in a paragraph below.

_____

_____

_____

_____

Terms To Review

Use each of the following terms, which you studied earlier, in a sentence that reflects the term's meaning.

impact
(Chapter 3, Section 2)

_____

_____

constant
(Chapter 8, Section 3)

_____

_____

Section Wrap-up

Now that you have read the section, answer these questions from Setting a Purpose for Reading at the beginning of the section.

What economic problems did independent African nations face?

_____

_____

_____

How have social tensions impacted African culture?

_____

_____

_____

Copyright © by The McGraw-Hill Companies, Inc.

Chapter 23, Section 2
Conflict in the Middle East

(Pages 711–716)

Reason To Read

Setting a Purpose for Reading Think about these questions as you read:
• How was the state of Israel created?
• How did Islamic revival affect Middle Eastern Society?

Main Idea

As you read pages 711–716 in your textbook, complete the chart below by filling in the important events in the history of Arab-Israeli conflicts.

Year	Event

Sequencing Events

As you read, place the following events on the time line below.
• **PLO is founded**
• **Iran frees American hostages**
• **Suez War begins**
• **Khomeini seizes control of Iran**
• **Six-Day War takes place**

◆ **1955**   ◆ **1965**   ◆ **1975**   ◆ **1985**

Copyright © by The McGraw-Hill Companies, Inc.

The Question of Palestine *(pages 711–712)*

Responding

As you read this lesson, think about the time when the state of Israel was created. Imagine that you are an Arab or Jew living in Palestine in 1948. Write a short paragraph describing your reaction to this event.

_____

_____

_____

_____

Academic Vocabulary

Use the following academic vocabulary word from this lesson in a sentence that shows you understand the word's meaning.

immigrated

_____

_____

Nasser and Pan-Arabism *(pages 712–713)*

Identifying Cause and Effect

As you read the lesson, complete the graphic organizer below by identifying the three effects of Pan-Arabism.

Pan-Arabism → (three boxes)

Terms To Know

Define of describe the following key term from this lesson.

Pan-Arabism

_____

_____

Copyright © by The McGraw-Hill Companies, Inc.

Terms To Review

Write the letter of the correct definition next to each of these terms that you studied earlier.

_____ **1.** behalf
(Chapter 5, Section 1)

_____ **2.** revenues
(Chapter 2, Section 2)

a. money that a government collects

b. money that a government gives to citizens

c. in support of

The Arab-Israeli Dispute (pages 713–714)

Sequencing

As you read this lesson, note the dates and events in the ongoing Arab-Israeli dispute. Then complete the time line below to show the sequence of events in the dispute.

1960—OPEC formed   1970   1980

Terms To Review

Write the definition of the following term that you studied earlier.

denied
(Chapter 10, Section 1)

_____

_____

The PLO and the *Intifada* (page 714)

Determining the Main Idea

As you read about the formation of the PLO, write the main idea of the passage. Review your statement when you have finished reading and revise as needed.

_____

_____

_____

Copyright © by The McGraw-Hill Companies, Inc.

 Key Points

 Notes

Terms To Know

Define or describe the following key term from the lesson.

intifada >

_____

_____

Terms To Review

Use the following term, which you studied earlier, in a sentence that reflects the term's meaning.

principle
(Chapter 1, Section 2) >

_____

_____

Revolution in Iran (pages 714–715)

Summarizing

Complete the following sentences as you read the lesson.

1. Devout Muslims hated Iranian civilization under the shah. They

   believed it was based on _____ .

2. The shah's opponents overthrew his government and helped establish

   an Iranian government run by _____ .

3. After Khomeini's death, a more _____ government

   allowed some _____ .

Terms To Review

Write the letter of the correct definition next to each of these terms that you studied earlier.

_____ 1. republic
(Chapter 2, Section 2)

_____ 2. respond
(Chapter 3, Section 4)

a. to react

b. a form of government in which the leader is not a monarch and certain citizens have the right to vote

c. a form of government in which a person or small group has absolute power

Copyright © by The McGraw-Hill Companies, Inc.

Iraq's Aggression (page 715)

Skimming

Read the title of the lesson and quickly look over the passage to get an idea of its content. Then write a sentence or two explaining what you expect the lesson to be about.

_____

_____

_____

_____

Terms To Review

Choose one of these terms, which you studied earlier, to fill in each blank.

resolved
(Chapter 10, Section 4)

1. Although Iraq and Iran were at war for nearly a decade, the war's basic issues were not _____.

2. The United States and its allies launched an attack in the _____ in order to topple Saddam Hussein.

region
(Chapter 3, Section 2)

3. Muslims in the _____ have long had an uneasy relationship because of religious differences.

Afghanistan and the Taliban (page 715)

Visualizing

As you read the descriptions of the changing regimes in Afghanistan, try to imagine what it was like to live under the rule of the Taliban. Then try to imagine how your life would have changed once the Taliban was driven out of Kabul. Record your response in a paragraph below.

_____

_____

_____

_____

_____

Copyright © by The McGraw-Hill Companies, Inc.

Key Points

Notes

 Copyright © by The McGraw-Hill Companies, Inc.

Terms To Review

Write the definition of the following term that you studied earlier.

> **imposition**
> (Chapter 6, Section 3)

_____

_____

Society and Culture *(page 715–716)*

Predicting

As you read the lesson, think about the role of women in Middle Eastern society and culture. Predict what role you believe women will play in the future of the Middle East. Write your answer in a paragraph below.

_____

_____

_____

Terms To Review

Use each of the following terms, which you studied earlier, in a sentence that reflects the term's meaning.

> **parallel**
> (Chapter 13, Section 4)

_____

_____

Section Wrap-up

Now that you have read the section, answer these questions from Setting a Purpose for Reading *at the beginning of the section.*

How was the state of Israel created?

_____

_____

_____

How did Islamic revival affect Middle Eastern Society?

_____

_____

_____

Chapter 24, Section 1
Communist China

(Pages 723–728)

Reason To Read

Setting a Purpose for Reading Think about these questions as you read:
- How did the Great Leap Forward and the Great Proletarian Cultural Revolution affect China?
- What were the major economic, social, and political developments in China after the death of Mao Zedong?

Main Idea

As you read pages 723–728 in your textbook, complete the graphic organizer below by listing communism's effects on China's international affairs.

Effects

```
┌──────────────┐        ┌──────────────────┐
│              │   →    │                  │
│  Communism   │   →    │                  │
│              │        └──────────────────┘
└──────────────┘   →    ┌──────────────────┐
                        │                  │
                        └──────────────────┘
```

Sequencing Events

As you read, place the following events on the time line below.
- **Mao Zedong institutes the Great Leap Forward**
- **A marriage law guarantees women equal rights in China**
- **China establishes diplomatic ties with the United States**
- **Mao Zedong launches the Cultural Revolution**
- **President Nixon visits China**

◆ 1950   ◆ 1960   ◆ 1970   ◆ 1980

Copyright © by The McGraw-Hill Companies, Inc.

Civil War and the Great Leap Forward *(pages 723–724)*

Determining the Main Idea

As you read this lesson, list the methods Mao used to redistribute land and increase food production in China.

_____

_____

_____

_____

Terms To Know

Define or describe the following key term from this lesson.

communes

_____

_____

Terms To Review

Write the definition of the following term that you studied in an earlier chapter.

collectivize
(Chapter 17, Section 2)

_____

_____

The Great Proletarian Cultural Revolution *(pages 724–725)*

Connecting

As you read this lesson, think about how Mao's Little Red Book was seen as the most important source of knowledge during the Cultural Revolution. In a paragraph, describe another book in history thought to be the most important source of knowledge.

_____

_____

_____

_____

_____

Copyright © by The McGraw-Hill Companies, Inc.

 **Key Points**

 **Notes**

Terms To Know

Define or describe the following key term from this lesson.

permanent revolution

_____

_____

Academic Vocabulary

Use the following academic vocabulary word from this lesson in a sentence.

professional

_____

_____

Terms To Review

Write the definition of the following term that you studied earlier.

eliminate
(Chapter 8, Section 3)

_____

_____

China After Mao (pages 725–726)

Monitoring Comprehension

As you read the lesson, think about the Four Modernizations. Why didn't the Chinese succeed with the "fifth modernization," democracy? Explain your answer in a paragraph below.

_____

_____

_____

_____

Terms To Know

Define or describe the following key term from this lesson.

per capita

_____

_____

Copyright © by The McGraw-Hill Companies, Inc.

Terms To Review

Use each of the following terms, which you studied earlier, in a sentence that reflect the term's meaning in this lesson.

violations
(Chapter 19, Section 1)

_____

_____

income
(Chapter 13, Section 2)

_____

_____

Chinese Society Under Communism *(pages 726)*

Summarizing

After you have read this lesson, write a brief paragraph summarizing four ways that communism influenced Chinese society.

_____

_____

_____

_____

Terms To Review

Write the definition of the following term that you studied earlier.

transform
(Chapter 12, Section 1)

_____

_____

China and the World: The Cold War in Asia *(pages 727–728)*

Clarifying

As you read the lesson, think about China in world politics during the Cold War period. Why did the Cold War affect China's attitude toward the Soviet Union? How did China's relationship with the Soviet Union change from the 1950s to the 1980s? Write your answers below.

_____

_____

_____

Copyright © by The McGraw-Hill Companies, Inc.

Key Points

Notes

Academic Vocabulary

Use the following academic vocabulary word in a sentence that shows you understand the word's meaning.

tension

_____

_____

Terms To Review

Write the definition of the following term that you studied in an earlier chapter.

armistice
(Chapter 16, Section 4)

_____

_____

Section Wrap-up

Now that you have read the section, answer these questions from Setting a Purpose for Reading *at the beginning of the section.*

How did the Great Leap Forward and the Great Proletarian Cultural Revolution affect China?

_____

_____

_____

_____

_____

What were the major economic, social, and political developments in China after the death of Mao Zedong?

_____

_____

_____

_____

_____

Copyright © by The McGraw-Hill Companies, Inc.

Chapter 24, Section 2
Independent States in South and Southeast Asia
(Pages 734–738)

Reason To Read

Setting a Purpose for Reading Think about these questions as you read:
- What policies did Jawaharlal Nehru put into effect in India?
- What internal and external problems did the Southeast Asian nations face after 1945?

Main Idea

As you read pages 734–738 in your textbook, complete the graphic organizer below by identifying the challenges India faced after independence.

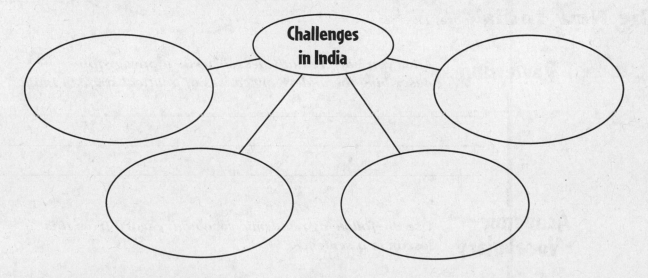

Sequencing Events

As you read, number the following events in the order in which they occurred.

_____ Hindu militants destroy Muslim shrine at Adodhya

_____ East Timor wins independence from Indonesia

_____ East Pakistan becomes independent Bangladesh

_____ France agrees to peace settlement in Vietnam

Copyright © by The McGraw-Hill Companies, Inc.

Key Points

Notes

India Divided (pages 734–735)

Summarizing

After you have read this lesson, write a brief paragraph summarizing the results of the conflicts between Hindus and Muslims in India.

_____

_____

_____

Terms To Review

Define or describe the following term that you studied in an earlier chapter.

migration
(Chapter 1, Section 2)

_____

_____

The New India (pages 735–736)

Reviewing

After you have read the lesson, write a paragraph describing the underlying causes of political strife in India.

_____

_____

_____

Academic Vocabulary

Use the following academic vocabulary word from this lesson in a sentence.

moderate

_____

_____

Terms To Review

Write the definition of the following term that you studied in an earlier chapter.

nuclear
(Chapter 20, Section 1)

_____

_____

Copyright © by The McGraw-Hill Companies, Inc.

Key Points

Notes

Pakistan *(page 736)*

Comparing and Contrasting

As you read this lesson, complete the diagram below showing the similarities and differences between East and West Pakistan.

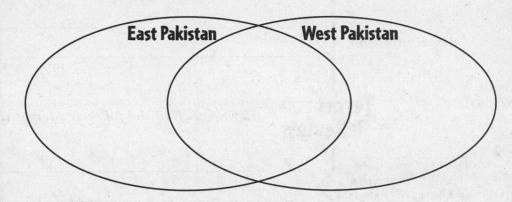

East Pakistan   West Pakistan

Terms To Review

Write the letter of the correct definition next to each of these terms that you studied earlier.

_____ **1.** attain
(Chapter 17, Section 3)

_____ **2.** stable
(Chapter 11, Section 2)

a. to keep

b. firmly established

c. to come into possession of

Southeast Asia *(pages 736–738)*

Identifying Cause and Effect

As you read the lesson, focus on the refusal of France to give up power in Vietnam after World War II. How did this decision affect the United States? Write your answer in a paragraph below.

_____

_____

_____

_____

_____

Copyright © by The McGraw-Hill Companies, Inc.

 **Key Points**

 **Notes**

Terms To Know

Define or describe the following key terms from this lesson.

> stalemate

_____
_____

> discrimination

_____
_____

Terms To Review

Define each of the following terms that you studied earlier.

> **republic**
> (Chapter 2, Section 2)

_____
_____

> **promote**
> (Chapter 14, Section 3)

_____
_____

> **gender**
> (Chapter 21, Section 4)

_____
_____

Section Wrap-up

Now that you have read the section, answer these questions from Setting a Purpose for Reading *at the beginning of the section.*

What policies did Jawaharlal Nehru put into effect in India?

_____
_____
_____

What internal and external problems did the Southeast Asian nations face after 1945?

_____
_____
_____

Chapter 24, Section 3
Japan and the Pacific
(Pages 739–744)

Reason To Read

Setting a Purpose for Reading Think about these questions as you read:
- What important political, economic, and social changes have occurred in Japan since 1945?
- What did the "Asian tigers" accomplish in Asia?

Main Idea

As you read pages 739–744 in your textbook, complete the table below by listing the key areas of industrial development in South Korea, Taiwan, and Singapore.

South Korea	Taiwan	Singapore

Sequencing Events

As you read, place the following events on the time line below.
- **Japan adopts new constitution**
- **Great Britain returns control of Hong Kong to mainland China**
- **General Chung Hee Park is elected president of South Korea**
- **Liberal Democratic party defeated in Japan**

♦1940   ♦1950   ♦1960   ♦1970   ♦1980   ♦1990   ♦2000

Copyright © by The McGraw-Hill Companies, Inc.

The Allied Occupation (pages 739–740)

Summarizing

As you read the lesson, record the changes that General MacArthur made in Japan after World War II.

_____

_____

_____

Terms To Know

Define or describe the following key term from this lesson.

occupied

_____

_____

Terms To Review

Use the following term, which you studied earlier, in a sentence that reflects the term's meaning in this lesson.

civil
(Chapter 2, Section 2)

_____

_____

The Japanese Miracle (pages 740–742)

Evaluating

As you read the lesson, think about the reasons for the "Japanese miracle." In your opinion, which factor had the greatest affect? Explain your answer in a paragraph below.

_____

_____

_____

_____

Terms To Know

Define or describe the following key term from this lesson.

state capitalism

_____

_____

Copyright © by The McGraw-Hill Companies, Inc.

Key Points

Notes

Academic Vocabulary

Use the following academic vocabulary word from this lesson in a sentence that shows you understand the word's meaning.

cited

_____

_____

Terms To Review

Write the definition for each of the following terms that you studied earlier.

export
(Chapter 11, Section 3)

_____

_____

innovations
(Chapter 4, Section 1)

_____

_____

The "Asian Tigers" (pages 743–744)

Synthesizing

As you read the lesson, think about the things that the "Asian tigers" have in common and list them below.

_____

_____

_____

Terms To Review

Write the definition of each of the following terms that you studied earlier.

coup d'etat
(Chapter 11, Section 2)

_____

_____

eventually
(Chapter 3, Section 4)

_____

_____

Copyright © by The McGraw-Hill Companies, Inc.

Australia and New Zealand (page 744)

Analyzing

As you read this lesson, recall that many British people settled in Australia and New Zealand in the 1800s. As a result, many people identified themselves with the British Empire. Is this changing today? Explain.

_____

_____

_____

_____

Terms To Review

Write the definition of the following term that you studied earlier.

derived
(Chapter 2, Section 1)

_____

_____

Section Wrap-up

Now that you have read the section, answer these questions from Setting a Purpose for Reading *at the beginning of the section.*

What important political, economic, and social changes have occurred in Japan since 1945?

_____

_____

_____

_____

What did the "Asian tigers" accomplish in Asia?

_____

_____

_____

_____

Copyright © by The McGraw-Hill Companies, Inc.

Chapter 25, Section 1
The Challenges of Our World
(Pages 751–755)

Reason To Read

Setting a Purpose for Reading Think about these questions as you read:

- What challenges face the world in the twenty-first century?
- What are the promises and perils of the technological revolution?

Main Idea

As you read pages 751–755 in your textbook, complete the table below.

Concern	Cause	Effect
Deforestation		
Loss of ozone layer		
Greenhouse effect		
Acid rain		
Weapons		
Hunger		

Sequencing Events

As you read, number the following events in the order in which they occurred.

_____ **Oil spill from tanker in Alaska devastates environment**

_____ **Toxic fumes kill 3,800 people in Bhopal, India**

_____ **Earth Summit in Rio de Janeiro takes place**

_____ **Indonesian wildfires destroy rain forests and endanger animals**

_____ **Nuclear explosion at Chernobyl releases radiation that kills hundreds**

Copyright © by The McGraw-Hill Companies, Inc.

The Environmental Crisis (pages 751–753)

Monitoring Comprehension

As you read, write down one question from each subhead for a partner to answer. Exchange questions and see if you can answer your partner's questions.

Impact of Population Growth

_____

_____

Chemical Wastes and Disasters

_____

_____

Terms To Know

Write the letter of the correct definition next to each of these key terms from this lesson.

_____ **1.** ecology

_____ **2.** deforestation

_____ **3.** ozone layer

_____ **4.** greenhouse effect

_____ **5.** acid rain

a. the clearing of forests

b. thin layer of gas in the upper atmosphere that shields Earth from ultraviolet rays

c. rainfall that results when sulfur mixes with moisture in the air

d. global warming caused by the buildup of carbon dioxide in the atmosphere

e. study of the relationship between living things and their environment

f. remnant of an organism from a past geological age

Academic Vocabulary

Define each of the following academic vocabulary words from this lesson.

layer

_____

_____

environment

_____

_____

Copyright © by The McGraw-Hill Companies, Inc.

 **Notes**

Terms To Review

Use each of the following terms, which you studied earlier, in a sentence that reflects the term's meaning in this lesson.

intense
(Chapter 4, Section 1)

_____
_____

chemical
(Chapter 21, Section 4)

_____
_____

The Technological Revolution (pages 753–754)

Connecting

As you read this lesson, think about all the advances made during the technological revolution. Which invention, discovery, or advancement do you believe has had the greatest affect on society?

_____
_____
_____
_____

Terms To Know

Define or describe the following key terms from this lesson.

biowarfare

_____
_____

bioterrorism

_____
_____

Academic Vocabulary

Use the following academic vocabulary word from this lesson in a sentence that shows you understand the word's meaning.

mental

_____
_____

Copyright © by The McGraw-Hill Companies, Inc.

Key Points

Notes

Terms To Review

Choose one of these terms, which you studied earlier, to fill in each blank.

network
(Chapter 1, Section 3)

access
(Chapter 12, Section 3)

1. _____ to satellites, cable television, fax machines, and cell phones allow people around the world to communicate with one another.

2. The Internet is the world's largest computer _____ .

3. The Internet provides users with quick _____ to large amounts of information.

Economic and Social Challenges (pages 754–755)

Analyzing

As you read, complete the table below by listing the differences between developing and industrialized nations. Then write a general statement summarizing the economic and social challenges each group of countries face.

Developing Nations	Industrialized Nations

General Statement

_____

_____

Terms To Know

Define or describe the following key term from this lesson.

global economy

_____

_____

Copyright © by The McGraw-Hill Companies, Inc.

 **Notes**

Academic Vocabulary

Use the following academic vocabulary word from this lesson in a sentence that reflects the term's meaning in this lesson.

 **sufficient**

_____

_____

Political Challenges (page 755)

Determining the Main Idea

As you read, write down the main idea of the lesson. Review your statement when you have finished reading and revise as needed.

_____

_____

_____

Terms To Review

Circle the letter of the word or phrase that is closest in meaning to the underlined word that you studied earlier.

identified
(Chapter 17, Section 3)

In the years after World War II, Asian and African leaders <u>identified</u> democracy as the defining theme of their political cultures.

a. separated   **b.** described   **c.** ignored

Section Wrap-up

Now that you have read the section, answer these questions from Setting a Purpose for Reading *at the beginning of the section.*

What challenges face the world in the twenty-first century?

_____

_____

_____

What are the promises and perils of the technological revolution?

_____

_____

_____

Copyright © by The McGraw-Hill Companies, Inc.

Chapter 25, Section 2
Global Visions

(Pages 756–758)

Reason To Read

Setting a Purpose for Reading Think about these questions as you read:
- What international organization arose at the end of World War II to help maintain peace?
- How have ordinary citizens worked to address the world's problems?

Main Idea

As you read pages 756–758 in your textbook, complete the pyramid below that depicts the structure of the United Nations. The Security Council is the most important advisory group of the United Nations.

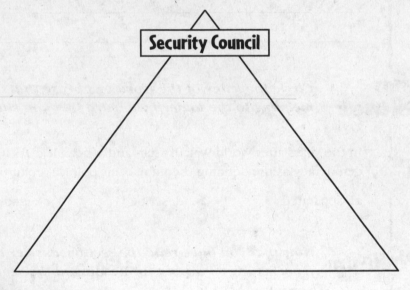

Security Council

Sequencing Events

As you read, write the correct date next to each event on the time line below.

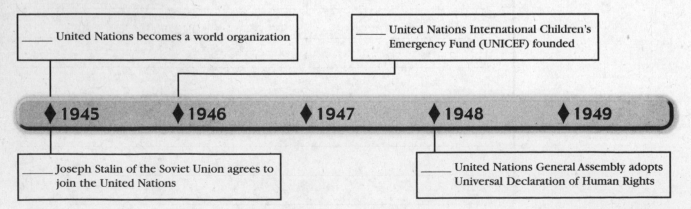

_____ United Nations becomes a world organization

_____ United Nations International Children's Emergency Fund (UNICEF) founded

♦ 1945   ♦ 1946   ♦ 1947   ♦ 1948   ♦ 1949

_____ Joseph Stalin of the Soviet Union agrees to join the United Nations

_____ United Nations General Assembly adopts Universal Declaration of Human Rights

Copyright © by The McGraw-Hill Companies, Inc.

The United Nations (pages 756–757)

Summarizing

As you read the lesson, complete the table below by summarizing the roles of the General Assembly, the Security Council, and the specialized agencies of the United Nations.

General Assembly	Security Council	Specialized Agencies

Terms To Know

Define or describe the following key term from this lesson.

peacekeeping forces > _____

Academic Vocabulary

Use the following academic vocabulary word from this lesson in a sentence.

neutral > _____

Terms To Review

Write the letter of the correct definition next to each of these terms that you studied earlier.

____ **1.** visible
(Chapter 5, Section 1)

____ **2.** fundamental
(Chapter 21, Section 4)

a. basic

b. recognizable

c. complex

Copyright © by The McGraw-Hill Companies, Inc.

Key Points

Notes

New Global Visions (pages 757–758)

Analyzing

As you read this lesson, think about the different methods taken to address global problems. Then develop a possible solution to one of these problems and write a paragraph discussing the issue and the solution.

_____

_____

_____

_____

Terms To Know

Define or describe the following key term from this lesson.

disarmament

_____

_____

Academic Vocabulary

Use the following academic vocabulary word from this lesson in a sentence.

institute

_____

_____

Terms To Review

Choose one of these terms, which you studied earlier, to fill in each blank.

professional
(Chapter 24, Section 1)

1. Some _____ shows that Canadian forests are affected by acid pollution from the United States.

research
(Chapter 21, Section 4)

2. NGOs include _____, business, and cooperative organizations, as well as religious and peace groups.

3. One approach to global problems is social movements led by ordinary citizens rather than _____ scientists, doctors, lawyers, and politicians.

Copyright © by The McGraw-Hill Companies, Inc.

 **Key Points**

 **Notes**

 **Section Wrap-up**

Now that you have read the section, answer these questions from Setting a Purpose for Reading *at the beginning of the section.*

What international organization arose at the end of World War II to help maintain peace?

_____

_____

_____

_____

_____

How have ordinary citizens worked to address the world's problems?

_____

_____

_____

_____

_____

Copyright © by The McGraw-Hill Companies, Inc.

Chapter 25, Section 2

421